W9-AVG-397

Voices from the Wild Horse Desert

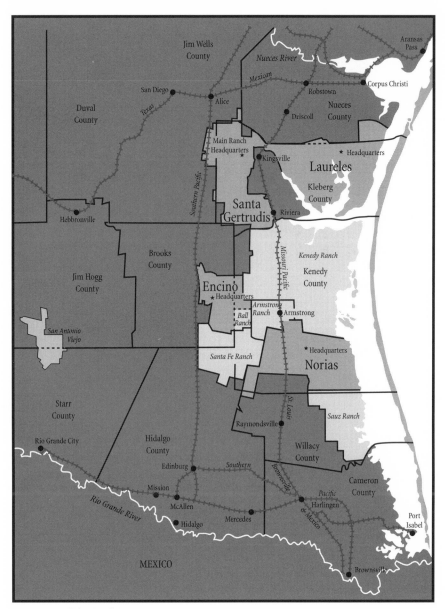

Map courtesy of King Ranch, Inc.

Voices from the Wild Horse Desert

THE VAQUERO FAMILIES OF
THE KING AND KENEDY RANCHES

Jane Clements Monday and Betty Bailey Colley

Foreword by Stephen J. "Tio" Kleberg

Introduction by A. Carolina Castillo Crimm

University of Texas Press, Austin

Requests for permission to reproduce material from this work should be sent to Permissions, University of Texas Press, P.O. Box 7819, Austin, TX 78713-7819.

⊗ The paper used in this publication meets the minimum requirements of American National Standard for Information Sciences—Permanence of Paper for Printed Library Materials, ANSI Z39.48-1984.

Library of Congress Cataloging-in-Publication Data

Monday, Jane Clements, 1941–
    Voices from the Wild Horse Desert : the vaquero families of the King and Kenedy Ranches / by Jane Clements Monday and Betty Bailey Colley.
        p.   cm.
    Includes bibliographical references (p.   ) and index.
    ISBN 0-292-75204-0 (cl : alk. paper). — ISBN 0-292-75205-9 (pbk. : alk. paper)
    1. Mexican American cowboys—Texas, South—Interviews.   2. Mexican American families—Texas, South—Anecdotes.   3. Ranch life—Texas, South—Anecdotes.   4. King Ranch (Tex.)—Anecdotes.   5. Kenedy Ranch (Tex.)—Anecdotes.   I. Colley, Betty.   II. Title.
    F395.M5M63   1997
    976.4—dc21   96-45639

Contents

Foreword

S everal themes wind through the remarkable histories of the King and Kenedy Ranches in South Texas: strong-willed, determined people; triumph over adversity; the building of successful businesses; working in concert with nature; and innovative problem-solving. Born and bred from outstanding human achievement, a cultural blend of Hispanic and Anglo heritages, these ranches exemplify Texas entrepreneurial spirit, ingenuity, and industry. And nowhere in these sagas is this spirit of ingenuity and industry better represented than in the lives of the people who have worked in the Wild Horse Desert. Working together, the extended families of the King and Kenedy Ranches have sustained them in a harsh, unyielding country through seven generations, forging distinct and unique ranching cultures.

This remarkable book is their story, voices that in many cases historians never expected to hear. Readers shall stand in debt to Jane Monday and Betty Colley for their enterprise in eliciting these family recollections by Kineños and Kenedeños; to Ana Carolina Castillo Crimm for an insightful introduction, which places these oral histories in historical context; and, most of all, to the ranch families themselves who recorded their memories of life in South Texas.

Los Kineños are my extended family. Having lived and worked almost my entire life on King Ranch, I am firmly convinced that the people and culture of this ongoing enterprise are its greatest asset. To them, and to the Mexican American culture which created the character and success of King Ranch, I conclude by repeating the dedication offered in Tom Lea's magisterial history, *The King Ranch,* published in 1957:

A todos aquellos hombres
Kineños de verdad
Se dedica esta obra
En reconocimiento de lo que
Les debe este rancho

Stephen J. "Tio" Kleberg
Vice President
King Ranch, Inc.

Preface

Voices from the Wild Horse Desert is the story of vaquero families who have lived and worked on the prominent King and Kenedy Ranches of South Texas for six generations. Vaqueros (Mexican cowboys) are the highly skilled work force that cares for and works the cattle day by day. Their families are stable support systems for this work. These remarkable stories of their contributions to the development of the cattle industry in the United States, and the settling of the Southwest, were gleaned from oral history interviews. This book is a forum for their voices, an opportunity for them to recount the expert skill, dedication to task, loyalty, and personal code that has characterized their lives for generations.

The origins of the vaquero can be traced to expert horsemen who brought their knowledge to the Americas with the early Spanish settlers and passed it on to the American Indians. From these two cultures evolved the Mexican vaquero, with his extensive knowledge of cattle and horses. Vaqueros came to South Texas in several waves: during the period of Spanish rule prior to 1821, during Mexican rule (1821–1836), in the period following the American Civil War (1861–1865), and during the Mexican Revolution (1910–1920). They came individually and in groups.

The King and Kenedy Ranches are located in South Texas on the Wild Horse Desert, between the Rio Grande to the south and the Nueces River to the north. The Wild Horse Desert was once a no-man's-land between Mexico and the United States. This land has seen the passage of many cultures. American Indians first tracked it for game and food as they traveled from the land of the iceberg toward the land of the sun to establish what would become the great civilizations of the Aztecs and the Incas. Next came Spanish conquistadores (conquerors) in search of gold and precious metals. With them they brought horses and cattle. They crossed this "wild desert" only to return empty-handed and disillusioned from their search for riches, but they left behind their animals, which would become the seed stock for the American cattle industry.

By the time that private cattle ranches were established in South Texas in 1750, the institution had been evolving for seven centuries in Spain and Mexico. The early Spanish settlers arrived in this arid land with knowledge and culture that allowed them to succeed at raising large herds of cattle. Anglo settlers adopted the Spanish/Mexican ranching institution, which became the primary social unit that would undergird the settlement of the Southwest and, finally, the West. According to George W. Saunders, who founded the Old Time Trail Drivers' Association in 1915, "these early cattlemen rescued a huge wilderness area . . . stocking, peopling and developing sixteen states and territories." The King and Kenedy Ranches were an early part of this movement and became two of the most famous ranches in the world.

Captains Richard King and Mifflin Kenedy were business associates as early as 1847, and they would maintain a close relationship all their lives. Their lucrative venture in steamboating on the Rio Grande included moving supplies for Zachary Taylor during the Mexican war with the United States from April 1846 to February 1848. Then, during the American Civil War in the early 1860s, they began shipping cotton from the Southern states to Mexico, moving the cotton on their steamboats to foreign ships in the Gulf of Mexico. They also carried supplies for Confederate troops. By this time, they had already begun looking to their new adventure: ranching on the Wild Horse Desert.

In 1852, King traveled on horseback north from his home in Brownsville, Texas, across the mostly uninhabited waves of desert grass on his way to Corpus Christi, Texas. He stopped by a creek called Santa Gertrudis, named by Blas María de la Garza Falcón for the patron saint of his daughter. Inspired with a vision for this land, King purchased it in 1853 and, along with his friend Gideon K. "Legs" Lewis, established his cow camp. Several years after Lewis was killed by an irate husband in 1855, Mifflin Kenedy joined King in his venture, and they set out to convert these vast resources of desert to a profitable cattle business. They succeeded beyond all expectations.

Following the acquisition of the land, the workforce was the next important consideration, and, to find workers to develop his ranch, Captain King would look south. In 1854, Captain King went into northern Mexico and persuaded the entire village of Cruillas (Cruias) to move their animals and belongings and come to Santa Gertrudis to make it their home. These villagers became the first Kineños (the people of King Ranch), the prototype for the Kenedeños of the Kenedy Ranch, who would come with Kenedy when he joined in King's ranching venture in 1860. Other vaqueros migrated to find work on neighboring ranches in the area, and some eventually worked for both Kenedy and King. This book is about the Kineños and Kenedeños, who became the steady, dependable work force that helped make these two great Ranches possible. They included both vaqueros, who worked with livestock from horseback, and ranch hands who worked the dozens of other jobs on the Ranches.

The vaqueros worked directly with the cattle and were key to the success of these Ranches. Some of the vaquero families were on the Wild Horse Desert even before Captain Richard King first viewed this wild expanse. The Treviño family received a land grant from Mexico in 1834, as did the Longória family for Los Sauces in 1831. We were fortunate to interview their descendants. During these talks, little interest was exhibited in the subject of land acquisition practices, and so this topic has been left for future inquiries.

No matter whether the vaqueros were on the range rounding up cattle, keeping a herd at night, roping, or branding, it was their skill and loyalty that made these ranches work.

Vaqueros on South Texas ranches were destined to be key players in the saga of the settlement and development of the American West from the Mississippi River to the Pacific Ocean. They were part of a complex, social organization adopted from the Hispanic legacy of *patron-peón* feudalistic rule. Often, the ties that existed between the families of the ranch owners and the families of the ranch hands grew stronger with the passing years. The employer-employee relationship at these ranches was characterized by a bond of faithfulness on the one hand, and of responsibility on the other. This reciprocal relationship became inherent in the continuing patterns of life and labor on the Ranches. If illness, misfortune, or trouble struck a loyal hand, responsible owners made sure that there was help waiting, according to the need, as they still do today.

These South Texas ranches became home for both owners and workers, and their characters and cultures derived from all the people who lived on them. This relationship is perhaps best captured in a local folk tale relating to the Kleberg family and King Ranch. A woman visitor approached an old man who was puttering around the Santa Gertrudis headquarters. She opened a conversation by asking him if he worked there; he acknowledged that he did. "Then you work for my friend Bob

Kleberg, president of King Ranch!" "No, Señora, I work for King Ranch. Mr. Kleberg, he work for King Ranch, too."

King Ranch has often been called the birthplace of the American ranching industry. Its contributions to the industry are legion. The story of King Ranch and its rise to become a world leader in many facets of ranching and agriculture has been told in books, magazines, and professional journals many times the world over. The Ranch founded the first major American beef breed, the Santa Gertrudis, and, recently, the King Ranch Santa Cruz. Here were bred the King Ranch Quarter Horses, recognized as some of the best in the world, and top Thoroughbred racing horses including Assault, one of only eleven Triple Crown winners. King Ranch is also the source of countless technical innovations. It was designated a National Historic Landmark in 1961.

King Ranch includes 825,000 diverse acres with four divisions: Santa Gertrudis, which is the location of the Ranch headquarters, Laureles, Encino, and Norias (see frontispiece).

Captain Mifflin Kenedy began amassing land for the Kenedy Ranch by establishing his La Parra Ranch in what is now Kenedy County (Ward 1993, 780). It is bounded by a division of the King Ranch on the south, Baffin Bay on the north, and the Laguna Madre on the east. By the time Kenedy died in 1895, the Ranch totaled 400,000 acres and was one of the largest and most successful ranches in Texas. The Kenedy Ranch located its headquarters at La Parra, which is divided into the Mifflin Kenedy Division and the Laurel Leaf Division (Graham 1994, 53). The Ranch has been a close business associate and adjoining neighbor to King Ranch since 1860.

Many of these vaquero families intermarried. Most of the stories included here were collected from the more than sixty members of their families and associates interviewed for this work. Some are fifth- and sixth-generation vaqueros. Their ages range from twenty to ninety-three. Some of the interviews were conducted in English, and some were conducted in Spanish, then translated. Several of the interviewees are now deceased, but their legacy continues on the following pages.

We gratefully dedicate this book to these vaquero families. We have recorded their words. This is their story. They spoke to us with light in their eyes, reflecting the pride and wisdom of their heritage. They talked of the good times and the bad, of their work, and of their lives. Always, they spoke with pride in who they are. They seemed genuinely pleased at interest in their stories. We hope that readers will enjoy getting to know each of them as their voices echo across the Wild Horse Desert.

Our intent from the first was to write about Texas heroes and potential role models whose stories have not been told. When we learned of the *Kineños* and *Kenedeños,* we were intrigued with their history. Our thanks go to Tom and Dorothy Shockley and Ron Kellet for opening the pathway to collecting these amazing stories.

To Mr. Stephen "Tio" Kleberg of King Ranch and to Mr. James McCown and the John G. & Marie Stella Kenedy Memorial Foundation goes our gratitude for their interest and cooperation.

With every successful project there must be people who believe in it to make it happen. Mr. David Maldonado of King Ranch and Mr. Juan Guevara, formerly of Kenedy Ranch, served as valuable contacts to our interviewees and helped to facilitate the interviews, and we express our deep felt appreciation.

To Mr. Bruce Cheeseman, King Ranch Consulting Archivist, Lisa Neely, King Ranch Archivist, and Jamene Toelkes, Assistant Archivist, we are deeply grateful for the many hours spent providing invaluable knowledge and advice, assisting with research, and most of all, for their dedication to quality and accuracy.

To our friend, Alberto "Beto" Maldonado, we say thank you for his advice, wealth of knowledge, and warm support. To Mr. Leonard Stiles goes our appreciation for his breadth of knowledge, his desire to have these stories told, and his willingness to facilitate a number of the interviews.

To the new generation of vaquero family members, represented so well by Sonia Maldonado Garcia, who believe in their families and helped us to convey the need for their stories to our interviewees, we say thank you.

Our gratitude goes to Dr. Donald Coers for providing technical assistance and support. Sincere thanks go to Jim and Fran Presley for their knowledge and encouragement so necessary in the early phases of the project. Janet Sisson was a continuous friend and expert technology consultant throughout the project, and we are grateful. Gary and Charlotte Collins were continuous sources of encouragement.

To Charlie "Poppie" and Dorothy "Dee" Monday go thanks for providing our home away from home, home-cooked meals, love, and support in this project.

Our deepest appreciation and love go to our families for their interest and support. To our Monday children, Kimberly, Julie, Buddie, and Jennifer, and to our Colley children, Carey, Jill, and Steffen, go our thanks for their belief in us as we worked with the project. Our gratitude goes to Burnham Jones for important technical advice and unfailing belief in the value of the work. And to Jane's husband, Charles, our most constant supporter, we can never say how much we appreciate your interest and your patience.

Finally, our deepest appreciation goes to our interviewees. They welcomed us into their homes, accepted the sincerity of our work, ignored the recorders and note pads, and spoke to us from their hearts. Our greatest hope is that we have accurately presented to you, our readers, their heartfelt stories of their contributions to our heritage.

Introduction

by Ana Carolina Castillo Crimm

W hen Richard King and Mifflin Kenedy established their ranches
on the lands of the Wild Horse Desert in 1854 and 1860, respec-
tively, their success was predicated not on their visions and dreams
alone, for neither was knowledgeable of the livestock industry, but on
the partnership which they formed with their Mexican labor force, the
Kineños and Kenedeños.[1] The wisdom and skill of their employees,
combined with the willingness of both King and Kenedy to give them
complete trust and responsibility, created the King and Kenedy Ranches
and crowned with success the efforts of both owners and employees.
This unity of purpose and melding of efforts by an unusual combination
of labor and management are rare among capitalistic ventures and are
rarer still in agricultural enterprises such as the Mexican haciendas from
which King's and Kenedy's ideas sprang.

Richard King and Mifflin Kenedy were familiar with haciendas.
During the years which they spent trading and steamboating on the Rio
Grande, they met and dealt with the agents and *mayordomos* of the Mexican cattlemen south of the river. These agents represented the elite and
wealthy owners of cattle ranches, the ranches better known and better
understood by their Spanish name of haciendas or *latifundios*. These
Mexican cattlemen owned millions of acres, hundreds of thousands of
head of livestock, highly profitable ranching and agricultural operations,
and enjoyed tremendous wealth, social prestige, and political power. In
order to develop a new profit-making venture, Richard King, the hard-
driving, Horatio Alger – entrepreneur with little education and no up-
bringing, and Mifflin Kenedy, the quiet, hard-working, well-educated
Quaker, formed a partnership much like those formed by many Eastern entrepreneurs who were then helping to create the new industrial
United States. The ranches which resulted were based on a mixture of
three cultures — Hispanic, Southern, and Western.[2]

Thus, the King and Kenedy Ranches form a kaleidoscope of cultures. In order to understand the development of the ranches and their evolving relationship with the Kineños and Kenedeños who worked for them, it is necessary to compare the histories of Mexico, the South, and the West. Although the ranches were born from the Mexican hacienda, they grew as Western cattle ranching grew. The patriarchal relationship between King and his Kineños and Kenedy and his Kenedeños derived as much from the Spanish patriarchal *latifundio* as from the paternalism of the southern plantation, and the Kineños and Kenedeños themselves were then, and are now, the quintessential Western cowboys, the reality behind the myth.

King and Kenedy formed their ranches based on the haciendas and *latifundios* that they saw across the border. The Mexican haciendas were the first livestock operations in the New World. The term *hacienda* was initially associated with any large rural estate which supplied the growing urban markets of colonial Mexico with beef, hides, and tallow as well as agricultural produce. Most of them existed in central and southern Mexico. A *latifundio* was an hacienda of immense size, most often found in the drier climates of Northern Mexico where a cow and calf often required hundreds of acres of grass to survive. A rancho, on the other hand, was usually a smaller rural property worked by the owner himself with the aid of his immediate family, and such ranchos were scattered throughout Mexico. Like the haciendas, the *latifundios* were economically oriented, profit-motivated capitalistic ventures involved in livestock raising. As an added benefit, the wealth from the production of cattle and sheep provided the landowner with prestige and elite standing. *Latifundios,* such as that of the Sanchez Navarro family in the northern Mexican States of Chihuahua and Coahuila, could encompass as much as sixteen million acres and be largely self-supporting. Most of their profits derived from extensive annual trail drives of sheep to Mexico City. The Sanchez Navarro agents also sold their diversified products in local, national and international markets, including the ports along the Rio Grande—where they may well have come to know the two Anglo traders. Other *latifundios* in Northern Mexico were equally large. The Urdiñola family, who became the Marqueses of San Miguel de Aguayo y Santa Olaya in 1682, held a *latifundio* grant that covered over fourteen million acres. The Vazquez Borregos controlled over a million acres on their *latifundio,* and the Garza Falcón family on the Sabinas River held a relatively small *latifundio* of only 457,160 acres. All of these families had enormous wealth, political power, and social prestige among the landed aristocracy of Northern Mexico. When Tom Lea, in his history of the King Ranch, suggests that in Mexico "the sale of meat was a local and small-scale affair," and that King proposed to "import the system, improve it, and make it pay," he was unfamiliar with the profitable hacienda agricultural production and distribution system that had existed in Mexico for three hundred years.[3]

Historically, haciendas and *latifundios* as economic endeavors developed from the arrival of the first Spanish settlers in the 1500s with their newly introduced livestock. The first cattle were landed by Gregorio de Villalobos along the Pánuco River near Tampico in 1521, six months before Cortéz captured Mexico City. These cattle, a combination of three different strains of Spanish cattle, were to become the famed longhorns which spread into Texas along the coast. The first hacienda was granted to Cortéz, himself, when he was given the title of Marqués and, along with it, the entire Valley of Oaxaca for his services in the conquest of Mexico. Like the many other new haciendas that were granted throughout Mexico during the sixteenth and seventeenth centuries, from its inception the Marquesado of the Valley of Oaxaca was economically oriented with the emphasis on finding profitable markets and cutting labor costs. Both Hernán and Fernando Cortéz were intent on generating profits by selling beef, hides, and tallow to markets in the rapidly growing city of Antequera (later Oaxaca City) and to distant Mexico City. Cattle and sheep, which the Spanish continued to import, flourished in the new climate where there were no predators and where the grassy valleys provided ample room for rapid growth. Livestock raising, therefore, represented a high-profit-potential/low-risk-venture.[4]

In the Valley of Mexico itself, many of the new hacendados, using Indian and Mestizo labor, profited from the production of cattle on their haciendas, often much to the detriment of the Indian corn fields nearby. Farther north, the rapidly expanding silver mines in Zacatecas and Guanajuato also demanded more livestock production to supply beef to feed the laborers; hides to produce harnesses, hinges, heavy belts, and straps for the mine machinery; and mules and horses to carry the silver to Mexico City. Haciendas, often owned by local merchants or the mine owners themselves, developed in the vicinity of the mines to supply the new market. Throughout Latin America, beginning as early as the 1600s, hacendados improved cattle and sheep breeds and developed new methods of handling and managing the livestock in order to increase profit margins. Landowners also diversified—both in the production of goods and in their use of labor—when markets or natural disasters demanded it. Wheat, a crop not known previously in the New World, was planted by Spanish hacendados to produce bread for the rapidly increasing urban Spanish market. Corn, produced by the native populations in the New World for thousands of years, remained a profitable commodity since it continued in use among the Indians for their native tortillas and tamales, foods that were gradually adopted by the Spanish. Therefore, when Richard King and Mifflin Kenedy chose to invest in cattle ranching, they could draw upon 300 years of history and trial-and-error knowledge.[5]

The Kineños and Kenedeños inherited a long tradition of service, but unlike their Mexican counterparts, their labor relationship with King and Kenedy evolved in a different and distinct direction. In Mexico, labor to work the haciendas and *latifundios* had always been readily available from the Indians and Mestizos. During the sixteenth century in New Spain, in order to provide the conquistadors with a livelihood, the Spanish created the *encomienda* system whereby Indian laborers and entire Indian towns were assigned to the Spaniards to provide labor and tribute (a form of taxation), much as the Indians had done under the Aztecs. In 1549, partly in response to protestations by missionary fathers such as Bartolomé de las Casas that Indians were being overworked and mistreated, the Spanish government abolished the labor requirement for Indians. The conquistadors, who were left with a minimal labor force and pinched profits, demanded more workers or, they warned, the King would not get his taxes. In response, the crown created the *repartimiento* system in which the government hired out Indians to labor on haciendas and assigned officials who ostensibly protected them from mistreatment. By the seventeenth century, however, European diseases had devastated the Indian labor force, and the hacienda owners were scrambling for workers. Tribute from individual Indians and from their villages had also shifted from in-kind contributions to monetary payments, and the government had gotten out of the Indian rental business. Indians in need of cash to pay their tribute sought jobs on the haciendas as wage laborers or sold their own crops in a market dominated by Spanish hacendados.

A system of debt-peonage developed through which the hacienda owner, perhaps seeking to retain tighter control over his laborers, advanced wages to the Indians. According to some scholars, this trapped them in debt and forced them to remain on the hacienda until the debt was paid off, which usually never happened. On the northern estates, such as the *latifundio* of the Sanchez Navarro family, the company store (*tienda de raya*) served the same purpose, and anyone trying to flee the debt was caught and returned to the hacienda. Scholars have found that some laborers, like credit-card debtors today, were indeed trapped, while others benefited from the system and learned to use it to their own advantage. Jan Bazant has argued that debt-peonage was often a convenience rather than a detriment. Laborers who lived on the haciendas on a full-time basis, whether indebted to the landlord or not, frequently perceived themselves as a privileged group who were protected by the hacendado from ill-fortune, inclement weather, and poor markets. Small independent farmers, tenants, and sharecroppers who had to subsist on small plots of their own were far more deeply in debt since they had no protective safety-net from market fluctuations and could not store grain to tide them over during times of drought or poor markets. Like the laborers of Jan Bazant's hacienda studies, the Kineños and Kenedeños were privileged and protected laborers, immune to depressions and lay-offs, and, although there was a company store, they never faced the evils of debt-peonage.[6]

The Kineños, according to oral tradition and studies carried out by Norma Martinez, originated in the town of Cruillas (or Cruias), Tamaulipas, in Northern Mexico.[7] In 1854 Richard King, who was in need of laborers knowledgeable about cattle ranching, paid for 100 settlers and their livestock to move from Cruillas to his newly acquired ranch on Santa Gertrudis Creek in Texas, where he built them homes and gave them jobs on the ranch.[8] These were not the first Mexicans to move to new homes near the Rio Grande. During the 1740s, the Spanish Empire in Texas faced threats from the expanding English empire, and Spain needed citizens to guard its exposed northeastern frontier. The Viceroy in Mexico City offered José de Escandón a noble title in exchange for bringing colonists to the new settlement of Nuevo Santander. Beginning in 1749, Escandón carried out what the Spanish called an *entrada,* or entrance, in which he used his own funds to move 6,000 colonists from the center of Mexico to the Rio Grande Valley, to supply them with livestock and tools for their new settlements, to establish towns and churches for them, and to grant each settler a portion of land. By 1755, Escandón had successfully established twenty-three towns and fifteen missions in northeastern Mexico and the settlers were in possession of small land holdings. Not all of the settlers were content with the size of their ranches. Some, such as Blás María de la Garza Falcón, negotiated with Escandón for larger grants and began to expand their holdings to the north side of the Rio Grande which would remain Spanish territory for another seventy years, until 1821. Others who expanded their holdings included Enrique Villareal, who owned most of present day Corpus Christi; José de la Garza, who claimed 59.5 leagues (over 263,000 acres) along the Rio Grande; and José Narciso Cabazos, who held 600,000 acres in what are now Cameron, Willacy, and Kenedy Counties, parts of which would one day be included in the King Ranch. The towns and ranches that Escandón's settlers established included, among others, Laredo, Dolores, Mier, Camargo, Reynosa, and perhaps even Cruillas—towns that Richard King, the steamboat captain and impresario, visited one hundred years later.

Mifflin Kenedy, rather than go to such lengths, simply hired skilled Mexican vaqueros from the Rio Grande area. Why, then, did Richard King go to such lengths to establish a labor force of Mexicans on his ranch? While hacienda owners had long made a practice of keeping whole communities of workers on their ranches, such an expensive practice did not make economic sense to Anglo businessmen or to the growing numbers of Western ranch owners who increased profits by retaining a labor force only during the periods of peak demand, the spring and fall roundups. By the 1870s cowboys throughout the West were laid off during the winter by ranch owners interested in cutting labor costs. On small ranches, where an owner might have only a few cowboys, one or two favored hands might live on the ranch year-round and develop quasi-familial ties to the owner. But on large spreads, cowboys were seasonal workers who were paid off after the fall cattle drive, and they drifted off to make their way as best they could during the cold winter months. King, however, developed a distinct and different relationship with his employees.[9]

Richard King needed his employees and their skills as much or more than they needed him. He had lived in big cities and had worked on steamboats most of his life and understood trade and markets, but King knew little of working longhorn cattle or training horses. Although he bought cattle from his Mexican ranch neighbors and picked up information from them about cattle raising, the only ones who could help him achieve his dream were the families from Cruillas. These Mexican vaqueros taught him to work cattle, trained his horses for him, showed him how to cull and keep the best stock, and helped him build the ranch itself. He handled the marketing and they handled the cattle. Their united efforts made them a family, a King Ranch family who adopted the name Kineños, a name which slowly grew to mean much more than merely one who worked on the ranch. The term was built on generations of loyalty, pride, mutual respect, and admiration. He provided housing and wages, and they taught him the cattle trade. He protected the vaqueros and their families, and they gave their lives to protect his. He celebrated their births and marriages with them as they celebrated his, and when one of the Kineños died, King grieved with them, as they did for him. Unlike the absentee landlords of the haciendas, King worked on the ranch with his vaqueros, relied on their expert knowledge, and gratefully accepted their training. Unlike the paternalistic southern plantation owners, he respected and admired his workers as they respected and admired him. Unlike the Western ranchers, he did not lay them off during the winter in the interest of profits, but kept them on the payroll, year in and year out, generation after generation. It was an unusual labor relationship. Together, they became King Ranch.[10]

Another part of the answer to the successful ranching operation may have been his wife, Henrietta King. Henrietta's father was a Presbyterian minister from Vermont who moved to the Rio Grande border to minister to the Mexican people. His daughter accompanied him, learned Spanish, and, evidently, developed a fondness for the people she met at her father's mission. When she married Richard King, she turned her attentions to the King Ranch cowboys. She became *La patrona*, a Mexican term which translates variously as patron, defender, saint, protector, master, employer, or boss. She was all of these things to the Kineños as she took over their welfare. As Lea describes it, "she dosed and nursed the sick, supplied the needy and . . . used her authority for good as she conceived of good."[11] She also saw to their education and encouraged those who showed promise by offering them opportunities to continue schooling and to rise in the ranks. She often joined in their lives and, during roundups, she and her children joined her husband and his Kineños for meals as they gathered the herds. In is unclear whether *La patrona* tried to convert her Kineños to Anglo ways or whether she and King protected their Mexican cultural beliefs. She did encourage them to learn English, but the Kineños continued to eat their own food, practice their own religion, enjoy their own customs, sing their own songs, and speak Spanish. Spanish became the working language of the Ranch, and it is evident that even Anglo foremen spoke Spanish or picked it up very quickly if they wanted to be successful. The Anglo owners, in fact, learned to eat Mexican foods such as tamales and tortillas, which the Kineños made for them. All of the King children and grandchildren grew up speaking Spanish.

Upon the death of her husband in 1885, Henrietta King continued to control the operations of the ranch for almost another fifty years through her son-in-law, Robert J. Kleberg, who married Alice, the youngest daughter. Henrietta, the proper, black-gowned, Victorian matriarch, and Kleberg, the quiet, hard-working, properly respectful, German attorney had a close-knit relationship which carried the Ranch and the Kineños through both good and bad times during the following decades.[12]

Mifflin Kenedy developed a similar close relationship with his employees. His wife, Petra Vela de Vidal, although a Mexican herself, did not develop a *patrona* relationship with the workers but left that to her granddaughter Sarita. Sarita Kenedy took over the care and well-being of the Kenedeños. Like the King children, she grew up speaking Spanish among the vaqueros and their families. She knew them all intimately and cared deeply for them. After the death of her father, it was not her brother who ran the ranch but Sarita herself who carried on the work, in Spanish, with the help of her Kenedeños. She expanded the ranch through the purchase of more lands, and with her husband, Arthur East, continued the tradition of cattle ranching that her father had learned from the Kenedeños. Unhappily, Sarita had no descendants, and today the ranch is under two trusts. The personal relationship to the Kenedeños is gone, although the vaquero families still retain their memories of *La patrona* and the good times they shared. Today the Kenedeños continue to preserve a sense of community in the town of Sarita and some still work on the ranches.[13]

The personal, patriarchal element in the relationship between the Kings and Klebergs and their vaqueros may have been the determining factor in creating a workforce whose loyalty, dedication, and fidelity was the envy of many western ranchers and corporate entrepreneurs. When Cy Yeary, in charge of hiring for the King Ranch, was asked by a reporter for the *Corpus Christi Caller-Times* what was done to weed out the surplus when a division of the ranch became overstocked with employees, he replied that there was no need. "There's always a few of the boys who decide early in life they want to follow other occupations."[14] In 1953, the ranch maintained 90% Kineño workers and only hired 10% from outside. As Yeary put it, the ranch grew its own employees. Over the generations, the Kineños and Kenedeños developed a feeling that they belonged to the ranch and the ranch belonged to them, and, evidently, the Kings, Klebergs, and Kenedys agreed.[15]

When Richard King rode across the lands of the *Llanos Mesteños*, he was crossing land which, as we have seen, had a long history of ownership. Why, then, were there no profitable haciendas or *latifundios*, as there were in Mexico, dotting the great stretches of grasslands from the Rio Grande to the Nueces River? The answer lies in fifty years of almost uninterrupted conflict and warfare. Landowners in Texas, in particular the descendants of the Escandón settlers who had spread onto lands of the Wild Horse desert, had not been able to enjoy their haciendas in peace. The Mexican Revolution for independence from Spain, although dimly heard this far north, had bloody repercussions. In 1810 and 1811, as Father Miguel Hidalgo y Costilla lighted the fires of revolution in the center of the country, revolutionaries favoring independence revolted in San Antonio, then the capital of Texas. They attacked the ranches and destroyed the possessions of those who opposed independence from Spain. Within the year, royalist forces under General Arredondo arrived in Texas to put down the revolutionaries and exact deadly vengeance for the destructions of the previous year. American filibustering forces under Augustus Magee and Gutiérrez de Lara, who supported independence from Spain, attacked Nacogdoches, La Bahía, and the ranches along the San Antonio and Nueces Rivers. It was not surprising that many of the landowners between the Rio Grande and San Antonio abandoned their ranches under the barrage of bloody attacks and counterattacks from 1811 to 1821 when Mexico at last gained independence. They were again forced off their lands in 1835 and 1836 during the Texas Revolution as marauding Mexican and Texian forces raided the ranches for food and supplies. Safety under the new Republic of Texas was even less likely. With no military—or money to pay for one—the Texas government had no way to protect its citizens, whether Texian or Mexican. Indians, in particular the Comanche, raided the abandoned haciendas and ranches from the Rio Grande to the Guadalupe River. By 1845, Texas had joined the United States. With the advent of the War with Mexico (1847–1848), American troops once again passed through the area on their way to Mexico, sometimes buying, sometimes stealing cattle from the few ranches that were left. By 1853, when Richard King bought his first parcel of land, warfare had moved south of the border, and it was better to move into Texas than out of it. Many Mexican landowners had lived precarious lives for the past forty years in the towns and villas in the Escandón settlements along the Rio Grande and in the Mexican state of Tamaulipas. Occasionally they would return to their ranches, sometimes for a few years at a time, to harvest and plant or collect a herd of horses or cattle to sell at the local markets. By the time that King began to buy up land, several Mexican families had moved back to their ranches, and he often turned to them for help in times of trouble.[16]

Anglo discrimination was another reason why Mexican rancheros did not return to their ranches. The Mexican ranchers could not understand the racism that they faced in the United States. As landowners, they felt entitled to a place in the society among the upper middle classes, a place to which their wealth entitled them. For three hundred years, landed elite Spaniards and Creoles (Spaniards born in the New World) had looked down on the Indians and Mestizos with European superiority. The lower classes were prevented from riding horses, which were reserved for *gente decente* (decent people). Even after the Spanish grudgingly allowed the Indians and Mestizos to mount horses in order to do the hard work of livestock handling, there was always a clear and distinct difference between the vaquero and the *charro,* or gentleman rancher. The *charro* was a landowner, a person of wealth, a person of prestige, a person who expected respect. When the Mexican ranchers did not receive the respect they expected from Anglos, some sued and won against disrespectful Anglos in court. Others demanded and received apologies from too-arrogant newcomers, while a few retreated onto their ranches or into their own Mexican communities in San Antonio, Victoria, or Corpus Christi.[17]

The Mexican vaquero, as a person without land, had faced discrimination in Mexico and faced it again in the United States. In Mexico vaqueros had an accepted place in society. In the United States they were interlopers who faced discrimination, violence, and racism. Despite the antipathy Anglos showed about working with Mexicans, they admitted, if only grudgingly, that vaqueros were the first cowboys and that they had excellent reputations as ropers and superior bronc busters. In fact, vaqueros made up over half of the cowboy workforce on most Texas and southwestern ranches, although few Anglos would acknowledge their preeminence in the field. Even the 1953 history of the King Ranch in the *Corpus Christi Caller-Times,* which goes to great lengths to detail the lives of the Anglo foremen, failed to mention anywhere that the workers on the King ranch were originally Mexicans. They remained the invisible cowboys in spite of attempts by people such as Richard King, Mifflin Kenedy, J. Frank Dobie, and others to correct the American biases against them.[18]

After 1848, Anglos and Mexicans in Texas were in disagreement over the questions of land ownership and legal titles. For Mexicans, land ownership was emotional rather than economic. As Malcolm Ebright has pointed out:

> This connection [to land] is on the visceral rather than the legal level. It is this feeling for the land in the heart and in the gut that guarantees that the legal history of land grants in the Southwest is not just something from the dim, dark past. Land grants and the law are as current as today's news and will continue to be so

as long as there are people who remember the land, and who remember their ancestors who received title to the land by means
of a *merced de tierra*.[19]

Some Mexicans, emotional over their perceived land losses to Anglos,
still continue to question the means and methods by which Anglos
gained access to these lands. Although some sales may have taken place
under duress, recent studies have indicated that Mexicans were canny
negotiators in their dealings with Anglo land purchasers. Mexicans,
more often than not, demanded and received the going price of $1 per
acre for their land. Neither King nor Kenedy were antagonistic toward
the Mexicans, nor did they attempt to cheat or steal the lands. Titles
were questionable not because of the ranchers' business practices but
because of the age-old difficulty of keeping track of ownership. Land
piracy, claim jumping, and outright land theft did exist, however, and
Mexicans who sold under market value to other less friendly Anglos
may well have faced pressure and racist discrimination. In some cases,
selling out was the better economic choice in order to make a quick
profit by getting rid of land that they did not use and for which they
were being heavily taxed.[20]

The amounts of land involved in the transactions were not small.
The Spanish and later the Mexican government had always believed that
livestock raising required much larger quantities of land than farming.
Grants to the early Anglo settlers in Texas, from 1821 to 1835, consisted of
a *league* and a *labor*. The league, for grazing cattle or sheep, contained
4,428.4 acres, while the labor was used for farming and contained 177.1
acres. The total price to the buyer for over 4,600 acres was the cost of the
paperwork and surveying, approximately $12. The standard land unit in
the United States in 1819 was a 640 acre section at a cost of $1.25 per acre
or $800, an amount beyond the reach of most small farmers. Anglos
flocked to Texas during the years of Mexican control to gain access to
these almost free, incredibly large amounts of land. Mexican impresa-
rios or land agents such as Stephen F. Austin and Martín de León carefully had each piece surveyed, registered the boundaries with the Mexican government, and provided each property owner with an original
title and three copies. One copy was retained by the impresario, one
copy went to the state files in Saltillo, and the third was sent to land
offices in Mexico City. The problem was that not all of those who came
to Texas prior to 1836, either Mexican or American, had been under an
impresario, and not all had verifiable land titles. For a land purchaser
such as Richard King, the importance of a secure title was paramount.[21]

By the Treaty of Guadalupe Hidalgo in 1848, the United States guaranteed the security of Mexican titles, or so the government said. The U.S. sent commissioners to Texas, New Mexico, and California to try to sort out the jumble of legal titles. Some Mexican landowners, especially those along the Rio Grande, had held their land for three or more generations and many did not have titles. Americans, many of whom had been drifting into Texas for twenty years, some legally and some illegally, did not have titles either. The commissioners, therefore, faced incredible problems. As William Carey Jones reported in 1852 from California, where many of the titles were in question:

> Any measure calculated to discredit or cause to be distrusted, the general character of the titles there . . . would, I believe also retard the substantial improvement of the country. A title discredited is not destroyed, but everyone is afraid to touch it, or at all events to invest labor and money in improvements that rest on a suspected tenure.[22]

Conditions in Texas were not much better. Commissioners Bourland and Miller were sent to the Rio Grande valley to determine the legality of the titles of local landowners. After months of interviewing, recording depositions from longtime landowners along the Rio Grande, and collecting documentation, the Bourland and Miller Commission lost much of their data and the legal titles of numerous landowners when their ship sank off the Texas coast. Richard King, therefore, had to choose his land purchases carefully, but even then some were inevitably questionable.[23]

All of King's hard work, the loyalty of his Kineños, and his investments paid off when the cattle business boomed after 1870. Three factors influenced the rise of the cattle industry. The first was land: the United States acquired Texas with its hundreds of thousands of cattle in 1845 and the Western states with their millions of acres of grasslands in 1848. After Western lands were stripped of their buffalo herds in the 1870s and the United States cavalry removed the Indians, vast acreages of excellent grazing land became available for profit-oriented cattle ranchers such as King and Kenedy. The second factor was the end of the Civil War in 1865. Northern businessmen, flush with victory, had capital to invest in new industries. King and Kenedy had also profited from the Civil War. They had made a fortune from their steamboating by shipping cotton out of the South, across the Rio Grande, and down to Matamoros where it was sold to British merchants. Now, like the Eastern entrepreneurs, they too sought a profitable return on their money. The final factor was transportation. For cattle ranchers to reach their full profit potential, cattle had to be moved quickly and with the least loss of weight to the urban centers of the Northeast and Midwest. There immigrants flowed in from Europe and Asia to furnish labor for the burgeoning factories. All of those people needed Texas beef and King and Kleberg were in the ideal position to supply it.[24]

Railroads were expanding across the country but few had made the cattle connection. Attempts to take cattle to the Eastern markets had been made in 1846 by Edward Piper, who drove cattle to Ohio, and in 1853 by an Illinois merchant who drove a herd from Texas to New York in only a year and a half. In 1867 Joseph McCoy of Illinois, after several disheartening rejections by both communities and railroads, finally convinced Abilene, Kansas, and the officials of the Hannibal and St. Joseph Railroad to provide pens and transportation for cattle from Texas. By 1870, over 300,000 cattle were being shipped out of Abilene and the boom was on.[25]

Richard King and Mifflin Kenedy were unusual among Texas ranchers in their purchases of large amounts of land, although certainly no different than the *latifundio* owners across the Rio Grande. Men who arrived in Texas with little money to invest were advised to buy cattle rather than land. Others who came with little or no funds were able to start herds of their own by working for other ranchers during roundups and branding a share of the calves for their own herds. Until the end of the Civil War in 1865, most cattle raisers in Texas had ranged their cattle on unoccupied public lands. By 1872, however, barbed wire was invented, and within a dozen years ranchers began to use the new wire to build fences and corrals all over the West. Fences and corrals meant that heavier cattle could be produced by selective breeding, and profits could be doubled or tripled. As profits skyrocketed, big Eastern and European investors bought up vast acreages, enclosed them with barbed wire fences, overstocked the ranges, and shut out the small rancher. Although small ranches (those under 10,000 acres, such as the SR Ranch) continued to exist, the market belonged to the huge ranches such as the Matador, Pitchfork, Swenson, Spur, Slaughter, and XIT, many of which had foreign owners or investors. King and Kenedy had been there first, however, and Richard King, now with over 600,000 acres (later to grow to 1.27 million acres under the tenure of Mrs. King) and a sound knowledge of the cattle industry, thanks to his Kineños, sent his first cattle up the trail on the long annual trail drives northward. Kenedy, overwhelmed by the potential profit, sold his entire ranch for over one million dollars to a Scottish syndicate. He reinvested his money in a second ranch and the Kenedeños continued to work for him, his son John, and his granddaughter, Sarita Kenedy East.[26]

Although Populists and small ranchers complained, "fearing that unscrupulous Capital would destroy man's liberty to compete,"[27] King and other ranchers, investors, and entrepreneurs kept the cattle flowing northward. Fattening centers were established in Ohio, where a symbiotic relationship developed between Western cattlemen, Ohio feedlot operators, and Midwestern corn producers. Gail Borden, also a big Texas rancher, attempted to create a meat biscuit so that cattle could be processed in the South and owners would not have to pay for shipping to the North. King himself tried "injecting salt brine into the veins of butchered cattle as a preservative,"[28] but somehow the idea of embalmed cattle didn't sell well in the Northeast. Investors demanded better management techniques, a greater emphasis on cost cutting, and even greater returns on their investment.[29]

By 1880, cowboys were beginning to attract the attention of the American public. Men on horseback have always appealed to the earthbound pedestrian, and cowboys were no exception. Horsemen have epitomized grandeur and glory, and statues often portray great heroes on rearing chargers. The term cowboy, however, had originally meant a simple Irish cattle herder, although Scottish highlanders who protected their owner's cattle were portrayed in a more noble fashion, "always ready to perform for their lords every kind of service."[30] During the American Revolution, the term cowboy was used to describe a Tory cattle thief, and in early Texas the cowboys were Anglo marauders who stole cattle from Mexican ranches during and after the Texas Revolution. By the 1880s, however, a dichotomy had developed. On the one hand, city dwellers read of the exploits of heroic Wild West cowboys while on the other hand ranch owners distrusted their cowboy workers as drunken, carousing drifters. Young men flocked to the West dreaming of glorious exploits. Teddy Roosevelt, drawn by the image of knights errant on horseback, spent part of his youth as a cowboy on Western ranches. Over 35,000 young men came West to drive herds to northern markets. They formed a distinct social group that held distinct cultural values. Although they did not always abide by them, their values included faithful service, willingness to risk life and limb, silence at injustice, honesty, stamina, and lack of fear. Cowboying was a young man's job, a challenging, demanding, and exhausting job. It provided exhilarating danger and exciting competition. As Will James commented, "The Cowboy's life can't be learnt in a day or even a year, it's a life you got to be raised at to understand." It was a life which appealed to the youth of America.[31]

On the negative side, however, cowboys were usually those who left the East because they had nothing to lose, and when they came West they found they had nothing to gain. By fencing the ranges and hiring seasonal help, there was less of a need for "labor units,"[32] as the corporate owners euphemistically called the cowboys. These laborers became expendable employees on Western ranches where corporate investors were concerned with the bottom line. Because many young men dreamed of being cowboys, ranchers had an overabundance of workers. Such labor surplus kept the wages low. Wages normally ranged from as low as $15–$20 per month in Texas and the South to as high as $40–$50 per month in the North. The highest wages went to full-time employees, while seasonal workers received as much as thirty percent less. Mexican cowboys, although they often had to train the tenderfeet Easterners, were paid one third to one half what Anglo cowboys were paid. Many Anglo ranchers hired vaqueros because they could pay the Mexicans $10–$12 per month instead of the $20–$25 expected by Anglo cowboys. Cowboys were required to furnish their own saddles, bridles, clothing, and bedrolls. When cowboys "paid $85 for a saddle, $20 for a bridle, $15 for spurs, $15 for a lariat and as much as $85 for a sombrero,"[33] a monthly paycheck did not go far.[34]

Compounding the problem for cowboys and vaqueros both—except, of course, for those on the King and Kenedy Ranches—was the seasonal nature of the work. Since cattle required little care during the winter, cowboys were laid off after the last roundup or cattle drive in the fall. They spent the winter "riding the chuck line"[35] in hopes of a free meal and a place to stay in exchange for chopping wood or doing other menial chores. Some moved in with relatives, others took advantage of ranches where absentee owners might not know of the generous hospitality they were providing. Since these young, improvident cowboys were often paid off in one lump sum for the five or six months of work, the few hundred dollars vanished in a matter of days into the pockets of gamblers, bar owners, and dance hall girls in the towns at the end of the trail. Cowboying did not look so glamorous after several days without food. A few cowboys tried to unionize to protect themselves by demanding year-round wages. Because the ranch owners could replace them almost immediately and often used violence and strike-breakers against them, because cowboys had difficulty getting together for meetings, and because many a young man believed that cowboying was a way of life and not a job, they failed. With no way to protect themselves or demand higher wages, the chances of a cowboy improving himself were almost nonexistent. It was little wonder that many turned to crime.[36]

The experiences of the Kineños on the King Ranch, and the Kenedeños under Sarita East, however, were very different. During the for-
mative years on both ranches, the vaqueros became the backbone of
the ranching operations. By the 1870s they received wages of between
$20 and $25 per month, just like the Anglo cowboys, with a bonus of
$5 a month on the trail drives, and the salary was paid year-round. The
younger boys in the families were also encouraged to earn money by
doing odd-jobs around the camps. The Kineños were not the only Mexicans working on the ranches. Menial jobs were not given to the Kineños
or Kenedeños but to Mexican labor from across the border. During the
years of the Mexican Revolution from 1910 to 1920 and again during the
Depression of the 1930s, both the Klebergs and Sarita East hired needy
Mexicans in search of jobs to dig out the plague of mesquite trees which
had infested the ranches. These Mexicans worked seasonally and many
returned to their homes in Mexico, but the Kineños and Kenedeños
were the elite of the cowboys. Although it is true that all of the top foremen, except Lauro Cavazos, who made foreman in 1926, were Anglo, the
second level of command, the caporales and *mayordomos,* were almost
exclusively Kineños and Kenedeños. In fact, the Mendietta family had
three consecutive generations of caporales. The vaqueros became the
cow bosses and horse bosses on different divisions of the ranch, taking
command, organizing work details, and making decisions. The vaqueros
were given responsibility for, and trusted implicitly with, extensive cattle
and sheep herds, with the prized Santa Gertrudis cattle, with the best of
the cutting and racing horses, with the operation and care of outlying
ranchos. As the story of Abios proves, King had the good sense to place
his entire year's trail herd, an investment of hundreds of thousands of
dollars, under the care of his trusted Kineño. The Kineños and Kenedeños worked hard for their pay, but unlike the Anglo cowboys, they
were never turned out at the end of the season. They were encouraged to
have families, often intermarrying with other Kineños or Kenedeños,
creating a closely knit community in which almost everyone was related
to everyone else. When the men were away, the women knew they could
count on each other and on the *patrona* for help. In their old age, the
men were kept on the payroll and given jobs which still helped the ranch
but allowed the older men to take life a little easier. It was with regret
that the men left the hard work of the round-ups and cattle drives, one
even apologizing for having to die. The men repaid the trust with un-
matched loyalty, and King and Kenedy repaid their loyalty with affection
and cradle-to-grave protection. No other Western cowboys would have
such a life.[37]

The Eastern image of the cowboy was not the Western reality. The Eastern press might view the cowboy as a paragon of virtue, far from the corrupting influence of the big cities, but, unlike Richard King, Western ranch owners usually saw cowboys as lazy, violent, immoral, low-class, lawless, drunken derelicts. The Cattlemen's Associations of Montana and Wyoming kept blacklists of cowboys who were prone to cause problems, and they updated and passed the lists around to their members frequently. Ranch owners warned each other of particularly difficult cowboys. Even cowboys who wanted to improve their lot had little chance to do so. Early Texas ranchers had allowed cowboys to begin their own small herds by branding one out of every four or five calves for themselves in exchange for their work during the roundup. Northern ranch owners, however, soon learned that a hired hand with his own herd could far too easily brand ranch cattle which had been missed during the roundup or alter the brands on his employer's cattle. Association members agreed not to hire cowboys who had their own herds. Ranch owners and lawmen found that the worst thieves and rustlers were often unemployed cowboys who were familiar with the ranges, knew that the cattle would be unattended during the winter, and needed money to survive.

Cowboys also lacked the opportunity to marry or raise a family. In addition to the problem of the limited number of women in the West, cowboys held seasonal jobs, drifting from ranch to ranch. Unemployed during the winter, they had no means to support a wife and family. Married cowboys could not take their wives with them to the ranches, and their pay was not sufficient to buy their own bit of land. And, finally, when a young cowboy was injured or became too old to work, his only options were to work as a cook or horse wrangler. The life of the cowboy, poor as it might be, was not to last.[38]

By 1885, the decline of the cattle boom was already looming and it only took a small nudge from mother nature to push it over the edge. After the panic of 1873 huge potential profits had brought hundreds of new investors into the market both from the eastern United States and from Europe. The overpopulation of cattle on the grasslands had forced the price of beef down from seven cents per pound in 1882 to two cents per pound in 1886. The costs of transportation and feed far outweighed potential profits. The increased number of cattle also had damaged fertile grasslands, and successful ranching now required more acreage, more fencing, and more outlay of capital. Finally, during 1885, with cattle prices already depressed, a drought destroyed much of the grass, forcing owners to send cattle to market early. That winter, terrible blizzards extended across the country and reached far into Texas, killing off thousands of head of cattle, and, in some cases wiping out whole herds along with the investors who owned them. The disasters of 1885–1886 forced hundreds of ranches into receivership and ended the cattle boom. Its demise marked the end of the era of the cowboy.

From this end was born the myth of the Anglo Nordic cowboy. Pulp novelists, authors, and screenwriters cleansed the cowboy of all evil, all sin, and all Hispanic traces, and created an image of the cowboy who was modest, truthful, brave, democratic, and a proud defender of Anglo Manifest Destiny. He appeared first in the form of Owen Wister's Virginian and was followed by thousands of similar apparitions, mirages which supplied a safety valve for the American culture, a John Wayne West where freedom, equality, and democracy for white Anglo males still existed. The American public never knew that vaqueros such as the Kineños and Kenedeños really were the true cowboys, quiet, hardworking, honest, faithful, law-abiding men with courage, stamina, tremendous skill, and a lack of fear.[39]

The King Ranch, under the widowed Henrietta King and her son-in-law, Kleberg, survived the end of the cattle boom by hardscrabble fighting for every dime. Kenedy, who had reinvested his money in ranching, also faced staggering problems. King, like thousands of other ranchers across the West, had over-stocked his ranges. The cattle had destroyed the grass, the drought killed what was left, and the low-growing, scrub-brush mesquite tree began to spread across the ranch and ruin any hope of grazing. King's death in 1885 left Henrietta and Kleberg with the job of pulling the ranch through the drought and the blizzards. They did so by following the ideas first used on the Mexican haciendas. They diversified into horses, sheep, and agriculture, cotton, in particular. They dug water wells to create irrigation for a cotton crop, and the wells saved them from disaster. The discovery of oil on King Ranch in 1939 solidified the ranch's financial position, and while many of the other large Texas ranches were closing their operations, the Klebergs and Kenedys received new business capital through the successful exploitation of their mineral interests. The Klebergs continued improving their cattle breed, eventually producing the Santa Gertrudis, and branched into horse racing and cutting horses.[40]

As for the Kineños, life on the Ranch was certainly good in comparison to the hardships faced by other cowboys across the United States. Their skill and hard work were acknowledged and rewarded by the Klebergs and Kenedys, although it seems surprising that not a single Kineño has ever been recognized or inducted into the National Cowboy Hall of

Fame. Indeed, the only Mexican in the Cowboy Hall of Fame is an Arizona ranch foreman from Sonora named Ramón Ahumada. On the ranch, the Kineños, unlike the drifting cowhands throughout the West, had their families, homes, medical care, schooling for their children, and steady, year-round jobs and paychecks. They preserved their culture, made Spanish the language of the ranch, and they ate their *pan de campo,* tortillas, meat, beans, and rice while other cowboys survived on cornbread, bacon and coffee. The descendants of the Kings and Klebergs and the Kineños created a ranch community which has lasted for five generations. The Kenedeños still exist in the small town of Sarita, and they still retain their pride in being Kenedeños but it is left to the Kineños to carry on a tradition of pride, prestige, and honor at being a Kineño, part of King Ranch, and the first of the cowboys.[41]

NOTES

1. The terms Kineños and Kenedeños are Mexican pronounciations of the words *King* and *Kenedy,* with the addition of the suffix *-eños,* or one who belongs to that person or place.

2. Tom Lea, *The King Ranch* (Boston: Little Brown and Co., 1957), pp. 89–95; Charles H. Harris III, *A Mexican Family Empire: The Latifundio of the Sanchez Navarro Family, 1765–1867* (Austin: University of Texas Press, 1975), pp. 70–75, 185. A debate has raged during the last two decades over whether cattle ranching as it existed in the American West, and in particular in Texas, was more influenced by the Spanish livestock methods or by the British cattle herding techniques introduced into the cowpens of the Carolinas. The leading proponent of the "cowpen school" which supports British influence has been Terry G. Jordan in his work *North American Cattle-Ranching Frontiers: Origins, Diffusion and Differentiation* (Albuquerque: University of New Mexico Press, 1993); and among many others Grady McWhiney and Forrest McDonald, "Celtic Origins of Southern Herding Practices," *Journal of Southern History* Vol. 51 (1985), pp. 165–182. Supporting the Spanish side have been scholars and authors such as Richard W. Slatta, *Cowboys of the Americas* (New Haven: Yale University Press, 1990); and Sandra L. Myres, "The Ranching Frontier: Spanish Institutional Background of the Plains Cattle Industry," in Harold M. Hollingsworth and Sandra L. Myres, eds. *Essays on the American West.* A third view has come from Jerome O. Steffen, *Comparative Frontiers: A Proposal for Studying the American West* (Norman: University of Oklahoma Press, 1980), who suggests that "superficial differences have dominated debate . . . detracting from the more fundamental similarities." (p. 54) He maintains that ranches should be studied as economic, entrepreneurial entities. This argument is one which has been debated in reference to haciendas among Latin America scholars for years (see next footnote).

3. George M. McBride, *The Land Systems of Mexico* (New York: The American Geographical Society, 1923), p. 82; William B. Taylor, *Landlord and Peasant in Colonial Oaxaca* (Stanford: Stanford University Press, 1972), pp. 111, 122, 144, 199; David A. Brading, *Haciendas and Ranchos in the Mexican Bajío: León: 1700–1860* (Cambridge and London: Cambridge University Press, 1978), pp. xi, 3, et passim; Eric Van Young, *Hacienda*

and Market in Eighteenth Century Mexico: The Rural Economy of the Guadaljara Region,
1675–1820 (Berkeley, Los Angeles and London: University of California Press, 1981);
Judith Francis Zeitlin, "Ranchers and Indians on the Southern Isthmus of Tehuantepec:
Economic Change and Indigenous Survival in Colonial Mexico," *Hispanic American
Historical Review* Vol. 69:1 (February 1989), pp. 23–60; Slatta, *Cowboys of the Americas,*
p. 225; Lea, *The King Ranch,* Vol. 1, p. 115 (all further references are to Vol. 1). Lea cannot
be faulted for his assumption that beef production in Mexico was small and local. For
most of the twentieth century, scholars have debated whether the hacienda was merely
feudal, undercapitalized, self-subsistent with a serflike labor force and small agricultural
surplus or whether it was a capitalistic enterprise whose owners were entrepreneurs interested in expanding their profit margin. David A. Brading, in the introduction to his
book *Haciendas and Ranchos* clearly and cogently explains the argument over the economic viability of the hacienda. The resultant scholarship has proved that hacienda owners, even as early as Cortéz, were entrepreneurial and capitalistic in their outlook although they may have also benefited both politically and socially as they used their
wealth to buy positions of political power and negotiated for marriages which helped
them move to prominence in the society.

4. John E. Rouse, *The Criollo: Spanish Cattle in the Americas* (Norman: University of
Oklahoma Press, 1977), pp. 191–192; Steffen, *Comparative Frontiers,* p. 55; William E.
Doolittle, "Las Marísmas to Pánuco to Texas: The Transfer of Open Range Cattle Ranch-
ing from Iberia through Northeastern Mexico," *Yearbook of the Conference of Latin
American Geographers,* Vol. 13(1987), pp. 3–11; Van Young, *Hacienda and Market,* pp. 1, 5;
Taylor, *Landlord and Peasant in Colonial Oaxaca,* p. 121; Lolita Gutiérrez Brockington,
The Leverage of Labor: Managing the Cortés Haciendas in Tehuantepec: 1588–1688 (Dur-
ham and London: Duke University Press, 1989), pp. xviii, xix.

5. Brading, *Haciendas and Ranchos,* p. 10; Steffen, *Comparative Frontiers,* pp. 58,
67–68; Myres, "Ranching Frontiers" in *Essays on the American West,* p. 33; Slatta, *Cowboys of the Americas,* pp. 16, 20; David Dary, *Cowboy Culture: A Saga of Five Centuries*
(New York: Alfred A. Knopf, 1981), p. 7.

6. Brading, *Haciendas and Ranchos,* pp. 4, 5, 6, 12; Brockington, *Leverage of Labor,*
pp. xvi–xvii; McBride, *Land Systems,* pp. 30, 31; Taylor, *Landlord and Peasant,* pp. vii, 131,
149; Michael C. Meyer and William L. Sherman, *The Course of Mexican History* (New
York and Oxford: Oxford University Press, 1983), pp. 130–131, 170; Van Young, *Hacienda
and Market,* p. 2; Slatta, *Cowboys of the Americas,* pp. 20, 107, 226; Charles Gibson, *The
Aztecs Under Spanish Rule: A History of the Indians of the Valley of Mexico, 1519–1810*
(Stanford: Stanford University Press, 1964), pp. 249–255; Jan Bazant, *Cinco Haciendas
Mexicanas: Tres Siglos de Vida Rural en San Luis Potosí: 1600–1910* (México D.F.: El Cole-
gio de México, 1975), pp. 132, 134. Like the haciendas, there have also been debates over
the relative good or evil of the debt peonage system. Scholars such as George McBride in
his *Land Systems of Mexico* argues that hacienda laborers, usually Indian or mestizo
(mixed blood), were trapped on the haciendas by advances on their wages or loans which
they would never be able to repay (pp. 30–31; *see also* Slatta, *Cowboys of the Americas,*
p. 107). Bazant, among others, argues to the contrary—that the advances were not a necessity, but a convenience that the laborers could use or not as they saw fit. Bazant even
argues that peons who lived permanently on the hacienda formed a privileged group
within the workforce of the hacienda much as the Kineños were to do on the King Ranch.

7. Tom Lea (*King Ranch,* p. 123) suggests that the name of the village from which
the Kineños came was "now lost without a trace." Norma Martinez, herself a descendant

of the Kineños, has studied the oral histories and traditions which have been retained among the families. Her research indicates that the Kineños came from the town of Cruillas, (also Cruias or Cruyas) Tamaulipas in Northern Mexico. Martinez describes the location of the town "at the foot of the Sierra Madres . . . go to Laredo and then go southeast of Monterrey four to six hours." Modern maps of Mexico show the town of Cruillas in the approximate location she gives. Tamaulipas and the Escandón colonies were areas where a number of Spanish immigrants settled in the 1740s and from which numerous Mexican settlers, including many among the Martín de León colony in Victoria, moved to the eastern towns of Texas. The settlers from San Antonio, on the other hand, appear to have come from Monterrey, Saltillo, and other inland cities and towns. See Jesús Francisco de la Teja, "Land and Society in Eighteenth Century San Antonio de Bexar: A Community on New Spain's Far Northern Frontier," (Ph.D. diss, University of Texas at Austin, 1988); A. C. Castillo Crimm, "Success in Adversity: the Mexican Americans of Victoria County, 1722–1880," (Ph.D. diss., University of Texas at Austin, 1994).

8. David J. Weber, *The Spanish Frontier in North America* (New Haven and London: Yale University Press, 1992), p. 194; Lea, *King Ranch*, p. 123; Myres, "Ranching Frontiers," in *Essays*, p. 32; Ricki S. Janicek, "Land Titles in Northern Mexico," (Ph.D. diss, Tulane University, 1989) pp. 18–19.

9. Slatta, *Cowboys of the Americas*, pp. 93, 96; Michael Wayne, *The Reshaping of Plantation Society: The Natchez District, 1860–1880* (Baton Rouge: Louisiana State University Press, 1983), pp. 197–198. Like debates over the seigneurial versus economic view of the haciendas, scholars have also debated the relative benefit of patriarchalism on Southern plantations. Writing in the 1930s, U. B. Phillips maintained that slavery was a kindly institution in which slave owners cared for their slaves out of a need for their services. Twenty years later, Kenneth Stampp responded to Phillips in *The Peculiar Institution* with the argument that slavery was a terrible institution in which paternalism was the ultimate form of control, that it destroyed the slaves' African culture and left them as empty vessels to be refilled with American culture. Stanley Elkins, in *Slavery: A Problem in American Institutional and Intellectual Life*, likened plantations to concentration camps where torture and cruelty destroyed slave personalities and left them no more than mindless, shiftless Sambos. By the 1970s, John W. Blassingame, in *The Slave Community*, Eugene Genovese in *Roll, Jordan, Roll: The World the Slaveholders Made*, and Leon Litwack, in *Been in the Storm So Long*, argued that slaves were neither mindless nor deprived of their culture. These authors maintained that slaves had retained their African culture, created strong family ties, maintained their religous independence, created their own music, demanded and frequently received better treatment, and often bought their own or their families' freedom. Some slaves even had their own businesses and owned slaves of their own. Lawrence Levine even argued, in *Black Culture and Black Consciousness*, that slaves created strong, supportive communities in which they could carry on creative, artistic, and even entrepreneurial pursuits. Therefore, patriarchalism, as it related to Southern plantations and the King Ranch, was not necessarily a destructive force but one under which laborers could create their own communities and form protective units of their own.

10. See the Preface to this work.

11. Lea, *King Ranch*, p. 131.

12. Lea, *King Ranch*, pp. 127–131, 150.

13. See Chapter 5, this work.

14. *Corpus Christi Caller-Times, King Ranch: 100 Years of Ranching, 1853–1953* (Corpus Christi, Texas, 1953), p. 99.

15. Slatta, *Cowboys of the Americas*, pp. 98, 222; Lea, *King Ranch*, p. 150; *Caller-Times, King Ranch*, pp. 65, 98–99; McBride, *Land Systems*, pp. 29–30.

16. Meyer and Sherman, *Course of Mexican History*, pp. 285–297, 299–309; Robert Calvert and Arnoldo De León, *The History of Texas* (Wheeling, Ill: Harland Davidson, Inc., 1996), pp. 44–47, 51–53; T. R. Fehrenbach, *Lone Star: A History of Texas and the Texans* (New York: Collier Books, 1968), pp. 119–131; Juan Carlos Garavaglia and Juan Carlos Grosso, "Mexican Elites of a Provincial Town: The Landowners of Tepeaca (1700–1870)," *Hispanic American Historical Review* Vol. 70:2 (May 1990), p. 292; Taylor, *Landlord and Peasant*, p. 122; Slatta, *Cowboys of the Americas*, p. 167.

17. Slatta, *Cowboys of the Americas*, pp. 29, 39, 43, 165–166, 203; see also Crimm, "Success in Adversity," for the court case of Fernando de León who sued and won three cases against the Anglo sheriff and the Victoria town mayor for stopping and frisking de León in the street without just cause.

18. Slatta, *Cowboys of the Americas*, pp. 29, 39, 40–43, 165–166, 173, 203; Lea, *The King Ranch*, pp. 90, 114, 118–119, 124; Marshall W. Fishwick, "The Cowboy: America's Contribution to the World's Mythology," *Western Folklore* Vol. 11:2 (April 1952), pp. 79, 80, 83–84; Mody C. Boatright, "The American Myth Rides the Range: Owen Wister's Man on Horseback," *Southwest Review* Vol. 36:2 (Summer 1951), pp. 162–163; *Caller-Times, The King Ranch*, pp. 64, 98, et passim.

19. Malcolm Ebright, "Introduction: Spanish and Mexican Land Grants and the Law," *Journal of the West* Vol. 27:3 (July 1988), p. 11.

20. Lea, *King Ranch*, p. 104; A. C. Castillo Crimm, *Persistent Community: The Mexican American Community of Victoria, Texas*, forthcoming; see also Armando Alonso's work on the Rio Grande Valley ranches, forthcoming.

21. Calvert and De León, *History of Texas*, p. 54–55; Edward Everett Dale, *The Range Cattle Industry: Ranching on the Great Plains from 1865 to 1925* (Norman: University of Oklahoma Press, 1930, 1960), p. 5; Martín de León papers, General Land Office, Austin, Texas; Archivos de la colonia de Martín de León, Instituto Estatal de Documentación, Saltillo, Coahuila, Mexico; Ramo de Tierras, Tejas, Archivo de la Nación, México, D.F., México.

22. Iris H. W. Engstrand, "An Enduring Legacy: California Ranchos in Historical Perspective," *Journal of the West* Vol. 27:3 (July 1988), p. 43.

23. Galen D. Greaser and Jesús F. De la Teja, "Quieting Title to Spanish and Mexican Land Grants in the Trans-Nueces: The Bourland and Miller Commission, 1850–1852," *Southwestern Historical Quarterly* Vol. 95:2 (April 1992), pp. 450–452, 463–464; Daniel Tyler, "Ejido Lands in New Mexico, *Journal of the West* Vol. 27:3 (July 1988), p. 34; Engstrand, "Enduring Legacy" *Journal of the West* pp. 42–45; Lea, *King Ranch*, p. 101.

24. Fishwick, "The Cowboy," *Western Folklore*, p. 78; Carlos A. Mayo, "Landed but not Powerful: The Colonial Estancieros of Buenos Aires (1750–1810)," *Hispanic American Historical Review* Vol. 71:4 (November 1991), p. 779; Slatta, *Cowboys of the Americas*, p. 25; Steffen, *Comparative Frontiers*, p. 55.

25. Steffen, *Comparative Frontiers*, pp. 57, 69; Dale, *Range Cattle Industry*, pp. 5–6; Myres, "Ranching Frontier," in *Essays on the American West*, p. 22; Boatright, "American Myth," *Southwest Review*, p. 163.

26. Steffen, *Comparative Frontiers*, pp. 53, 55–56; J. C. ("Cap") McNeill, III, *The McNeill's SR Ranch: 100 years in Blanco Canyon* (College Station: Texas A&M University, 1988), pp. ix, 13–14.

27. Boatright, "The American Myth," *Southwest Review*, p. 163.

28. Steffen, *Comparative Frontiers,* pp. 55–56.

29. Fishwick, "The Cowboy," *Western Folklore*, p. 78; Mayo, "Landed but not Powerful," *Hispanic American Historical Review*, p. 779; Slatta, *Cowboys of the Americas*, p. 25; Steffen, *Comparative Frontiers,* pp. 55, 57, 69; Dale, *Range Cattle Industry*, pp. 5, 6; Myres, "Ranching Frontier," *Essays on the American West*, p. 22; Boatright, "American Myth," *Southwest Review*, p. 163.

30. McWhiney and McDonald, "Celtic Origin," *Journal of Southern History*, p. 172.

31. Slatta, *Cowboys of the Americas,* pp. 1, 4, 6, 49, 93, 99, 100, 141, 231; Fishwick, "The Cowboy," *Western Folklore*, p. 78; McWhiney and McDonald, "Celtic Origin," *Journal of Southern History*, p. 172; Dary, *Cowboy Culture*, pp. xi, 13; McNeill, *SR Ranch*, p. 19; Boatright, "American Myth," *Southwest Review*, pp. 157, 159; Will James, *Cowboys North and South* (New York: Charles Scribner's Sons, 1931), pp. viii–ix.

32. Slatta, *Cowboys of the Americas*, p. 68.

33. Louis Pelzer, *The Cattlemen's Frontier: A Record of the Trans-Mississippi Cattle Industry, 1850–1890* (Glendale, CA: The Arthur H. Clark Co., 1936), p. 246.

34. Pelzer, *Cattlemen's Frontier*, pp. 166, 246–247; Slatta, *Cowboys of the Americas*, pp. 82, 101, 166; Dale, *The Range Cattle Industry*, pp. 49–50; Ernest S. Osgood, *The Day of the Cattleman* (Minneapolis: University of Minnesota Press, 1929, 1954), p. 104; McNeill, *SR Ranch*, p. 19.

35. Slatta, *Cowboys of the Americas*, p. 93; McNeill, *SR Ranch*, p. 19.

36. Slatta, *Cowboys of the Americas,* pp. 93, 96–99, 101, 108, 222; Osgood, *Day of the Cattleman*, pp. 104, 148, 150; McNeill, *SR Ranch*, p. 19; Pelzer, *Cattlemen's Frontier*, pp. 246–247; Boatright, "American Myth," *Southwest Review*, p. 158; Dale, *Range Cattle Industry*, p. 49.

37. Slatta, *Cowboys of the Americas,* pp. 39, 166; Nora E. Ramirez, "The Vaquero and Ranching in the S. W. United States, 1600–1970," Ph.D. diss. Indiana University, 1970, pp. 70–75, 104–105, 135.

38. Boatright, "American Myth," *Southwest Review*, p. 158; Slatta, *Cowboys of the Americas*, pp. 28, 46, 93, 97, 99, 221, 229; Osgood, *Day of the Cattleman*, pp. 148, 150, 229; Dale, *Range Cattle Industry*, p. 49; Pelzer, *Cattlemen's Frontier*, p. 277.

39. Steffen, *Comparative Frontiers,* pp. 66–67; Fishwick, "The Cowboy," *Western Folklore*, pp. 78, 80–82, 91; McNeill, *SR Ranch*, p. 19; Slatta, *Cowboys of the Americas*, p. 221; Boatright, "American Myth," *Southwest Review*, p. 157.

40. See Chapter 2, this work.

41. Slatta, *Cowboys of the Americas*, p. 93; Steffen, *Comparative Frontiers,* pp. 66–67; Zeitlin, "Rancheros and Indians," *Hispanic American Historical Review*, p. 23.

NOTE: For purposes of clarification, the authors use "Ranch" (capitalized) to refer to the King and Kenedy Ranches, and "ranch" (lowercase) to refer to all other ranches. Kineños and Kenedeños refer to people who worked at various jobs on the Ranches and who became valued participants in their operations, usually for generations. Some were vaqueros working the cattle and some were family members or other workers. Not all vaqueros were Kineños and Kenedeños, and not all Kineños and Kenedeños were vaqueros.

Round 'Em Up, Move 'Em Out

Since the founding of the King and Kenedy Ranches in the mid-nineteenth century, the greatest challenges have been to locate, round up, and brand cattle, the basic activities of the ranching industry. They consume more of the effort and skill of the rancher than any other endeavors, for they represent the process whereby the Ranch's product is made ready for market. King and Kenedy had no prior experience in ranching. Vaqueros came from an established tradition of working cattle and horses, and, because of their knowledge, were chosen by King and Kenedy for this vital work from the time the Ranches were established.

When King first came to the Wild Horse Desert in 1852, the cattle ran free, many of them wild Longhorns. Unmarked cattle could be claimed by placing a brand on them. Possession really was nine-tenths of the law. Rustling abounded, especially by bandits from across the border, and many cattle were lost each year both to rustlers and to the hardships of the land.

At first, these Longhorns were valued not for their meat, but for their hides and tallow (fat). Large barns were constructed to slaughter these animals after they were rounded up, and the hides and tallow were sold and shipped east, often from Corpus Christi or Brownsville, Texas.

Captains Kenedy and King were friends and business associates for years before King established his Ranch at Santa Gertrudis in 1853, and the partnership was to continue. In 1860, Kenedy bought in to the Santa Gertrudis acreage. Soon Kenedy and King began bringing in finer lines of cattle, particularly British breeds, to upgrade the quality of their cattle and to increase their market value. In 1868, Kenedy sold his interest in Santa Gertrudis and purchased Laureles Ranch at Flower Bluff, Texas. He owned Laureles until 1882, when he sold it to a Scottish syndicate and purchased La Parra, which means grapevine. The Ranches have continued in a close association ever since.

King and Kenedy and Their Quest

When Captain Mifflin Kenedy established the La Parra Ranch in the dusty, hot, deserted Wild Horse Desert, he put together thousands of acres of ranch land for himself. He also acted as business mentor, friend, and sometime associate to Captain Richard King, who started the mammoth King Ranch located both north and south of the Kenedy Ranch. Even though the two men, who were both highly intelligent, were partners in Santa Gertrudis at one time, they were dissimilar in nature. Still, they forged a remarkable friendship that survived two wars, bandit treachery, droughts, floods, and swiftly changing political scenes.

King was generally unschooled, except through experience. He was apprenticed as a jeweler in Manhattan at age nine, and at age eleven he slipped aboard as a stowaway on a ship headed for Mobile, Alabama. He would spend his early life becoming expert at steamboating, his first profitable venture. Though he was considered to be a rough man, he was known to possess an excellent business sense combined with great vision. To conceive of building King Ranch in the Wild Horse Desert is an obvious example of his farsightedness (Cheeseman 1994, 89).

In contrast to King's brawny build and gregarious nature, Kenedy was of small frame with a somewhat prim disposition. Born in Chester County, Pennsylvania, of Quaker parents, Kenedy was educated in a Quaker school and was, for a brief time, a teacher. A few years later, while working steamers in Florida, he met Richard King (*Corpus Christi Caller*, September 23, 1984).

The Demand for Beef

After the Civil War, there was an enormous demand for beef in eastern cities. Entrepreneurs, like King and Kenedy, saw a fortune to be made moving their great herds up the trails to Sedalia, Missouri, and, later, up trails to Abilene and Dodge City, Kansas. Animals that could be purchased in 1870 for as little as $11 a head in Texas could be sold for twice that price in Abilene, and double the Abilene price in Chicago (Lea 1957, 1:297).

Sometimes King bought cattle from other ranchers in the area, then, with his own cattle, sent them "up the trail." Julian Buentello of King Ranch related the following story:

Captains Richard King (left) and Mifflin Kenedy were friends and business partners. King established Rancho Santa Gertrudis in 1853 (King Ranch) and Kenedy established La Parra in 1882 (Kenedy Ranch). They were leaders in the founding of the American cattle industry. Courtesy of King Ranch Archives, King Ranch, Inc.

In the 1870s and 1880s, there was a pasture with some old pens where all the cattle people would bring their cattle together before they started up the trail. They weeded out the cattle they didn't want, and then the Captain [King] would buy what he wanted, and they would put the cattle together to take up the trail. There were hold[ing] pens in the pasture. One time lightning struck and killed many of the cattle before they could start the drive. I remember stories of trees with slick wire around them where the pens used to be.

Antonia Quintanilla Buentello of King Ranch remembered hearing similar stories:

I remember stories from my father. They would herd the cattle to a central pasture called the partida *[cattle drive holding pen] where they would be divided. This was in the 1870s and 1880s. He said they would have to herd the cattle at night to keep them together. They worked shifts. All the cattlemen would bring their cattle to the* partida *on the Ranch. The Captain [King] made the decision which went on the trail, which to slaughter, which to send back. He bought the ones he wanted to go on the trail.*

The Trails, Both Far and Near

We had to keep the cattle quiet at night. . . . and I liked to sing.
George "Chorche" Mayorga (King Ranch)

During the time of the trail drives, Captain King sent cattle numbering in the tens of thousands up the trail to these markets. The April 12, 1933, issue of the *Kingsville Record,* under its "Fifty Years Ago" column, reprinted an 1883 story that told of the annual spring cattle drive of King Ranch that was underway with eighteen thousand head of cattle.

King sometimes hired private contractors to take his herds north. At times, his own Kineños were chosen to work the drives up these troublesome trails. Ramón Alvarado was one of those men in whom King had great confidence. Ramón "made many trips with herds to the North as boss, and continued to do so up to the year 1880" (Alvarado 1937, 6). John Fitch, King's foreman at his Agua Dulce Ranch, was one of his contractors. Fitch's account book details expenditures during a drive of approximately five thousand steers to Abilene, Kansas, in the spring of 1875. Fitch was given no salary, but he and his partner, A. C. Allen, signed a contract with King in which King paid Fitch and Allen $12 a head and agreed to split the profits from the sale of the cattle, with King taking 50 percent. Fitch and Allen realized about $5,000 each, and King cleared about $50,000. The vaqueros on the drive were paid at least $25 a month, considerably more than the $10 to $15 a month they received on the Ranch (Young 1992, 42).

Ramón Alvarado was one of the first vaqueros on King Ranch. He helped his father build the first jacales on the Ranch in 1854. In the 1880s Ramón was one of the cow bosses.

On another occasion around 1882, King contracted with a man named North to take cattle up the trail. When North encountered difficulty and the cattle stampeded, King dispatched Ramón Alvarado with his *remuda* (a group of fifteen to twenty-five horses used to work cattle) by train to Corpus Christi. From there, the remuda and their supply wagons were loaded on the train, thereby arriving on the trail as quickly as possible to round up the remaining cattle.

King made many trips up the trail as he moved beef to these northern markets. Many stories have been told of the challenges and romance of life on the trails, but seldom has the business basis of these drives been noted. During the thirty years following the American Civil War, 5,800,000 cattle, 1,000,000 horses, and 35,000 men went up the trails from Texas (Lea, "The Mighty Ranch of Richard King," 42).

The *corridas* on the Kenedy Ranch also made several *partidas* in the mid-1880s. They, as well as *corridas* of King Ranch, usually drove the animals to Alice, Texas, then contracted with other crews to take them north; however, several times the Kenedy crews took them all the way to Kansas. On one such drive, one of the vaqueros, Martín Acuña, drowned while crossing the river. "Acuña was pushing the cattle across the river, when suddenly he and his horse disappeared under the water. The horse came up, but the vaquero did not" (Villarreal 1972, 21).

In *Cow People,* J. Frank Dobie recounted a fictitious story based on a characterization of one of the famous vaquero families, the Alvarados. The story of Abios illustrates why Captain King's ultimate trust was always with his own Kineños to bring his herds safely up the trail. Dobie's story related that, in the spring of 1880, King had a herd "shaped up" to go up the trail to Dodge City, Kansas. Abios was late. Finally three days had passed. Still no Abios. Young Richard King II was very impatient and wanted to know why his father, the Captain, was waiting on that old drunk. Finally, Abios showed up, and he took charge of a herd worth thousands of dollars.

Captain King and his son went on ahead to Kansas to await the herds. As the other trail bosses arrived in Kansas, the Captain would ask them how the trail had been. The first trail boss reported that he had trouble at Cimmaron, and some of his cattle had drowned. The second trail boss replied, when asked, that it had rained and stormed through the Indian territory, and he had lost some cattle in a stampede. The third trail boss said that the Indians had run off his horses. Several days later Abios arrived. Captain King asked him how his drive had been. He said, "Oh *muy bien, Señor.* No trouble at all. We came along *despacio, despacio,* slow, slow. I picked up 130 King Ranch cattle lost out of other herds. We are 130 cattle long. Look how the cattle have gained in weight. Look how contented they are." Captain King turned to Richard and said, "Now do you know why I wait for Abios?" (Dobie 1964, 219–222).

Mifflin Kenedy, like King, counted on his sons to help him on the trail drives. After working in New Orleans, John Gregory Kenedy (born

1856) returned home to help his father on cattle drives to Fort Dodge, Kansas. Another of Kenedy's sons rode the trails also.

In the summer of 1878, James W. "Spike" Kenedy was completing a trail drive from his father's ranch to Dodge City, Kansas. Because of his attention to a dance hall girl named Dora Hand (alias Fannie Keenan), he was thrown out of a saloon by James H. "Dog" Kelly, who owned the saloon and was also the third-term mayor of Dodge City. Kenedy left Dodge City but then returned on October 4 in the middle of the night and fired a gun into Kelly's house with the evident intent of killing him. Kelly was out of town, but two of the dance hall girls were in the house. The bullets missed one of the girls, but killed the second, Dora Hand. James fled the town and was pursued by a posse sent out to track down the killer. On his trail were Bat Masterson, Wyatt Earp, and Charles Bass, three of the most famous lawmen in the West. Kenedy was shot in the arm, captured, and returned to Dodge City to stand trial. His father, Mifflin Kenedy, got the news and hurried to Dodge City. The charges were dropped. James died in 1884 at the age of twenty-nine (*Corpus Christi Caller*, September 24, 1984.)

The legendary trail rides to the great northern markets finally ended around 1885 following the invention of barbed wire in 1872. This single invention virtually closed the open range. The railroad became the cattleman's salvation. The struggle to get the railroad into South Texas was a great one, and its realization changed forever the future of the Wild Horse Desert. The railroad solved the problem of getting cattle to market, and it enabled the Rio Grande Valley to become a viable supplier of vegetables and fruits, as well as cattle, for markets in the rest of the nation.

The King and Kenedy Ranches soon built large shipping pens. King Ranch built theirs, called the Caesar Pens, near Kingsville, and other pens were built at points up and down the railroad lines, some located at communities named for King family members, such as Alice and Ricardo (Richard). These two Ranches were as big as some states; the December 1933 issue of *Fortune* magazine reported that King Ranch was larger than the state of Rhode Island and four-fifths the size of the state of Delaware. Roundups still took weeks to complete. Cattle would be gathered at these pens for shipping during the next sixty years.

We brought Mexican steers—Longhorns—from near Rio Grande City to the Kenedy Ranch. Mexican Longhorns are smaller and meaner [than most cattle]. It took a week. We used two or three horses a day. There were two hundred horses in the remuda.

Sometimes we had camp set up, sometimes we slept in the open. We used pens built along the way.

A group of vaqueros went ahead and got permission to cross the plains and use water wells and holes. We would string them [the cattle] out and water about twenty at a time. The cattle ate grass on the trail. We would stop every two or three hours to graze them. The dust was bad. We used bandannas and rotated sides for the wind. New guys got the bad side.

The Ranch furnished all our equipment. My father had to buy all of his. He was paid seventy-five cents a day. It was in the 1930s in the Depression and it was [considered] a good job. Housing, food, and school were free. Enemorio Serna (Kenedy Ranch)

The cattle were like Santa Gertrudis, commercial. It would take about a month to drive cattle from the Ranch to San Antonio. Seferino Gutierrez (Kenedy Ranch)

I helped drive cattle. When we got to the Ranch we placed the cattle in corrals. When the cattle were going to be shipped, there was a man who came with the wagons. He brought like forty or fifty wagons. There were like twenty to twenty-eight cows in each wagon. The wagons took the cattle to the train. Nicolas Rodríguez (King Ranch)

George Mayorga of King Ranch described his experience:

We brought the cattle from Santa Rosa to Alice. We had to keep the cattle quiet at night and guard them around, and I liked to sing. I would sing "Stila Song," "The Purple Bull," and others. The cattle liked it. Kleberg liked "El Rancho Grande."

I play the harmonica. I played it around the chuck wagon—songs like "Una Noche" and "Alissia." Everybody sang. I was the only one with a harmonica. My father bought it for me. He played, too. He was a cowboy and worked on all sections. I taught myself to play. My son has my harmonica.

The early Kineños also served as guards for Captain King during the days when he traveled on the road between the Ranch, Corpus Christi, and Brownsville. He often took four or five armed vaqueros with him. Stagecoach camps were set up at twenty-mile intervals with guarded corrals of fast horses and strong mules in case there was trouble and fresh mounts were needed. Nicolas Rodríguez remembered stories about those camps being located on the Ranch. The Kineños accompanied King when he carried the payroll, which could amount to as much as $50,000. He transported it in a secret steel box built into his road coach.

These loyal vaqueros also took good care of King's family. During the 1870s, the family made many trips to San Antonio. King's daughter, Alice, remembered fondly the campfires by the road at night and the guard of armed Kineños. She remembered the rumble of the moving wheels of the King Ranch wagon train, paced by the statuesque outriders sweeping through high grass on fast horses with manes and tails flowing (Lea 1957, 1:326).

Faustino Villa was a vaquero whose loyalty to the King family was legendary. He was a deckhand for Captain King while King was running *Colonel Cross,* his steamboat purchased for $750, on the Rio Grande. At one hundred years of age, Faustino swam a half-mile across the flooded Santa Gertrudis Creek to deliver the mail to El Abogado (the lawyer), Robert Kleberg.

Villa refused to accept a pension from the Ranch. His explanation was: "When Faustino Villa gets so he can't earn grub, he'll be ready to go." He got his wish and remained on the payroll, riding horseback until two weeks before his death (Lea 1957, 2:785).

The following story about Ignacio Alvarado further illustrates this dedication to the King family. After Captain King died, his son-in-law, Robert Justus Kleberg, was managing the estate. Ignacio was still the caporal and was late to take charge of a herd and move it. Two days went by. Finally, Ignacio's son appeared and said, "My father says to tell you he was sorry he could not come. He had to die" (Lea 1957, 2:515).

"On March 20, 1875, the Kineños met the ultimate test. An Army telegram . . . was relayed by General W. T. Sherman to Secretary of War Belknaps stating that King's Ranch was surrounded by a large party of Mexican bandits asking for aid. Border tales related that the raiders were attacked and were given a good beating by the Kineños with some of the raiders being hung" (Lea 1957, 1:271–272, 277).

In March 1916, the bandits again crossed the Rio Grande to raid the Kenedy and King Ranches and other ranches. The Klebergs were warned that the bandits had captured family member Alice East at San Antonio Viejo and had not harmed her, but that they were in the area. Bob Kleberg had high-powered rifles and ammunition carried to the roof of the Main House at Santa Gertrudis. He issued guns to the Kineños to defend the Rancho (Lea 1957, 2:589). On a humorous note, some of the older interviewees remembered that many of the men didn't know how to fire those guns.

The Kenedy Ranch, also, was fortunate to have dedicated, dependable employees. The September 26, 1984, *Corpus Christi Caller* reported that "cowboys and locked gates still guarded the family and their cherished privacy."

Sometimes the owners were required to protect themselves:

Mifflin Kenedy, the quiet Quaker, was asked to command a citizens' group in February of 1860 to protect the citizens from an invasion by Juan Cortina. The citizen army was called "The Brownsville Tigers." As a verification of the rough and tumble times, Kenedy wore a thirty-pound bulletproof vest. . . . A story is also told that, on one of her trips between Corpus Christi and Brownsville in a custom-built Concord stagecoach, Mrs. Kenedy [Petra Vela] was guarded by armed vaqueros. While the party was sleeping under a thicket of mesquite trees, they were awakened by rustling in the brush. Mrs. Kenedy asked, "*Quien viene?*" ["Who goes there?"] The *bandidos* replied, "*Paisanos*" [fellow countrymen] and stepped out of the bushes. Captain Kenedy responded "*pasé*," meaning to enter. Mrs. Kenedy jumped up from the floor of the stagecoach and said, "No, no, you mean to retire, not to enter." Then she looked at the bandits and recognized one, and told them firmly to go away because she recognized one of them and, when she got to Brownsville, she would tell his mother. (*Corpus Christi Caller,* September 23, 1984)

Petra Vela Kenedy had a mud wagon, or a horse-drawn coach, for her journeys from La Parra in Kenedy County to Corpus Christi, seventy-five miles away. The coach bore the same crest that Mrs. Kenedy had placed on her china. The heavy-duty passenger coach was once popular because of its durability and because the unsurfaced roads often splattered mud on the coaches (*Corpus Christi Caller-Times,* December 18, 1992). Petra Kenedy's mud wagon is now on display at the Corpus Christi Museum of Science and History in Corpus Christi, Texas.

José María Morales was one of the most trusted Kenedeños. He was a *mayordomo* (boss) of supply wagons, a caporal, and, because of his knowledge of the area, he often served as a guide to those unfamiliar with the pastures. He was even trusted with taking the Ranch payroll from San Antonio, where the Ranch conducted banking transactions, to La Parra. Though he was followed and had some close calls, José was always armed and was never successfully robbed (Villareal 1972, 19–20).

Though many of the vaqueros worked as armed guards at times, their primary function was to take care of the cattle.

The Workforce

This is where most of the boys learned . . . by helping to throw cows. Martín Mendietta Jr. (King Ranch)

The Kineños and Kenedeños possessed skills acquired over several generations. They provided almost all of the labor for the development of these Ranches. There was a well-defined chain of command; the workforce was disciplined and highly organized so that every vaquero knew exactly where he fit into the work structure. There was considerable trust between the workers and the owners. This trust was fostered by the owners' practice of treating the workers as individuals. In return, the owners received reliable work (Villarreal 1972, 75).

The number of vaqueros in a *corrida* (the basic cattle work unit) varied from about ten to thirty men. The work was divided between the remuda (horses), the *corrida,* and jobs not directly involving animals, such as brush clearing, windmill repairing, fence mending, and general repairs. The owner–family member was the chief administrator. Each division on both the Kenedy and King Ranches had a cow camp and a "workers on foot" section, those who did not work from horseback. The cow camp section had a caporal (boss) and a *caudillo* (second in command to a caporal). The vaqueros who worked with or on animals were directly under the caporal's command. The workers in the foot section had a *mayordomo* (boss), a *segundo* (second in command to a *mayordomo*), and from ten to twenty-five men in labor crews. The *corrida* also had a *remudero* (worker in charge of horses) and a *cocinero* (cook). The caporales and *los mayordomos,* some of whom were fifth- and sixth-generation vaqueros, had direct responsibility for getting the work done. In key positions, they were expected to exhibit leadership, skill, and knowledge and usually to possess some ability to read and write. They also had the authority to fire a worker who was unable to handle the job or who did not work (Villarreal 1972, 32, 46, 65).

The caporales on the Kenedy Ranch were Anglo family members

and extended family members until about 1916, when Lucio Salinas followed Edgar Turcotte as caporal of one of the *corrida*s (Villarreal 1972, 66). At about the same time, Lauro Cavazos had become the first Mexican American to hold the position on the Santa Gertrudis Division of King Ranch.

Jesse Salazar, a Kenedeño in the 1950s, mused: "The life of a vaquero is very interesting, almost romantic, never dull, but not one to make a man rich."

During the Great Depression, Kenedeños were paid $.50 a day, or about $15.00 a month. By 1960, they were being paid $90.00 a month, and by 1972, $125.00 a month. Housing and some food were also provided (Villarreal 1972, 44).

The working situation of the Kenedeños and the Kineños, who frequently became permanent residents of the Ranches, was quite different from that of the common laborers from Mexico, who were transients. Many of these migrants, sometimes hundreds at a time, worked clearing brush in the early 1900s. The vaqueros, on the other hand, were secure in the knowledge that at least they and their families would be housed and fed. Their situation was more advantageous (Currie 1915, 3).

Even so, owners and workers sometimes had difficulty getting along with each other. Mrs. Sarita East at La Parra Ranch had a reputation for showing kindness to the workers, and she often worked alongside them. A story in the September 26, 1984, *Corpus Christi Caller* recounts that Sarita East supplied the brains to the Ranch operations, and the heart. "If somebody had a problem, they knew where to go. She paid to get the babies born, bury the dead, and feed the hungry. She was called the *Madrina*—godmother—because it seemed she always had something for the children."

Reports by some of Sarita East's workers about her administrators were sometimes different, though. On one occasion, Edgar Turcotte, a caporal with the *corrida*s, and José María Morales had a dispute about a saddle. The Ranch rule was that each vaquero was required to furnish his own saddle. John Gregory Kenedy Sr. had given the saddle to José, who was reluctant to turn it back to Turcotte on demand. In fact, Morales said he'd "rather turn in his job than his saddle." He appealed to "Don Gregorio," and was not only allowed to keep his saddle, he also received a pair of untamed mules to keep him happy (Villarreal 1972, 71). Though disputes were usually settled by the immediate boss, longtime vaqueros would sometimes appeal to the owners.

On King Ranch, the cattle grazed on large pastures of eight to ten thousand acres; the largest pasture on the Norias Division of King Ranch was about sixty thousand acres. Fifteen to twenty cowboys made up this *corrida*. On the Norias Division they would spend the week before roundup day riding the dunes, searching the low, thick vegetation, including the mesquite and oak mottes, for the elusive cattle. The *corrida* would scour the prickly pear from early morning until dark, locating and bringing in the herd. The cattle were often "lost" or hiding in this thick brush, posing a frustrating challenge to those responsible for bringing them to the place where they would begin the long trail to market, and, later on, to shipping pens or to the Ranch breeding headquarters. No animals were to be left behind. They represented dollars on the hoof. In fact, cattle were not even killed for fresh meat on the trail unless they were injured. A complete roundup was also a matter of pride with the vaqueros.

One fact was in the vaqueros' favor: cattle have a social structure. They usually belong to a small group with an older cow or bull as its leader. They stay together, away from the others, and water together in the same place every day. So if a group of cattle could be found watering at one of the tanks, every member of that group could be corralled at one time into a holding pen. Some of the more seasoned cows knew how to hide from the *corrida* and would lie down in thickets or depressions until the *corrida* had ridden past. The vaquero *literally* had to learn to "think like a cow." This contest between man and beast occurred twice a year. All the skills, cunning, and physical strength the vaquero could muster were needed to outwit these animals and complete the task. Julian Buentello recalled:

> When we got ready to round up a pasture, we would start off at a fast lope and drop the men off around the cattle in a big circle. When they were all in place, we would holler one to the other, and then we would start running the cattle into the wind because it was cooler. It would take most of the morning. Then the men with the lead steers would rope them, and the rest would follow us to the pens or to the rest of the herd. We would then cut the cattle out and drive those to the shipping pens that were going to be shipped. There were nine sets of pens on the Santa Gertrudis Division.
>
> During a large roundup, we would have to ride the herds at night to keep them calm. We would take the cattle to holding traps and work until the pasture was clear. Then we would send a message to the boss that the cattle were ready. He would come, and we would cut the cattle.

The Work Was Brutal

Maybe the sun wasn't quite up when we started, but it sure was down when we quit. Daniel Morales (Kenedy Ranch)

The hours were long and often left little time or energy for recreation or other pursuits. On the Kenedy Ranch, the workday generally started about 4:00 in the morning and ended at approximately 8:00 in the evening. The work week extended from Sunday evening to the next Saturday evening. Gradually the hours were shortened. By the 1950s, the regular day started at sunup and was over by 5:00 or 6:00 in the evening, and the vaqueros were finished by noon on Saturday (Villarreal 1972, 47).

As on King Ranch, some of the vaqueros on the Kenedy Ranch worked after dark, taking turns watching the cattle. The work was strenuous.

We used to wake up very early and ate lunch around 4:00 P.M. One worked all day. After sunset, around 8:00 or 9:00 P.M., they brought the cattle to be held. We stayed up very late at night and woke up before sunrise. We worked very, very hard in that time. Today it is not like that—everything is easier and nicer.

There were no camping houses then. We used two tents. That was the hardest job for me, because I had to do all the job of fixing the tents, picking them up, folding the beds, and putting everything in the cars. We had beds made of bull skin—I made one myself.

The tents were very heavy, the worst when they were wet. It sometimes took lots of time to go from one place to another, because there was too much to carry, and nobody wanted to help me carry everything. Don Ubenze, my father-in-law, was the only one to help me sometimes. I really worked hard there.

We washed our clothes ourselves at night. Sometimes we wore the clothes wet the next day. There were some men who would just wait longer to wash, or, if not, until they got home.

At first I got paid $12 a month. That was in 1913 or 1914. Then $15 and then $18 a month. Today it is much better. Nicolas Rodríguez (King Ranch)

When we worked the cattle, we took bedrolls. We ate [breakfast] and saddled the horses by 5:00 or 5:30 A.M. We brought cattle from maybe eight or ten miles away. Then we had lunch. We separated the cattle and branded [them] after lunch. We could brand one hundred [head of cattle] per hour. We worked in threes in case one wanted to rest. Manuel Silva Sr. (King Ranch)

Bedtime was 9:00. After supper we slept. We slept in tents on the ground. We put salt grass on the ground during cold weather and slept under the saddle blanket. Our saddle was our headrest. The tents blocked the wind and rain. Jesus Gonzales (Kenedy Ranch)

I slept at camp on the ground in tents or in the camp house for about twenty-five years. Wagons pulled by six mule teams would bring the supplies and bedrolls. Enemorio Serna (Kenedy Ranch)

The Kenedeños slept in the open and did not use any type of shelter in the camps until the 1920s. Faustino Morales remembered using canvas to protect himself against the winter elements of cold and rain. Living conditions were still harsh, even after tents were issued. There was no heat in winter except for the campfire, and no cooling for the hot summers. Facilities for personal hygiene were almost always lacking (Villarreal 1972, 42).

Moving to the right pen or pasture was a challenge on the huge spreads comprising thousands of acres. According to Leonard Stiles, a former cow boss at the Santa Gertrudis Division, the vaquero Julian Buentello could always be counted on to be in the right place with the lead steers. The men would head down a trail or creek bed and turn their cattle to stay with Julian because he would know the way. "He was a natural navigator," said Stiles. "He could always navigate. He always knew where the fences and gates were, even at night. His son, Raul, had the same sense of direction. His father and grandfather did, too."

Martín Mendietta Jr., of both the King and Kenedy Ranches, is a fifth-generation vaquero and an expert on horses and range operations. His family members have been caporales on the Ranches for years; he followed his father as head of the cow outfit at the Santa Gertrudis Division. Martín described a typical day during roundup:

5:00 A.M. Get up, saddle up, and at light round up the cattle. Have a cup of coffee and maybe a piece of camp bread with beans in it. Didn't want a lot in our stomach.

To round up the pasture, we would lope around the pasture and post people all around at different locations. We would start moving the cattle. When we saw the man next to us, then we would move our group.

8:30–9:00 After we got the cattle to where we wanted them, we took turns going in to eat breakfast while other vaqueros would hold the herd. They would have set the chuck wagon up where the cattle were to be worked, and breakfast would be ready. Breakfast was eggs, beans, bread, and coffee. After breakfast we would separate the old cows and the dry cows and cut them out. We watered the rest of the herd, and the old and dry cows were moved to the corral to be shipped. When finished, we came back to the chuck wagon for lunch.

12:00 At lunch we had good meat—beef. We would kill a calf for lunch. The boss would cut out a spotted heifer—one that had white above her belly line could not be classified as a Santa Gertrudis. She would be dinner. There would be thirty to fifty people or more. We had the *corrida,* cooks, family, and visitors, and people who came from headquarters and other sections of the Ranch. They cooked ribs, steak, liver, intestines, guts, and kidneys. Also stew. They took iceboxes, and sometimes used the meat the next day. The men would sometimes cut off some of the leftover meat and take it home to their families when they started going in each night.

After lunch. In the hot summer, we worked again at about 2:30 or 3:00 P.M. The wind would come up from the south off Baffin Bay. We would get the fire hot and get the brands ready. Then we would rope and heel. We worked nine cattle at a time and would rope, throw them, brand, and vaccinate, and run them back to the herd, or separate them from their mothers and put them in a separate area. We put the newly weaned calves with an older cow with a bell on her neck. We would throw three to four hundred in an afternoon.

Mr. Bob would cut out a cow with horns that had grown wrong and we would heel her, throw her, and the boys would pile on her and use a wire device, or a small meat saw, to cut her horns. We worked 'til it was too dark to see.

This is where most of the boys learned. They started by helping to throw cows. I started this way with my Dad [Martín Mendietta Sr.].

Day's End. Supper was usually eggs, rice, meat, bread, and they made it different each day. Before we began going home at night, we slept at the camp house. We brought sleeping bags and rolled them out. Sometimes we sang songs like "The Purple Bull" and about wild horses and mean horses that we had ridden. Or we played dice, poker, and dominoes until 9:00 or 10:00. Then at 5:00 A.M. we were up again.

Leonard Stiles added the following perspective to roundups on King Ranch:

Martín was excellent with a knife, in castrating. Only one man would castrate, one would brand, and one would tattoo and that way we knew who was responsible if it didn't go right.

No one wanted to carry the bucket with the lime and grease in it. The men used a brush and put the mixture on new brands or any wound to keep down infection.

One man carried a bucket for testicles. They would put them in a sack and divide them at the end of the day to take home. They also cooked them at the camp and ate them.

Ghosts on the Wild Horse Desert

A lady appeared in a white gown and followed me. Jesus Gonzales (Kenedy Ranch)

The Kineños and Kenedeños possess a rich multicultural heritage that is heavily influenced by their Spanish and American Indian ancestry. Colorful stories steeped in these cultures have been passed from generation to generation. The Kineños, like their ancestors, have vivid imaginations fostered by long hours spent mostly alone on horseback on King Ranch's 825,000 acres. The Kineños seem readily to accept the existence of the supernatural (Neely 1993, 5). Lonely hours on the range often lead to ghostly sightings. As Seferino Gutierrez claimed, "A ghost accompanied me to the next ranch many times, step for step."

Yes, there are ghosts. A man dressed in black appeared on the way to my father-in-law's house many times. A lady appeared in a white gown and followed me 'til I finally lost her. I also saw a lady in a white gown with hair to her waist. I followed her, and she disappeared.

We would see campfires in the distance in the early morning and, when we got there, there would be nothing.

There was a man dressed in black by the water tower who would appear and disappear.

On another ranch, I saw a fire three or four feet high. I would ride to it and find only ashes, nothing apparent to burn. Jesus Gonzales (Kenedy Ranch)

There was a ghost story at Laureles. Where the colony is now there used to be a pasture near House #36 where there would appear a headless horseman.

    Another story is that there was a gentleman who found a bone in the Ojo de Agua Pasture and he took it home, and a lady dressed in white appeared to him and asked him to put her son back. Ofelia M. Longória (King Ranch)

We had a camp house on the prairie, and we could hear a man in the house walking around with his spurs. One night a man grabbed a cowboy by the neck with his hands, and we all left. Enemorio Serna (Kenedy Ranch)

Tools of Their Trade

Throughout the history of American ranches, certain tools have been critical for the work of the vaqueros, and it was the vaqueros themselves who developed most of these tools, along with techniques for their use.

THE VAQUERO'S HORSE—KEY TO SUCCESS

Next to the vaquero's skill in using his rope, his horse was the most critical element in the success of the roundup. The King Ranch Quarter Horse was so named because of its reputation for speed when running one-fourth of a mile. It was bred and perfected to perform nimble cuts and turns to head off any calf trying to hightail it back to the brush. This ability of a vaquero's horse to turn on a dime guaranteed the vaquero dominion over any bovine.

THE REMUDA

The job of *remudero* was a responsible one, because horses were so important to the work. As in the herds of cattle, the remuda had a leader, and this dominant horse was often fitted with a bell around its neck. Just at dawn, the lead horse would bring the others to water at a circular concrete trough, about thirty feet in diameter, that was filled by a nearby windmill. The men would stand in the center of the pen with their lariats held by their sides, and the horses would begin circling the pen counterclockwise. The cowboys would select one of their horses (each had several in the remuda to use during the day) and throw their lariat over the horse's head. The animal was trained to stop and wait for the vaquero. The horse was then taken to be saddled and was ready to go to work (Cypher 1995, 28).

> *Every cowboy had twenty-five horses. We had a horse caretaker. We would change horses every two or three hours to rest the animals.* Jesus Gonzales (Kenedy Ranch)

> *Each man rode several horses in a day—one to roundup, one to work cattle, another to ride back to the ranch. Different horses were used to ride the brush. We kept the good horses out of the brush. We wore chaps and brush jackets.* Seferino Gutierrez (Kenedy Ranch)

> *I had twelve horses, some old, some young. When I got in the co-*rrida, *each cowboy gave me a horse. There were many cowboys and others who got the best horses. They gave me the oldest horses, the ones that could not even gallop any more. Afterwards, when I started taming horses, I could choose the horses I wanted, and I could get good ones.* Nicolas Rodríguez (King Ranch)

> *The work was tough—chasing wild cattle in the brush. Now everything hurts in the morning.*
>
> *You gave the horse who knew the most to the young kid so he could learn from the horse. He just had to stay on and the horse would move the animal.* Martín Mendietta Jr. (King/Kenedy Ranches)

The brush was so thick that even those vaqueros who worked in it frequently had great respect for it. Julian Buentello told the following story:

> *José Lopez was a little man, and one time his horse started to fall, and he just came off it and hit the ground running. Another time we looked up, and his horse started bucking and running through the brush under limbs with him. He came right by us, and when we saw him again we said, "Why didn't you buck off?" He said, "I didn't know where I would end up, and it was too far to walk, and I might get lost, so I wasn't about to get off."*

Roundup was tough duty for horses, too, especially those working the brush. Leonard Stiles recalled treating the horses' injuries: "The best medicine was kerosene. Old horses would have thorns in them, or they would run over stobs [short, portruding tree stumps], and their ankles and knees would be swollen up. We would take a can of kerosene and pour down the leg, and it would relieve the swelling."

SADDLES

Quality saddles were a must for this work. Most were made on King Ranch and are still being made today. Martín Mendietta Jr. described the saddle trees: "Mr. Bob and Mr. Dick [Kleberg Jr.] would have saddle trees made for us. We used Mr. Bob's tree. It came in fifteen or sixteen inches long, depending on your size, and you could order it like that. You picked size fifteen, sixteen, or seventeen, and the caporal would order for his men."

DOGS IN THE ROUNDUP

. . . sometimes they would bite the mouths of the cattle to make them turn. Nicolas Rodríguez (King Ranch)

Often two or three dogs would work roundups with the *corrida.* They were especially helpful in tracking strays in the acres and acres of thick brush. Nicolas Rodríguez described how the dogs accomplished this:

We worked with dogs in the corrida. *They used to catch the cattle because they were all wild cows. The dogs would follow the cows [while] barking, and the cowboys would follow behind the dogs. There was one time when they were bringing like fifty head of steers, and one of them [the steers] got scared and jumped to another pasture. Well, it was not until the next day that a cowboy could go to look for it. He took a dog with him, and the dog tracked the steer from the place it had jumped to almost a quarter of a mile away. He [the dog] found the steer and brought it back.*

The dogs would bark at the cattle, and sometimes they would bite the mouths of the cattle to make them turn. There was a very good dog that used to wait in the pasture until a cowboy called her name, and she would stand on two legs next to the horse. The cowboy would grab her onto his horse and take her to the place where she would track the lost steer. This dog was very close to the cook, and she slept next to his bed. The cook woke up at 3 A.M. every day.

It was the little dog who at 3 A.M. would move his bed to wake him up. The cook would pet her for a while, and then get up. He fixed her food, and she was ready to go.

THE VAQUERO'S ROPE

I made my bull whips and quirts from deer skins and cow skins.
Miguel Muñiz (King Ranch)

The vaquero's pride and his rope were often closely related; the quality of his work depended on the quality of the rope and his skill in using it. Next to his horse, it was the most important tool in the roundup. The ranches furnished reatas (ropes), but it was not uncommon for the vaquero to buy a rope of his own liking. In the early days, the rope would always be of manila fiber. He sometimes greased it with linseed oil or *sebo* (tallow) to keep it supple, for dampness would cause these ropes to become almost as stiff as wire.

Shorter ropes, of perhaps twenty-five feet, were necessary for use in the brush. With luck, a vaquero might eventually get a chance to swing a loop if he followed the critter long enough and the brush was not too dense. But he was most likely to get a chance to rope the back legs by throwing the rope low, or he might lean over and throw the rope upwards, which he hoped would result in his roping at least half the animal's head. Ropes of forty or forty-five feet in length could only be used in the open range.

The men who aspired to be great ropers developed unusual skill. One such man on the Kenedy Ranch was Felipe Alegría.

Alegría could do everything well, but he was especially famous for his ability to throw horses using the *mangana* (lariat) to rope the front feet. He added a daring novelty to the *mangana* by tying the rope around his waist before throwing the loop. If he roped the horse the wrong way he could be dragged by the horse, but he never missed. One time his *mayordomo*, Morgan Chandler, tried to do the same thing and was dragged on his very first try. He was lucky to escape serious injury (Villarreal 1972, 47).

Once during a visit to King Ranch, Will Rogers observed the roping skill of the Kineños in the brush. At the suggestion of Bob Kleberg, he tried his hand at it. Rogers later said, "Lord, I was in there swinging around and messing things all up. I would hit where the calf had been just previously" (Lea 1957, 2:626).

Julian Buentello of King Ranch described a particular roping technique, called a "heeler":

In the brush, if you were roping and swung your rope above your head, they yelled "You should be working with the windmill crew." You didn't swing your rope in the brush. You used a small loop and threw it where he would step on it, and you could drag him or get 'em down and get another rope on him. It's called a "heeler."

Chorche Mayorga was one of the best heelers at the Ranch. He could stand in the middle of a corral and pick up two heels with no problem at all.

Each calf had to be roped for branding, inoculation against disease, and castrating. Timing was everything. Precise judgment and great skill acquired from countless hours of practice were used to throw the rope at just the right instant and in exactly the right way.

The Ranches continuously looked for ways of making this hazardous work as safe as possible. Leonard Stiles described one invention:

We used a special device developed at King called a botón. *It was a leather loop attached to the end of a new rope. It fitted over the saddle horn and made it easy to get the rope off if necessary. We did not tie the knot fast until the cow was on the other end. At King you might lose the rope but not the man—you could untie it from the horn if the cow got hung up or if your horse got caught in the rope. We tied fast on the range, but not in the brush.*

About the *botón,* Martín Mendietta Jr. said, "These kept you from being dragged."

After roping, the vaqueros sometimes had help getting the cattle in. Enemorio Serna said: "I liked to rope wild steers. I would tie them to a tree and then tie them to an ox, and the ox would take them out. I would use about twenty oxen on a drive. It would take the oxen about a day to bring them in. Then they were turned in to the herd.

Miguel Muñiz was ninety-three years old when he was interviewed. In his younger days, he was in charge of the King Ranch Quarter Horses, including Peppy, Rey del Rancho, and Little Man. He also became a master braider and plaiter. Using horsehair, he was well known for his ropes, bridles, and quirts. He was also noted for his plaited, decorative hat bands, one of which he displayed during the interview. Miguel explained:

I started plaiting at about age thirty. My father taught me. I helped him make ropes. I made my bull whips and quirts from deer skins and cow skins. I tanned them myself. I treated the skins by rubbing salt and baking soda on them. I hung them to dry. They would be as soft as your skin.

In later years, I could make two or three ropes a day with help. They were made from cotton and wrapped in braided horsehair. They were six or seven feet long and five hundred pounds strong.

Other vaqueros made *cabrestro,* or hair rope. Alberto "Lolo" Treviño of King Ranch still makes these using a wooden invention of his own to hold the hair while he braids the strands. The ropes are woven from the manes and tails of horses, and thus may be designed with patterns devised from a wide array of colors including silver, black, white, and all shades of brown and red. Lolo said: "These ropes are soft and unsuitable for lassoing, but may be used as a stake rope."

Lolo also makes fancy hat bands and bolo ties (plaited, rope-like necklaces). During the interview, he was wearing a straw hat decorated with one of his own horsehair bands; it was brown-and-black checked with a red border running along the lower edge. He also wore one of his own bolos. It held the tip of an animal horn with the initials "AVT," through which he pulled a red bandanna. Once a necessity for shielding his face from grit during roundup, it had now become a decorative item of his outfit worn while visiting with guests of the Ranch. He related the symbolism of his quirt (short whip with a handle):

It [the symbolism] has been in my family for seven generations. You see, it begins with four braided strands representing Mary, Joséph, [my] Mother, and Daddy [family], then goes to three strands representing grandchildren in red, black, and brown, then finally braided down to two strands representing Jesus Christ. My daddy taught me what it meant and how to do it [plait]. My daddy taught me, "A cowboy without a rope is like a man without arms."

Vaqueras

I was not afraid of anything . . . María Luisa Montalvo Silva (King Ranch)

The *corrida* was almost exclusively a man's world. There were, however, some vaqueras, or cowgirls.

María Luisa Montalvo Silva was born into a family with a long,

Albert V. "Lolo" Treviño's family traces its roots back to the Blas María de la Garza Falcón family that lived on the Wild Horse Desert before the arrival of Captain King. Lolo is a retired vaquero working in the Visitor Management Department of the Santa Gertrudis Division of King Ranch. He is an expert plaiter of quirts and ropes.

proud history on King Ranch. She grew up with a love of horses and, as a young girl, had the opportunity to work side by side with the vaqueros as an equal. María said:

> *I started working with Mr. Dick [Jr.] and Mr. Burwell in the* corrida *when I was about fourteen or fifteen. This was about 1940–41. I was not afraid of anything, and loved working the cows. The men at the* corrida *would pick out a horse for me. The men were very respectful. My nickname was "Wicha." I held the cows during branding and helped bring them in. We would change horses about two or three times a day. I wore a bush jacket, chaps, men's boots, a hat, and spurs. I wore a handkerchief over my face. I remember how dusty it was when I was behind the cows. I remember having glasses on, and my face was solid dirt, and, when I took off my glasses, my eyes were two white circles.*

Josefina Robles Adrián of King Ranch also worked as a vaquera with her family out on one of the *ranchitos*, which were homesteads located in remote areas of the Ranch, usually near windmills throughout the Ranch's vast acreage. The vaqueros living out in these lonely areas were in charge of managing that area of the Ranch, including stock, windmills, and fences. Josefina rode the fences and helped to bring in stray cattle. She said that when her father died, they moved the family off the *ranchito* the next day because it was too dangerous for the family to stay out there in a remote location by themselves without their father.

After the Roundup

Once the cattle were rounded up, the concentrated, critical work began. It was during this phase that the vaqueros truly got to demonstrate their skills, and it was here, too, that the young vaquero sons, and occasionally a daughter, had their first chances to prove themselves worthy of the name Kineños or Kenedeños.

CULLING

The first critical task was culling, or removing non-productive cows. When a cow went more than a year without bearing a calf, she was considered a liability and was removed from the herd and sold to market. Older cows producing less than desirable calves met the same fate. These animals had to be spotted as the cattle moved in circles around the vaqueros. The caporal or owner made instant decisions in the midst of about 450 head of cattle. They would spot the cow that needed to be removed and begin moving her to the outside of the circle, sometimes by force. As Julian Buentello said, "The *capitan* [caporal] made the decision which went on the trail, which to slaughter, which sent back."

It has been said that King Ranch president, Robert Kleberg Jr., knew better than anyone on King Ranch when a steer was as fat as it was going to get and should be shipped, or when a cow had begun to fail as a calf-producer and should be slaughtered. He could, in a split second, pick a calf to be saved for breeding, and select the ones to be sold, by pointing them out to the vaqueros while they were riding in the midst of the milling crowd of bawling animals (*Time,* December 1947, 89). Making correct decisions was a critical point in the operation of the King and Kenedy Ranches, for the Ranches' profits would be directly impacted.

The skill of the cutting horse was critical in heading off a cow that was attempting to turn back into the herd, and then "cutting" the cow toward the outside. The cow would then be picked up by another rider further out on the edge of the milling circle of cattle and finally moved to an outrider, who would "assist" her in joining a group of lead steers. Another cull would already have been selected and be on the way out. This process was repeated until all the undesirable cattle were separated from the main herd.

CUTTING THE BIG CALVES

By 9:30 or 10:00 A.M., the culling was finished. The vaqueros then turned their attention to the remaining cows and their seven- or eight-month-old calves. These calves, branded at the last roundup, were separated from their mothers in exactly the same way as the culls. By roundup time, they would weigh between five and seven hundred pounds. They would be younger and faster than the culls, and thus, even more difficult to control and move to the outriders than the younger calves. They darted, slipped, and challenged even the most talented vaqueros in their determination to return to their mothers' milk. According to Miguel Muñiz, the vaqueros "would cut seven or eight hundred head of cattle from seven or eight thousand [head]."

BRANDING

I knew when the iron was ready . . . it would turn red. Nicolas Rodríguez (King Ranch)

Young calves several months of age were marked and numbered for identification purposes when they weighed about 150 pounds. This was necessary for proper record keeping in the breeding programs and for retrieving cattle that might have strayed with other herds, especially before fencing was widely used. It also simplified the reclaiming of cattle taken by rustlers, a recurring problem in the far-flung pastures. As on most ranches, branding—or burning the marks on the animal with hot irons—was the practice whereby cattle were identified as belonging to The King and Kenedy Ranches. This method is still used today.

"On King Ranch," said Lolo Treviño, "cattle are marked with the Running W, the division identification, the cattle number which begins with the sire number, and the year dropped [born]. The numbers begin with #1 annually and can go to the 1600s."

Nicolas Rodríguez performed many tasks on King Ranch, but his specialty was branding. When branding cattle, the necessary expertise is in judging just how long to leave the redhot branding iron on the skin of the calf; the iron needs to be left on long enough to leave a visible mark but not long enough to burn the flesh to the extent that it becomes infected, endangering the animal's life. Nicolas had this gift:

I did all the branding myself because they trusted me very much. Whenever somebody else did the branding, the cattle's skin usually peeled off. I was very careful to make sure that the brand was just painted or stamped on the cattle, but not to burn them or hurt them. Sometimes, I got some help, because it was too much cattle, and I would get very tired.

After branding the animal, one applied lime and water to cool off the burn. One had to be very careful not to burn the cattle when branding because they would bleed and get sick. The problem was that nobody could help me because Don Caesar [Kleberg] would not allow anybody else to do the job.

Nicolas knew just how to build the fire for branding and how to judge when the temperature was right: "We used wood. We had to take the firewood on a cart pulled by mules. We also carried on that same cart the water and everything needed for the branding. All these were taken to the place where the cattle would be branded. I knew when the iron [for branding] was ready. It would turn red."

A number of other vaqueros described their branding and roping experiences:

I did a lot of roping. I roped to brand. The first brand I remember is the MK brand. Jesus Gonzales (Kenedy Ranch)

I branded at Sarita. I put oil on it afterwards. I did the ears, too, at the same time. We branded at about five or six months. Enemorio Serna (Kenedy Ranch)

I rounded up cattle and branded all year round. During the roundup, we would spot the cows and make a circle around them. There would be twenty-three or so cowboys. We cut out what would be shipped. Some were castrated to make steers.

I used a manila rope and a turnover loop. I threw the rope overhand instead of windup. I was the head roper. Seferino Gutierrez (Kenedy Ranch)

I roped cattle. I tied three legs and they branded. George Mayorga (King Ranch)

By mid-morning, the vaqueros also had another challenge. The winds began picking up, sending clouds of fine dust into eyes, ears, and noses, coating the weathered faces of the riders. The younger, less experienced men bore the brunt of the dust bath as they were placed downwind of the herd. Sometimes, the older men drew the same lot, as their muscles and joints could no longer stand up to the more vigorous assignments. Hats were pulled down, and bandannas were inevitably pulled up to just below eye level, against the swirling dust.

But the vaquero and his horse were highly skilled and even more agile than their target. The calf usually lost the cutting battle and was separated from the herd. If a calf should break and try to get away, quick retrieval by his pursuer was a certainty. So were good-natured hoots and cat calls from the other vaqueros.

Owners Stayed Involved

She was good people. Seferino Gutierrez (Kenedy Ranch)

The owners on the King and Kenedy Ranches often worked closely with this phase of the roundup also; they did not ask the Kineños and Kenedeños to do anything they would not do, and they usually did everything with equal skill. Every animal represented investment and prospective profit or loss. The owners also wanted to be with the vaqueros to share in the results of their success. Richard "Dick" Kleberg Sr. was one of the owners who enjoyed working alongside the vaqueros, and he was not above pulling a prank on them. Julian Buentello explained:

Mr. Dick [Sr.] was constantly doing something and always trying to keep us alert. He would wait 'til we looked busy, and he would cut out a heifer and run it through the camp, and we would have to rope it there or get back on our horses and get her before she got back to the herd, if we were going to have meat. We would cut her throat, bleed her, skin her, and cook the meat. The best part of it was the ribs.

The Kenedeño interviewees spoke respectfully of Sarita Kenedy East. According to Seferino Gutierrez of Kenedy Ranch, "Sarita East went on the range to supervise. She was a very good rider and helped cut the cattle. She was good people."

Mealtime

Before the all-weather, black-topped roads were built on King Ranch following World War II, the vaqueros working in the *corridas* on the far reaches of the pastures were fed from chuck wagons. When travel became less troublesome and time consuming, their meals were prepared at the camp house.

THE CHUCK WAGON

Mules pulled it. Jesus Gonzales (Kenedy Ranch)

The chuck wagon was the cook's kitchen on wheels and the cowboy's home away from home. It carried the food supply, the eating and cooking utensils, tools for building fire trenches, and tools for any other need that might arise, like horseshoeing. It carried whatever bedding and medicine there was, and it was the center of activity after work was done.

The chuck wagon was born of necessity during the fabled trail rides to northern markets following the Civil War. The drives took eight to twelve weeks and usually traveled in remote areas far from food supplies. The men needed plenty of nourishing food to support this physically demanding life. The Texas rancher Charles Goodnight gets credit for devising the chuck wagon in 1866 for this purpose, and it evolved and remained an important fixture on large ranching operations well into the 1990s (Rosenblatt 1994, 26).

The typical chuck wagon had a bed with bottom and side boards made of wood. Usually, there were metal bows bent up over the bed and fastened on either side from which a wagon sheet, or tarpaulin, could be stretched as protection from the sun or rain. It contained a chuck box for holding the cook's equipment. The rear wall sloped outward from top to bottom and was hinged at the bottom, so that when it was swung down and supported with a heavy prop, it made a table on which the cook could prepare his fare. This chuck wagon was like a kitchen cabinet on wheels (Adams, 1952, 12). As Felipe Garcia, a former cook at King Ranch, described, "In the wooden trunk we carried the utensils—stainless steel cups, plates, spoons, and forks—for forty people."

Jesus Gonzales of Kenedy Ranch, a cook's helper and trainer, described his demanding schedule and duties:

> The chuck wagon was wooden and had wooden wheels with metal spokes. Mules pulled it. We traveled about ten or fifteen miles a day from the camp to the roundup site. It took one-and-a-half or two hours to get there. We washed dishes in hot water and [used] bar soap. We made wood fires and used kerosene to start them.
>
> I got up at 3:00 or 4:00 to cook breakfast of refried beans, coffee, and bread. For lunch we cooked beans, rice, fried meat, bread, and coffee. I fed twenty-five [vaqueros] at a time. They all ate at once.

Since the cook was often the doctor and dentist while the *corrida* worked in the far-flung pastures, the drawers might also contain such remedies as quinine, calomel, black draught, an assortment of pills, horse liniment (for both horses and men), and kerosene for snake bites.

Captain King walked with a limp, and the Kineños name for him was El Cojo, The Lame One. The Kineños tell the story, although never verified, of how King was bitten by a snake and that one of them treated him with kerosene and saved his leg, and he walked with a limp after that.

According to Felipe Garcia, the chuck wagon might even hold sewing gear.

> I mended the clothes and carried a needle and thread. You had to be nice to me if you wanted your clothes repaired. And I sometimes was the banker—held the bets for the men.
>
> Our chuck wagon had all four sides that went down to work from. It was designed and built for use on King Ranch. It was built by the men who built the fences. It had the tank in back for

This cook's camp is typical of those set up during roundups on King Ranch. Camp bread and various pots of food are cooking over coals and the open fire. Courtesy of King Ranch Archives, King Ranch, Inc.

water—it held 250 gallons, enough for one day. The men filled their canteens from it. This wagon has been used for thirty years or more on King Ranch.

I had to clean the chuck wagons in the spring. We scrubbed them down with ash and sand and lye soap. We really worked on them to get them ready to pack for roundup.

Chuck Wagon Etiquette

Usually, the important meal of the day at camp was supper. While breakfast and lunch were hurried, the evening meal could be more relaxed. There was sometimes the opportunity to sit down and eat and spin yarns around the campfire, maybe hear one of the hands sing or play a little music, or just rest until bedtime, which was usually around 9:00. During this time, the cook cleaned up his "kitchen," washed the dishes, and made preparations for the next day's meals.

The cowboy selected a plate, cup, knife, and fork from the chuck box lid at the wagon, then went from pot to skillet and helped himself to food and coffee. The dining table was anywhere the cowboy could find a place big and clean enough to squat or sit. He often crossed his legs and used his calves to balance his plate while his coffee cup sat on the ground.

He could even cut his meat while sitting in this position. Sometimes his bedroll was his "table."

The cook was strictly in charge of mealtime. As Felipe Garcia explained, "We allowed no animals near the chuck wagons—horses or anything else. And they [the vaqueros] ate everything on their plates."

The cowboy's social etiquette on the King and Kenedy Ranches was no different from that of any other ranches and was closely observed:

1. The hands ate as they came in instead of waiting for everyone. It was more polite to go ahead and serve themselves than to have the others stand in line waiting.
2. Even if everyone was there at once, there was no crowding, shoving, rushing, or overreaching. These were not tolerated.
3. The Dutch oven lids were kept away from the sand, and the cowboys were careful to put the pots back on the fire so that the food would be hot for those still to come.
4. A cowboy did not take the last serving unless he was sure everyone else was finished eating.
5. There was no waste. He left no food on his plate. He either ate all the food or scraped it off for the animals and birds to eat. He might put it in the "squirrel can," a can for leftovers that would be fed to animals later. He would then place his dirty dishes in the huge dishpan for washing.
6. It was a breach of etiquette to tie a horse to a wheel of the chuck wagon, or to ride into camp so that the wind blew sand in the food the cook was preparing.
7. The men dared not eat until the cook called it ready.
8. If he found the water barrel empty, the cowhand's duty was to fill it.
9. To leave a bedroll unrolled and unplaced was a serious breach of etiquette. This might cause it to be left behind when the cook packed up.
10. Around the campfire, an unwritten law was that a song or fiddle piece or story was not interrupted.
11. A stranger would always be welcome at the wagon and ate with the cowhands. The unwritten code was that he was expected to dry the dishes. (Adams 1952, 123)

As the railroads came to South Texas and the roundups were closer to home, the Ranches erected camp houses on each division. These were concrete-block, one-room houses that were used for cooking, sleeping, and bathing. The men often came here for their meals, many times eating in shifts, and slept here during the roundups. These camp houses were strategically placed throughout the Ranches in the major pastures.

THE COOK

I started with ten pounds of flour. Felipe Garcia (King Ranch)

The cook held a unique role, and a good cook was considered absolutely necessary to keep the men in the outfits satisfied. If the men were not well fed with plenty of fresh, hearty food, they could not work the rigorous schedule required of them to perform the tasks of the Ranches. Even though any man who did not work in a saddle was looked upon with skepticism by the vaqueros, the cook demanded, and got, their respect.

Felipe Garcia learned how to be a cook very quickly from necessity and had the chance to learn from one of the last range cooks, "La Chista" Villarreal.

> *I was a vaquero. One day the boss told me the* corrida *needed a cook, and, if I would take the job and learn to cook in thirty days, I could have a house. I learned in two weeks.*
>
> *I learned to cook from Holotino "La Chista" [Little Bird]. He was called this because he was always hopping around like a little bird. There is even a little bird painted by the vaqueros on the side of his chuck wagon.*
>
> *La Chista had been cooking for King Ranch for thirty years and was at home cooking in the* corrida *or in the kitchen on the second floor of the Commissary.*

Leonard Stiles told some humorous stories that well illustrate the feeling of fun and kidding that existed in the *corrida*, especially where the cook was concerned:

> *La Chista was a funny little man. If anyone got bucked off a horse, he would pick up the bottom of his apron and say, "Just bring that horse over here and I'll ride 'em."*
>
> *One of the funniest La Chista stories was about one day when he was moving through the pasture in a truck with the chuck wagon tied on behind it to go set up for the noon meal. The vaqueros were waving at him and trying to get his attention to get him to stop. He just kept waving at them and didn't stop because they were always joking with him. The vaqueros couldn't leave the cattle so they couldn't tell him that he had lost his chuck wagon. It*

wasn't until several miles later that he turned around and realized that his chuck wagon had been disconnected, and he had to turn back and retrieve it.

No doubt La Chista returned the prank at some future time when the vaqueros least expected it. The unwritten code was that anyone who played a prank could expect one in return—and it must be accepted in good humor. Those who did not do so were ostracized until they conformed (Villarreal 1972, 73).

Felipe Garcia's first cooking lesson was *pan de campo* (camp bread), a staple of the vaquero's diet. He had no recipe to follow when he learned:

> *La Chista knew just how much flour, baking powder, salt, milk, warm water, and shortening to add to get the bread just right. I had to learn to feel when the dough was the right consistency, to just know when the bread was done, brown on the bottom and on the top.*
>
> *Other lessons followed on building and burning down the fire to the right temperature, and how to cook beans, rice, fried steak, and tortillas. After two weeks, I was willing to go it alone. Later, I learned to cook specialties. I made pouches of dried fruit and dough, and fried them. I made sweet breads—like doughnuts. And if the day was quiet with little wind, I would make cakes, both vanilla and chocolate.*

Cooks had to have other types of expertise to get the men fed on time. Felipe explained:

> *What a lot of people miss is that the cook had to be an expert driver to move that wagon and those mules around. We used six mules hooked together. The cook did not ride the wagon, but instead the back left mule and reined the rest from that position. They were tough to work with. The cook had to know all the roads and gates. If you think about it, the gates were a problem because you had to know where to enter the pasture as well as which one. The cook made more money than anyone else.*

Felipe Garcia's Workday

By 1991, Felipe began his workday between 6:00 and 7:00 in the morning when he drove out on paved roads from Santa Gertrudis headquarters to a nearby camp house. This schedule was in stark contrast to La Chista's day, which began at 3:00 A.M. in the camp before paved roads were built. "I served breakfast between 7:30 and 8:00," said Felipe. "Sometimes the cowboys had the fire going—they had been at work for a few hours. If I did not notice the smell of pungent smoke, I knew my first task was to build a fire. We used mesquite. It is the best wood because the flavor comes through."

The next task was to put on the coffee. There was always plenty of hot, fresh coffee for the vaqueros, whether they ate at the *corrida* or at the camp house.

In the early days, we made the coffee over the open fire. I used two big pots and put 1½ cups of coffee to a coffee pot half-full of water. The pots hung on a hook over the fire. I let it boil twenty or thirty minutes. When the white smoke formed on the top I knew it was ready. Then I added cold water enough to make the pot three-fourths full and to settle the coffee grounds. The coffee was ready.

In some outfits, the bread of choice was sourdough biscuits, but on the King and Kenedy Ranches, *pan de campo* was the staple. The round dough discs were cooked in black iron Dutch ovens placed over coals, with additional coals placed on the indented lid. Felipe described the technique:

Next, I made the camp bread. I started with ten pounds of flour. After the dough had rested ten or fifteen minutes, I rolled it out about a half-inch thick and put it in the greased Dutch ovens with a lid. I set the skillet on an iron triangle with fire [coals] under it and on top of the lid. I kept three going at once. If the fire was right, it took six or seven minutes to cook the camp bread.

For breakfast I used chorizo [sausage] browned in oil, then mixed with eggs. I also served refried beans. These beans were left from the day before and fried in grease in a skillet.

To clean up after breakfast, we heated the water and washed all the dishes in Ivory or Joy [dish soap] and hot water. It took a lot of big bones to carry those pans and water with the dishes.

After breakfast at the base camp, we were told the location for lunch, sometimes five miles away, and we moved camp, wagon, and sometimes the equipment truck there. Then we came back to the base camp in the evening. We used two locations and three fires.

When we got to the lunch site, we started the fire for barbecue. We used about twenty pieces of wood, and it would take anywhere from twenty minutes to two hours, depending if the wood was wet

*or dry. We seasoned the beef with corn oil, spices, salt, and pepper.
We cooked round steak, T-bones,* charra *[skirt steak or fajitas],
and ribs. We covered it and cooked it for an hour and a half. I
made gravy with flour, salt, pepper, and water. We used no pork;
we had plenty of beef. We cooked the rice and beans, and made
hot sauce. We used mainly canned tomatoes. We had iced tea or
Kool-Aid.*

*We usually took a siesta after lunch after cleaning up again.
Back at base camp, we might have beans and bread and molasses,
and sometimes sweet breads or fruit pouches. I would clean up and
get home about 6:00 or 7:00.*

Beef Every Day

Fresh beef was definitely the meat of choice. The men in the outfit
would butcher a yearling; there was no refrigeration on the range, so
meat might only last two or three days before spoiling. The meat was
sliced, seasoned with salt and pepper, and fried in grease, or it might be
battered with flour and water or milk, then fried. Julian Buentello described the butchering procedure: "The steer was selected, roped, and
the throat cut. Then it was hung, probably from a tree limb. Then it was
cut up and cooked."

And Then Ranch Beans

Beef and bread were the original staples of the cowboy's diet on the
trail and the range. Later, beans became a part of the cowboy's daily
menu. Then rice was added, then potatoes. The beans were picked over
to remove any small rocks or gravel, then washed and soaked overnight
in water. Jesus Gonzales remembered: "I added salt bacon to beans and
some onions and cooked them about two hours."

A Favorite Treat

José Alegría of both the King and Kenedy Ranches was famous for
his cooking at the Main House as well as in the camps. A special treat in
his camp was cow's head, cooked whole. He explained the process:

*The preparation began on Monday night. First, I dug a large
round hole and built a fire in it. I then skinned and dehorned the
cow head, seasoned it with salt, pepper, and garlic, then wrapped it
in a cloth, then a tow sack. I wet the whole package with water.
When the fire had burned down to coals, some dirt was spread on
the coals, then the cow's head was placed in, then more dirt and*

then more coals. The head cooked all night. The next morning the head was unwrapped and ready to eat.

The Kineños considered the brains, jaw meat, and tongue to be special delicacies, and they relished splitting a piece of *pan de campo* like a pocket and filling it with the steaming hot morsels.

THE LONE WOMAN COOK

The men would steal my tortillas and take them with them.
Ofelia M. Longória (King Ranch)

The cooks in the camp houses and in the *corrida* were men. Interviews revealed only one exception: Ofelia M. Longória had a job as a cook at one of the camp houses, where she fed as many as ninety men in a day. She explained: "As far as I know, I was the only woman to ever serve as a regular cook for the men working the ranches. Bobby Cavazos hired me. He told me the men would respect me . . . I had a face like a lemon."

Ofelia was about forty years old when she started this job and worked for seventeen years, until about 1983. The people she fed included residents at Laureles and the Mexican laborers. She described her routine:

I had two gas stoves, and one person helped me at breakfast and one helped at lunch. I got to the camp house at 3:00 A.M. I made tortillas in the morning and camp bread [pan de campo] at noon. In the morning I served French fries, eggs, chorizo [sausage], tortillas, coffee, and tea.

Breakfast was served at 6:30. I went home to rest for about an hour before lunch.

I served lunch at 12:00. I served carne guisada *[beef stew], rice, beans, camp bread, Kool Aid, and tea. After lunch I took a siesta.*

Supper was at 5:30. I would rotate serving meat and stew between lunch and dinner. I also served camp bread, tea, and Kool Aid. It took a half-sack of flour to make the seven or eight rounds of camp bread for each meal.

The men would steal my tortillas and take them with them. I would hear them talking on the radio about eating them and how good they were.

My first camp boss was Reynaldo [her husband], and then Felix. I got a week off for vacation and was paid $600 a month. I started learning to cook when I was ten [years old].

And There Were Other Challenges

THE BRUSH

Before we used the Caterpillars they used axes and hand cut.
Manuel Silva (King Ranch)

A major recurring obstacle to the orderly development of the King
and Kenedy Ranches began emerging in the early 1900s. At first, the land
was open prairies with wide expanses of lush, green grasses. Here and
there trees dotted the horizon between the Nueces River and the Rio
Grande. Then wild cattle and horses began spreading the mesquite
beans in their droppings. Other flora specimens cropped up to create a
thick, almost impenetrable vegetation that seriously hindered the King
and Kenedy Ranches' efforts to use the land for ranching. The fight
between the ranchers and the brush had begun—and the brush was
winning.

The initial method of brush clearing was axes and grubbing hoes
wielded by transient Mexican laborers who periodically arrived from
Mexico looking for work. Barton Currie's article in the August 28, 1915,
edition of the *Country Gentleman* reported an interview with Robert
Kleberg Sr.:

> We have cleared 10,000 acres of this mesquite range, and we are
> clearing 6,000 acres more northwest of Kingsville. All the clear-
> ing is being done by Mexicans. We have 500 of them at it now. . . .
> Mexican families came to us in droves. They were in pitiable
> condition—practically on the verge of starvation. . . . We di-
> vided the refugee Mexicans into camps and put them to work
> clearing the land. We provided food and shelter and clothing.

Robert Kleberg Sr. in his speech to an organization called the Farmers of Southwest Texas in 1911, spoke about these laborers:

> I want to say something for the little Mexican; I do not see
> many of them here; they are not here, they are out there in the
> heat, out there among the bushes and the thorns, and I ask you
> what you, or I, or any of us could do here in clearing away this
> brush if it was not for the little Mexican? Gentlemen, they are a
> great people, and you know it and I know it; they fill their place
> and they fill it well. (King Ranch Archives)

Brush clearing was a problem in the entire area. Around 1925, José Morales of Kenedy Ranch and his family moved to a nearby ranch for a year. He told of the laborers' efforts to clear the land. A brush-removal contractor named Desiderio Montez brought in as many as 160 Mexicans of both sexes at one time. The women's job was mainly to stack and burn the mesquite, but sometimes they used the ax and grubbing hoe in a never-ending, backbreaking effort to free the desert of brush. Children worked, too. The laborers usually worked in families, starting in the early morning and working until sunset. The pay was around $14 an acre, per family member (Villarreal 1972, 28).

A succession of inventions evolved to deal with the ever-encroaching brush, including Caterpillar tractors with cables, and stump pullers with gasoline engines. Manuel Silva of King Ranch directed the Caterpillars when the vaqueros cut the mesquite: "Before we used the Caterpillars, they used axes and hand cut. The machine replaced what twelve to fifteen men did before."

By 1951, the giant funnel dozer and root plow were developed, and the brush was finally brought under control. The device weighed fifty-two tons and destroyed four acres of brush jungle per hour. Until then, rounding up animals from this tangle was one of the vaquero's greatest and most exhausting challenges.

FENCES

Fencing has been a major component of the Ranches since Captains King and Kenedy faced the challenge of enclosing their pastures for protection against rustlers and the intrusion from peripheral animals — and sometimes their owners — into the Ranches' breeding programs. The following letter from Mifflin Kenedy to one of these intruders in the *1874 Kenedy Ranch Ledger Book* describes the need for fences:

> Brownsville, Texas   April 20, 1874
> Dear Sir,
> I am informed you are now establishing a ranch at a place and the point known as the "Burros" on the tract of land known as the Concepción Carricitos in this County of Cameron. The land where you are building your Ranch belongs to me, and has been in my possession some twelve years — I am also informed you are bringing or have sheep now at that point.
>   This is not a friendly act, as you are well aware that sheep

are injurious to the range, and particularly so where horses and cattle are raised—I have to ask that you will withdraw your sheep from my land, and also cease enacting any *cucado* cutting of timber or interfering in any way with my rights—as the land where you have located is mine, and I will take all legal means to defend it.

Yours Respectfully

M. Kenedy

King and Kenedy began fencing in 1868. Rogerio Silva of King Ranch said that cypress posts and hard pine planks were shipped from Louisiana and hauled overland to Laureles Ranch.

Kenedy first began fencing operations in 1868 on Laureles Ranch, with Captain Henry Howley in charge. Laureles was located on a peninsula in Nueces County, bounded by the Oso Creek on the north and Laureles Creek on the south, making it easier to fence than most ranches in the area. By the end of the year, Kenedy had fenced approximately thirty-six miles across the neck of his peninsula, enclosing about 131,000 acres. It was one of the first fences in Texas. Because there was no native lumber or stone in the area, and all materials had to be shipped in by water, fencing was very expensive. Kenedy used lumber for his first fencing, but soon turned to using No. 5 Bessemer steel galvanized round wire run through posts for the last few miles of the fence. These six-inch by six-inch by eight-foot posts of cypress wood, used for five-strand fencing, were spaced twenty feet apart and sunk three feet into the ground. They were imported from Louisiana. The advantages of fencing became obvious in 1873 when a severe drought occurred in South Texas, and Kenedy did not lose any stock, whereas most ranchers were losing thousands of cattle from starvation and exposure (*Corpus Christi Caller*, January 18, 1959).

After Kenedy had sold Laureles to a syndicate from Dundee, Scotland, in 1882 and purchased the La Parra (or Grapevine) grant, he constructed a pier, called Pasadizo Landing, at Baffin Bay for the use of the Ranch in importing materials for building fences and the Ranch headquarters (*Corpus Christi Caller*, January 18, 1959).

King would later purchase the Laureles property. It remains a division of King Ranch today.

After the death of Mifflin and his son, John Gregory Kenedy Sr., Mifflin's grandson, John Gregory Kenedy Jr. was in charge of Kenedy Ranch operations. He altered the organization of the work units on La Parra, disbanding the fence crews. The fences soon fell apart from disrepair. His sister, Sarita East, bought his stock and leased his part of the Ranch (Villarreal 1972, 29).

Captain King had a more difficult time fencing his land, because his land was not surrounded by water on three sides as Kenedy's Laureles was. King began by first fencing off the Santa Gertrudis Division.

Both Ranches eventually changed to cedar posts and smooth, heavy-gauge galvanized net wire that would not damage animals. In the twenty years from 1934 to 1954, King Ranch put up eight hundred miles of fencing (Lea 1957, 2:684).

The work was grueling and grimy. For years, trees were felled with axes that were swung all day long. Trimming and finally cutting posts from the trunks were part of the backbreaking process. Special crews were responsible for this work. During less demanding seasons, or during times of great need, vaqueros from the *corrida* would join these crews. At any rate, sweat poured.

Catarino Moreno of the Norias Division of King Ranch worked on the fence crews around 1945. He recalled: "The fences were mostly straight wire; little barbed wire was used. We used mesquite posts—cut lots of trees, sometimes seventy a day."

Nicolas Rodríguez of King Ranch was a member of the fence crews from time to time. He remembered: "Sometimes we got five or six posts from a tree. We used an ax and we cut them close to the ground. We worked from sunrise to sunset."

One of the most trusted *mayordomo*s on the Kenedy Ranch was Guadalupe Morales. He had unusual organizational skills. An incident in 1940, involving his fence crew, illustrated his knack for figuring out the most efficient way to accomplish the task. Guadalupe was constructing a fence at the rate of about a mile a day. Before he finished, he became ill and had to be placed in a tuberculosis hospital. The *mayordomo* who took his place accomplished considerably less than a mile a day. The difference was in the way each man organized the work crew.

Guadalupe had divided his twenty-five men into eight separate groups, each with a different function. The first crew set up the two end posts and attached flags to them to facilitate the aligning of the fence, and then marked the spots for the posts using a chain. The second crew, which consisted of four men (all other crews consisted of three men each) dug the holes. The third group set up the anchor posts (*tirones*) at quarter-mile intervals. (Each spool contains a quarter-mile of wire.) The fourth group would line up and set up posts every eight holes. The fifth group would align and set up posts every four holes. The sixth group would align and set up posts every two holes, the seventh crew would align and set up posts in the remaining holes, and the last crew drilled the holes in the posts. Nobody had to stand and wait on someone else in order to accomplish his assigned task (Villarreal 1972, 69).

WINDMILLS

Water has always been a critical necessity on the King and Kenedy Ranches. Windmills were necessary to bring artesian water to the surface for the cattle and horses to drink. Of the 381 wells on King Ranch in the late 1950s, 101 were flowing wells, 14 were worked by power pump, and 266 used windmills (Lea 1957, 2:685). Though windmills were drilled by professionals, special ranch crews kept them in top condition, and still do so today. On the four divisions of King Ranch, there are currently 320 windmills, 175 submersible pumps, and 10 solar wells. Maintenance of the windmills is contracted today.

Rosendo Rodríguez of King Ranch, the son of Nicolas Rodríguez, worked with the windmills at Norias. He recalled:

> Some of the windmills are named after famous cowboys like Macario Mayorga, one called Scotch because they drank Scotch whisky there, one for my grandfather, one for Ed Durham, and one because they found a man hanged on it.
>
> They also named pastures for people, like the one named Roberto for Bob Kleberg and one for Mr. Bob's wife.

One time in 1919, a major hurricane hit the area destroying or se-verely damaging many windmills and cisterns. Water was an immediate necessity for the animals. "The Ranch [Kenedy] had to form extra wind-mill crews to put all the windmills and cisterns back into operation" (Villarreal 1972, 26).

BUILDING CONSTRUCTION

One of the many jobs Kineños and Kenedeños did was building construction. John Gregory Kenedy Sr. began building a new ranch house at La Parra headquarters in 1913. Materials were brought in by rail to Sarita and were moved from there to La Parra by wagon. The building crews were all Mexican Americans except for the bricklayers, who were Anglos. Manuel Alaniz was a carpenter. Santos Hernandez and Mace-donio Salinas helped build forms for the foundation. The house took fifteen months to build (Villarreal 1972, 23).

José Morales moved building materials from Sarita to La Parra on wagons. After his father was killed by Anglos at the raid at La Atravesada on the Kenedy Ranch in the mid-1870s, José became head of the family at age twelve or thirteen. He began to acquire livestock of his own. In about 1880, Mifflin Kenedy fenced a pasture where José's cattle grazed. The pasture was owned by Mrs. Eulalia Tijerina, José's employer. Not wanting José's animals in the pasture, Kenedy bought them from José and offered him a job.

According to Villarreal, "José acquired a wagon and some mules and went to work hauling material for the headquarters building that was being constructed at La Parra. He was in charge of the four or five wagons used to haul the supplies and made two or three trips a day from Sarita to the building location at La Parra" (1972, 19).

In 1938, King Ranch added new housing for the vaqueros at the Norias Division. Catarino Moreno remembered the work: "I helped build twenty-one houses at Norias. I drove a *vagón* [wagon] which had rubber tires like a trailer and was pulled by horses. I carried the material for the houses."

When motor vehicles became common, the men switched from wagons to trucks. Antonio Salinas, on Kenedy Ranch, was one of these drivers: "I picked up lumber, supplies, four-strand wire, paint, and building supplies, and moved them around the Ranch."

In 1950 and 1951, King Ranch erected new housing for the vaqueros, called the New Colony, on the Santa Gertrudis Division. Today it still houses vaquero families, as well as retirees, in one-, two-, and three-bedroom houses. At the Kenedy Ranch both the active and retired Kenedeños still live side by side on the streets of Sarita, Texas, which is named for Sarita Kenedy East.

TICK ERADICATION

As far back as the 1870s, the cattle disease called "Texas fever" was a major challenge to the King and Kenedy Ranches and to ranches across Texas. It was a critical concern to the Klebergs and Kenedys during the time of the trail drives because it stymied the market, causing formerly reputable cattle to be turned back toward home. Winchester quarantines, bands of armed men standing on the roads to divert Texas cattle from an area, were set up by northern cattlemen, causing fights and further detours for the herd bosses from Texas (Lea 1957, 1:352).

Robert Kleberg Sr. and his son, Bob, led the effort to identify the culprit, which turned out to be a tick (boophilus annulatus). In 1891, Robert Kleberg Sr. invented, built, and began using the world's first cattle-dipping vat (Graham 1994, 51). Solutions developed for use in the vats killed the ticks on the cattle, and the ticks were eradicated from the land by keeping it free from the host cattle for a year. Finally, in 1928, after thirty-nine years, King Ranch was declared tick free by the U.S. Department of Agriculture (Lea 1957, 2:613).

Enemorio Serna remembered how tick eradication was done back then, when dipping vats were used, and he described how he does it today: "We spray and don't dip any more. We spray several times a year for flies and ticks. We wear long-sleeved shirts and pants in boots so that if ticks get on our necks or face, we can feel them and pick them off. If they get on me, she [his wife Olga] picks them off."

OTHER JOBS

In addition to backbreaking work with the multiple phases of ranch operations, these men, and sometimes women, worked closely with the owners and were expected to be on call as needed. Some of the vaqueros spent a great deal of time taking care of the needs of the owner family members, such as baby-sitting, food preparation, cleaning, collecting gear for hunting, or tending to any difficulty that might arise. According to Villarreal:

> He [John Gregory Kenedy Jr.] and his wife, Mrs. Elena Kenedy, had gone hunting and had got their hunting car stuck in the mud. Guadalupe [Morales] and José [Morales] had to unload their wagon [used for hauling firewood] and try and free the car. In bitter cold with rain falling the ropes broke, the mules and wagon got stuck too, and they finally gave up. Demencio [Bueno] went to the nearest *ranchito* and telephoned the ranch headquarters for someone to come and take the Kenedys home. José put the Kenedys in one of the wagons and took them to meet the rescue car. Guadalupe went back to camp to warm up by the fire. (1972, 27)

Rosendo Rodríguez at Norias served as a driver for Ed Durham, a Norias foreman. Rosendo said: "I took care of him. I knew when quail hunting time came the 'hunt was on.'"

Bob and Helen Kleberg loved to hunt, and Rosendo helped them and took care of their dogs. His father, Nicolas, also helped with the hunting trips, tracking deer. Nicolas said, "The family killed wild turkeys, deer and hogs."

According to the September 26, 1984, *Corpus Christi Caller,* "Johnny

Kenedy [Jr.] . . . loved to hunt and camp with 'Los Amigos' [friends] Bob Kleberg [Jr.] and Major Tom Armstrong. They often spent long campouts hunting." When asked what the vaqueros could kill, Nicolas Rodríguez said, "We could kill hogs, javelinas, and rabbits, but not deer, owls, or birds."

On the Kenedy Ranch, Antonio Salinas also worked the hunts: "At Christmas time, Robert Kleberg [Jr.] and John Kenedy [Jr.] would drink and hunt coyote and deer. I would be their driver."

Probably the closest vaquero to Bob Kleberg was Adán Muñoz.

Adán, born in an outcamp on the ranch, was a versatile phenomenon: an outstanding, all-around cowboy, horse trainer, chauffeur, mechanic, valet, bartender, gate opener, gun bearer, dog handler, chaperon, and dispatcher of any number of other duties that he carried out with tact and finesse. He, too, was on call twenty-four hours a day, seven days a week; from before dawn to the quiet hours before the next dawn, he never seemed to tire or get out-of-sorts. His thoroughness spoke for his dedication; the boss was never without food, a full liquor hamper, ice, the proper shotgun, rifle, pistol, ammunition, warm jackets, foul-weather gear—in short, provisions for every contingency. English butlers are renowned for their fidelity to their high-born masters. It's doubtful that any of them provided service the equal of homegrown Adán's. (Cypher 1995, 42).

Thus the vaqueros served the Ranches and their owners in every phase of their existence. They have been a supporting presence for births, marriages, and deaths—in good times and bad—with the Kenedy and King families.

From Longhorns to King Ranch Santa Cruz, Mustangs to Quarter Horses

S ince biblical times, livestock has been an important staple in people's lives. Beasts of burden have been valued, not only for human survival, but as a measure of wealth and prosperity. The world's great ranches are still judged by this standard today.

The expeditions of Christopher Columbus brought the first cattle and horses to the Americas around 1494 (Montejano 1987, 51). Other Spanish explorers followed, bringing the first cattle to North America at Vera Cruz around 1521 (Lea 1957, 1:39). Obviously well-suited for the terrain and climate, these tough, hardy cattle ran wild and multiplied; they are the ancestors of the Texas Longhorn.

The ranching tradition in Mexico evolved from a mix of Spanish and American Indian knowledge. This led to the emergence of the Mexican vaquero, who would develop the equipment and techniques needed for working the large haciendas. The vaqueros brought their knowledge of animals and terrain, their skills, and their work ethic across the Rio Grande. They tamed the Wild Horse Desert, with its diverse areas of palmetto thickets, live oak, black loam, and prairie. These early vaqueros were the prototype of the vaqueros who would become the heart and soul of the King and Kenedy Ranches.

Some of the early vaquero families lived in the vicinity of Santa Gertrudis Creek and were ranching on their Spanish and Mexican land grants before Captain King purchased his first grant in 1853. (The de la Garza, Cavazos, Longória, and Treviño families were land-grant owners in the area King was to select for his Ranch.) They possessed the necessary skills to assist King in establishing the operation that was to become the foundation of the industry in the United States.

In 1852, the founder of the Kenedy Ranch, Mifflin Kenedy, married Petra Vela Vidal, the beautiful and intelligent widow of a Mexican army captain. She was twenty-six years old and had six children. Her father,

Petra Vela de Vidal married Mifflin Kenedy on April 16, 1852. She was the widow of Colonel Luis Vidal of the Mexican army, with whom she had six children. She was the daughter of Gregorio Vela, the provincial governor of the Wild Horse Desert under the Spanish crown. The Kenedys lived in Brownsville and Corpus Christi. This oil painting was completed in 1875 when Petra was approximately fifty years old. Courtesy of the Corpus Christi Museum of Science and History.

Gregorio Vela, was the provincial governor under the Spanish crown for all of the territory between the Nueces River and the Rio Grande. Thus, Mrs. Kenedy had a strong connection to the Wild Horse Desert even before she married Kenedy. With her help, Kenedy was soon able to prosper in a political climate that was continually volatile. Thanks to Petra

Vela's connections, Kenedy was able to ship Texas cotton through Mexico, which the Union forces could not blockade. Soon he was shipping through Mexico the majority of cotton grown in Texas. Realizing that the days of steamboating were numbered, he took the profits from the sale of his steamboating business and invested in railroads and ranching (*Corpus Christi Caller*, September 23, 1984).

King expedited his fledgling Ranch's development when he persuaded an entire village from Mexico, called Cruias (Cruillas), to relocate with their livestock and work on the new land that he had purchased on the rise of the Santa Gertrudis Creek. The year was 1854.[1] In December 1854, Captain King brought his bride, Henrietta Chamberlain King, to live in a modest jacal in his cow camp. The daughter of a Presbyterian minister and carefully educated in boarding schools, she brought gentleness and culture to the Wild Horse Desert. She would later demonstrate amazing strength and business sense as mistress of King Ranch for seventy-one years. The Kings moved into their first ranch house in 1858, which was located on a site selected by King's friend, Robert E. Lee (Nixon 1986, 10).

Land ownership in the Mexican tradition had many meanings, some associated with the preservation of traditional ways of life, particularly of the family. In Mexican culture, land and cattle were for inheritance purposes, but to the Mexicans' Anglo neighbor, ranching had another meaning: it was also considered to be an investment with the potential for profit.

Richard King and his lifelong friend, Captain Mifflin Kenedy, were prime examples of this philosophy. Though they borrowed heavily from the Mexican ranching tradition, they also saw it as a financial enterprise and spent their lives devising systematic ways to add monetary profit to that family ranching tradition. As a component for financial success, both were committed to keeping their huge land holdings intact. According to the September 26, 1984, *Corpus Christi Caller*, ". . . John [G.] Kenedy Sr. passed the philosophy of his father [Mifflin Kenedy] on to his children [John G. Kenedy Jr. and Sarita Kenedy]: Never, under any circumstances, split up the 400,000-acre ranch, the father preached to his children." Mifflin Kenedy's legacy continues and the Kenedy Ranch remains an identifiable entity and is operated as a unit today. All stockholders of King Ranch are family members. Despite droughts, hurricanes, searing heat, litigation, and countless other adversities, each of these two great ranches remain viable forces in the cattle industry.

Cattle

Longhorn steers played a big part . . . Alberto "Beto" Maldonado
(King Ranch)

The history of cattle on King Ranch, generally recognized as the birthplace of the American ranching industry, is divided into four phases. The first of these involved the native Longhorns who, like the vaqueros, were Spanish descendants. These wild-running cattle were on the Ranch location before its establishment in 1853.

King also brought many Longhorns out of Mexico to begin his empire. These seed stock cattle quickly multiplied in this wild area and were tough enough to survive droughts, disease, and sometimes even evade cattle rustlers. During this period, there was little market for beef in Texas. Even if there had been more demand, Longhorn meat was considered stringy and, therefore, not particularly desirable. King continuously attempted to introduce better breeds of cattle to upgrade his herds. The numbers of these improved cattle continued to increase, and, by the end of the Civil War, the demand for meat in the North and the East led to the great trail drives. Finally, King Ranch Longhorns began to turn huge profits.

Shortly before his death in 1885, King suffered a personal tragedy in the loss of his nineteen-year-old son, Robert E. Lee King, to pneumonia. This loss almost jeopardized the future of King Ranch. After the boy's death in March 1883, Captain King entertained an offer from a British syndicate to buy him out.

King called his cattle bosses, Ramón Alvarado and Jaspar "Jap" Clark. He told them he wanted a roundup by 9:00 the next day in the Presa de las Tranquitas pasture. King looked out the window the next morning and, through his field glasses, could see all was ready. He put the buyers in a stagecoach, and he rode in a buggy to the roundup. He had the buyers stand on one of the vehicles so that they could see the herd of about twelve thousand animals. King asked Ramón why they had gathered so small a herd. Ramón told him it was because the roundup was so early, but the next day he would be able to have a larger one. The buyers wanted to know if King had more cattle than what they saw. He told them he could give them four or five roundups equal to this one. The buyers realized that they could not afford to buy the cattle in one roundup, much less the other roundups, so they left (Lea 1957, 1:357).

Like King, Mifflin Kenedy also endured the death of his son and a stepson: Thomas Kenedy, Mifflin's son, was attending a dance in Matamoros in celebration of his thirty-fifth birthday. He was accompanied by Elvira Lima, who was separated from her husband. Her husband was also at the dance, and trouble started. When Kenedy crossed back to the U.S. side at Brownsville with Elvira Lima, the husband (José Esparaza) shot Thomas Kenedy, and he died (*Corpus Christi Caller,* September 25, 1984).

Adrián J. Vidal was a stepson of Captain Kenedy's from Mrs. Kenedy's previous marriage. The stepson had a reputation as a notorious bandit. He had joined the Confederate army in October 1862, and, a year later in November 1863, he and his men left the Confederacy and joined the Union forces near Brownsville. He served as a scout—the eyes and ears of the Union army in South Texas. The next year, in 1864, he resigned his position with the Union forces and went to Mexico, where he joined the Juaristas (supporters of the exiled President Benito Juarez against the Imperial forces of Emperor Maximillian). Vidal was executed by the Imperialists in Camargo, Mexico, in 1865, as Captain Kenedy watched helplessly (*Corpus Christi Caller,* September 24, 1984).

After Captain Richard King's death in 1885, his trusted attorney and friend, Robert J. Kleberg, took over the management of the Ranch with King's widow, Henrietta King, giving advice and counsel. The next year, in 1886, he married their daughter, Alice Gertrudis King. With little knowledge of cattle ranching from the operational side, he needed and received experienced help from vaqueros. Among these were the cow boss Ramón Alvarado, in whom he had great confidence, and two expert horse bosses, Luís Robles and Julián Cantú. Also, José María Alegría had charge of the large sheep herds. Among other Kineño families already a part of the Ranch's operation were the Alegría, Alvarado, Barrientes, Cantú, Castañeda, Cavazos, de Luna, Flores, García, Garza, Gutierrez, Longória, López, Mendietta, Montalbo, Muñoz, Pérez, Quintanilla, Rodríguez, Silguero, Silva, Treviño, and Villareal families, who were all ready to help Kleberg move the Ranch forward (Account Book for Rancho Santa Gertrudis, 1854–1855, King Ranch Ledger Books).

Victor Alvarado described an example of this support in his memoirs:

> The camp or *corrida* that Ramón [Alvarado, Victor's father] brought were under orders of boss William Doughty, named Mac Doughty. Then Mac was the boss. All the cowboys wanted to quit but Ramón didn't want them to, said we should go on

with Mac, perhaps he would soon make a good boss and that's the way it turned out. Mac didn't know much of the workings of a ranch, but I and Manuel Mendietta and all other friends taught him. Mac worked and learned quickly. (Alvarado 1937, 9)

Likewise, vaquero families remained for generations as faithful workers on the Kenedy Ranch, thereby assuring its success. Members of the Encarnación Morales family were already in the area when Mifflin Kenedy set up his Ranch headquarters at the La Parra Division. Encarnación was no longer living, but his sons and stepsons, the Buenos, began working for the Kenedy Ranch more than a hundred years ago when one son, José María Morales, unloaded boats and brought supplies to the Ranch. Over twenty of his grandsons, two grandsons-in-law, fifteen great-grandsons, and seven great-great-grandsons have worked for the Kenedy Ranch. Most have been vaqueros (Villareal 1972, 11).

Kleberg continued to look for ways to upgrade King Ranch herds in an effort to meet the demands of a beef-hungry nation. Better suited to the rugged life of the desert than to supplying beef, Longhorns were soon used mainly as lead steers for handling newly branded or wild cattle (Lea 1957, 2:483).

Alberto "Beto" Maldonado of King Ranch described the uses to which the Longhorns were put:

Longhorn steers played a big part working cattle in the open. We would halter-break them. Then, as the calves were branded, we would send them to the steers and they would hold them there. At the end of the day we started the steers toward the pasture or pen where we wanted the calves, and they followed the steers. Can you imagine eight hundred just-weaned calves, trying to drive them? The steers did it for us.

We also used them to lead young cattle from one pasture to another. And we used them in the wild to bring in wild bulls. We would rope a wild bull and tie him to one of these steers and leave them alone. Eventually, the steer would take him to the trap or pens. There was a trap at the water hole. The only way the wild cattle could get to water was to go in and, once in, the gate swung shut and they couldn't get out.

Before the invention of the [bump] gate, my dad would sit on top of the windmill all night and, when the wild ones were inside, he would shut the gate. He had to stay very still and hope they didn't smell him—they were very smart.

Robert Kleberg Sr. turned to other breeds for his beef upgrading. Longhorns were eventually removed from the breeding loop and ceased to be a part of King Ranch's herd, but today they are again being bred for sale purposes. Julian Buentello recalled: "Mr. Kleberg [Robert J. Sr.] cleared out all the Longhorns at one point, and then, in 1951 and 1952, he [Bob Jr.] reintroduced them, and they have stayed in the Longhorn pasture ever since."

At the same time, Mifflin Kenedy was also improving his herds and phasing out Longhorns on the Kenedy Ranch. Bulls and cows were shipped to Alice where José Morales picked them up and brought them in carts to Kenedy Ranch (Villareal 1972, 22). As reported in Villarreal's private interview with Guadalupe Morales: "They brought in white-faced cattle, but they did not work out. Then they tried some other breeds that did not fare much better, but eventually they brought in 'red cattle' and Brahmas and slowly got rid of the Mexican cattle [Longhorns]."

Robert Kleberg Sr. began the second phase of cattle breeding on King Ranch by importing purebred British shorthorns and Herefords and eliminating the Longhorns. Before he could accomplish this, he had the challenge of ridding the pastures of the wild cattle that had been allowed to run unchecked in the years immediately preceding King's death. Ramón Alvarado's *corrida* was asked to handle the dangerous bulls. Many horses and men were injured, but Victor Alvarado remembered that they managed to find fun in this dangerous process. At the end of the day, they would take a wild bull and cut off his horns. They used canvas sacks as fighting capes and fought the bulls, to the delight of the other vaqueros (Alvarado 1937, 11).

The crossbreeding on King Ranch continued, but despite purchasing prize bulls from national shows, the breeds deteriorated. This may have been because of the differences between the hot, dry, windy climate of the Wild Horse Desert and the moist climate of the British Isles, combined with the English breed's lack of resistance to insects and thorns.

The third phase of King Ranch's remarkable cattle history was to result in the first recognized new breed of cattle in this country, and the first anywhere in over a hundred years—the Santa Gertrudis. Brahmans, cattle native to India, were crossed with carefully selected English-bred shorthorns. In 1920, an extraordinary bull named Monkey, because of his curiosity as a calf, was born on the Laureles Division. Monkey was sired by an A. P. Borden Brahman bull and a shorthorn milk cow. He combined the Brahman's ability to withstand heat and pests with the table-beef qualities of the shorthorn. The Santa Gertrudis was recognized as a new breed by the United States Government in 1940, after more than thirty-five years of meticulous breeding and crossbreeding. Monkey was the foundation sire; he would produce more than 150 useful sons.

Rogerio Silva of King Ranch remembered the special treatment Monkey received: "When he was two years old, they took him to Santa Gertrudis. They walked him to Santa Gertrudis so he would not get hurt. It took three days to walk and let him graze."

Valentín P. Quintanilla Jr. is a third-generation vaquero who also worked with the development of the new breed. He was the caporal in charge of the big *corrida* at Santa Gertrudis for seven years. Leonard Stiles said of him: "Valentín took care of the 'A' herd, which had about a thousand cattle in it. It was the foundation herd and was kept on the loop road. He focused on the five to six thousand commercial pure bred cattle, and he knew those bulls."

Manuel Silva of King Ranch tells of the dangerous work of penning bulls, a basic task required for the breeding and crossbreeding program:

> We had these cattle in the corral and had to put the bulls in a separate corral. Then we had to lasso them and cut the cuacos [horns]. The first bull we lassoed got so mad that nobody wanted to get near him. So I told Don Ricardo [Richard "Dick" Kleberg Sr.] that I would do it. He asked me how, and I said I would bring the truck and force him with it. He said, "It will break the lights of the truck." I said it wouldn't because the bull would have to bend his head in order to attack with his horns, and the truck bumper was too big and high.
>
> So the bull did attack the truck and hit the bumper and had no choice but to move where we wanted him, because he was hurting. We lassoed the bull from within the truck at a distance of about fifty feet. Two other cowboys ahead of us were ready to lasso his legs. We did that and took the bull to the pasture where he would stay.
>
> I say that, for cowboys, this is the most dangerous thing to do, the lassoing of bulls. Even with a truck. The nylon rope was attached to the truck's front bumper, and each bull weighed two thousand pounds. So if it slipped to one side of the truck, it would turn it over, or the rope would break.

The Master Showman

Dad showed the first Santa Gertrudis cattle in 1928. Alberto "Beto" Maldonado (King Ranch)

Beginning in the early 1920s, prize King Ranch animals were transported to major livestock shows, first in Texas, then around the country, and finally across the world. The name Maldonado became synonymous with expert cattle showmanship. The master showman was Librado Maldonado Sr.

JERSEYS

Librado Maldonado's skill in handling animals at shows was first perfected when he was hired at King Ranch in 1925 to work in the Jersey barn. He soon became the undisputed expert at training and grooming these milk-producers for the show ring, thus establishing an enduring family tradition that continues today.

Beto Maldonado, Librado's son, recalled:

Mr. Kleberg [Bob Jr.] would pick out twenty-five Jersey heifers and twenty-five Jersey bulls for him [Librado Sr.] to train. They would be eight or nine months old and weigh from 550 to 700 pounds. From these, they would pick six outstanding ones from each group, and we would show them for a year. Then they went back to the herd. My dad gave them all names.

Beto's older brother, Plácido Maldonado III, tells of his dad's first trips out of Texas to show King Ranch Jerseys: "In 1928 he [Librado Sr.] showed in Memphis, Tennessee. The Texas herd won first place. It included the King, Taft, Lasater, and Rio Vista Ranches."

SANTA GERTRUDIS

Beto Maldonado closely observed the master and became a famous showman in his own right. He showed with his father for the first time at the Dallas Fair in 1950. They showed Santa Gertrudis cattle and King Ranch Quarter Horses, and they also exhibited a display of King Ranch saddles. Still with the Ranch in the Visitor Management Department, Beto weaves some of his stories into the guided tours he gives:

Dad showed the first Santa Gertrudis cattle in 1928 in Houston [Texas] under a tent. Everyone wanted to know if they were for sale. He took their names and gave them [the names] to Mr. Bob [Kleberg] when he got back [to the Ranch]. Mr. Bob told him, "I will sell Santa Gertrudis cattle, but not until you can see nothing but red cattle around the Ranch headquarters and cowboys working them on sorrel horses."

We also showed at Austin, San Antonio, Fort Worth, and Dallas. I began showing with him in Dallas at the Texas State Fair in 1950.

The Maldonado family tradition of showmanship is continued at present by Librado Sr.'s twenty-two-year-old great-granddaughter, Sonia Maldonado Garcia. In 1992, she described some of her early experiences showing cattle:

I've never ridden horses. I just show cattle. I started 4-H in the third grade. We had a Black Angus cow. She dropped a Brahman-cross calf out of her, and I showed that calf in the fourth grade, and she won first place.

I learned to bathe and exercise her and how to have her stand correctly. I learned how to present myself and the animal.

My grandfather was the one who taught me, "Don't take your eyes off the judge and never let go." The first Showmanship Award I won was in the seventh grade. I had tried so hard, and finally I won. I went blank for a minute, but I didn't take my eyes off the judge. There've been some times when I've been dragged, but I never let go. This year, I had the Grand Champion at the Kleberg-Kenedy County Fair.

The Show Travels

The first day only the King of Morocco and his staff were allowed at the Fair. Alberto "Beto" Maldonado

The Santa Gertrudis breed has been shown in the far-flung reaches of the globe. Whether in Texas, another state, or on another continent, Librado always focused on the cattle. The pace of the King Ranch cattle show circuit was often strenuous. Beto and Plácido recounted the absolute dedication of their father to the welfare of the animals:

He never got tired and always worried about the animals first. We would leave a fair at midnight, or maybe 1:00 in the morning, and start to drive to the next fair so the animals would be there one or

In 1976, in honor of the U.S. bicentennial, Librado Maldonado Sr. showed a registered Santa Gertrudis bull, #1776, on the third floor of the Adolphus Hotel in Dallas, Texas. The former Texas governor John Connally is in the background.

two days to get accustomed to it. If we were to get to the fair at 3:00 in the afternoon, he would not let us stop for lunch, because the animals were thirsty. We took care of them first. You can imagine how late it was before we ate. We learned to eat when we could. We had to have the animals ready by 7:00 in the morning, and then we could have breakfast. Beto Maldonado

My dad traveled in wagons, then trucks, railroad cars, and, finally, airplanes in his lifetime. He loved railroads and fairs. We would load at Young's Siding or Caesar Pens. Dad rode with the cattle, even slept with them. Sometimes it was very hot or very cold. We took canned food: sardines, salmon, beans, and crackers. When the train stopped, we got hot coffee. Plácido Maldonado

The showings sometimes took on a flamboyant air as opportunities for publicity for the new American breed became available. Television was becoming the sensation of the media world. Beto described one such media event:

In the 1950s, we showed at the International Fair in Chicago. They wanted to show a bull on TV. So my father and Mr. Marshall

found a trailer and loaded Buen Amigo, a big, over two thousand-pound bull, and took him on the elevator to the twenty-first floor to be on TV. There were no remote cameras then.

Following the official recognition of the Santa Gertrudis as a new breed, King Ranch was in the position to transplant its adversity-resistant breed to other tropical regions of the world. Under the direction of Robert "Bob" Kleberg Jr., Cuba, South America, Australia, Spain, and Morocco were selected as expansion sites. Beto described a visit to Morocco:

In 1969, Mr. [Bob] Kleberg told my father he was going to send those bulls to Morocco and said [to me], "I want you to go with them." I was thirty-nine [years old] and got to go with my father. We were to take twenty-one two-year-old bulls, their chutes, feed, and everything. We took a special airplane. The plane load was the bulls, the air crew, and the group from King Ranch. It had special compartments that would hold two or three bulls each. Mr. Michael Hughes was the manager in Morocco, and he said he heard the plane coming—it was so loud he knew we were there. When we got there, we put the special chutes out, unloaded the bulls, and took them to special pastures where the Ranch crew had put up fences.

We were in Morocco for three weeks. We were there to introduce the Santa Gertrudis breed to the Mediterranean. The language was a problem, but we found a young man who was very helpful.

People came down from the mountains to see the Santa Gertrudis. They could not believe what they saw. My father would call, "Hey Babies," and these two thousand-pound bulls would come to him. He spoke to them in English—he said his bulls were bilingual because he spoke both English and Spanish to them.

After a few days, they [the cattle] settled down. We loaded them in trucks and took them to Casablanca for a two-week International Livestock Fair. The first day, only the King of Morocco and his staff were allowed at the fair. His father had visited Mr. Bob [Kleberg] at King Ranch, and a picture of his father [dressed] in khakis was in the booth when the King came by. My father was seventy-one at the time. It was the trip of my life.

The successful handling of these beautiful, sleek animals in a variety of places and circumstances did not just happen. Weeks and weeks of training and grooming were required, and there was no equal to the patience and expertise of Librado Maldonado in preparation for his show-ring magic.

Plácido Maldonado III left the Ranch to serve in the U.S. Army in World War II as a surgical technician. He shipped out to Africa, saw combat in Italy, and was awarded the Bronze Star for heroism. Beto Maldonado remained on the beef-producing Ranch, a critical industry for feeding troops as part of the war effort. Both sons had clear recollections of the exacting routine devised by their father for taming and grooming the show cattle, beginning with the Jerseys. They, too, followed his procedure:

TAME THEM

- Bring them into the barn and tie them to the stall fence. Check on them all during the night to be sure that they do not get tangled up.
- Untie and lead them to water.
- One month later, put a halter on. (According to Beto, his father "made the halter himself to get the right fit. He used a wooden piece to keep the halter from coming off.")
- Let them drag the halter rope and self-break themselves.
- Grab the halter rope, and tie them to the fence.
- Leave them there.
- Walk by to get them accustomed to people.
- Begin bringing them through a chute. Scratch their legs and head with a curry comb while they are in the chute.
- Use a comb with a long handle so you don't get kicked.
- Turn out the bad ones.
- Lead them to a fence, and tie them there.

GROOM THEM

- Use a giant nut or bolt and screw it into the horns and attach leather straps so it can be pulled tight to shape the growth of the horns.
- Brush them all over starting at the head and working back. Put blankets over them to make them sweat to shed old hair. Use a curry comb and get the old hair out.
- Condition their hair. Use a heavy rag and wipe from one end of the animal to the other. ("The rag," said Beto, "would get lanolin on it from so much use on the natural hair. Everyone wanted to know what kind of oil we used. It was the natural oil of the cattle.")

- Clean the horns with a small rasp; smooth with emery cloth, shine with a little oil. (Beto said he wished his dad could observe present methods because "today we use a sander and emery cloth and do in fifteen minutes what it took him an hour to do.")
- Clip ears, flanks, and switch-tails.
- Manicure hooves.
- Massage the udder and nipples of the females with oil.
- Teach them how to stand.
- Give them lots of tender loving care.

Plácido said:

Dad was a master at training. He taught them [the cattle] to stand and raise their heads. The Jerseys were gentle, except for the males, sometimes. Dad got hooked several times.

To discipline them, he used a halter with a chain under the chin and a ring in the nostril. The ring was the best. It was like a show collar on a dog.

The grooming of the Santa Gertrudis followed a similar pattern as the Jerseys, with some refinements. Beto said: "We sponged their ears and eyes and washed their tails with Ivory soap—he [Librado Sr.] wanted them to be clean and puffy. We had a hydraulically operated machine that would lay the animals on their side so we could clip and trim their hooves."

When not engrossed in the show circuit, Librado was noted for his many contributions to the youth of Kingsville and the surrounding communities. "Dad would help all the Kingsville 4-H kids," said Beto. "He would go teach them to groom, and he went to all of their shows." Beto does the same thing. He said, "I go to watch and help teach when I can."

The Auctions

People came from Africa, Australia, and South America . . .
Alberto "Beto" Maldonado

In 1950, auctions were initiated at King Ranch starring prize-winning King Ranch livestock. Instead of taking famous King Ranch animals to the world, the world would now come to King Ranch. With uncanny control and pride, Beto and Librado Maldonado showed the Ranch's best to a variety of notables from faraway places. Beto described the auctions:

In 1950, we began selling Santa Gertrudis cattle and Quarter Horses, first under a tent. At first, we just walked them through the ring. Then we halter-broke and taught them to show in the ring.

We began working eight or nine months ahead of the sale, when the individuals were chosen for auction. We began halter-breaking and training at this age—we also kept up their health certificates.

The Ranch mailed out catalogs with pictures and pedigrees and also had updated information available at the auction. People were curious and anxious to buy these outstanding individuals.

We would have a big barbecue, and people would come in their airplanes. People came from Africa, Australia, and South America. The King of Morocco came. Mr. Sid Richardson came from Dallas, and Mr. Nelson Rockefeller, and the du Ponts from New York. I have a picture of Bing Crosby with my dad. George Bush came before he was president.

At retirement, Beto moved from the show ring to the Visitor Management Department. Often driving the hourly bus tours the Ranch offers, he can answer virtually any question a visitor asks about the history or operation of the Ranch. "Last year," said Beto, "I helped guide the White House press corps when President Bush spoke at the Texas A&I (now Texas A&M University–Kingsville) commencement. Lauro Cavazos Jr., then U.S. Secretary of Education and a King Ranch descendant, was here with his aide, whose home is also Kingsville. The White House photographer was also from Kingsville."

An Era Ends

It was to be his final appearance . . . Falfurrias Facts

In 1980, Librado Maldonado suffered a stroke that would prove to be fatal, and with him a legend died.

The following cutline appeared in the February 17, 1983, *Falfurrias Facts* at the time of Librado Sr.'s death: "The Crowd at the 1979 King Ranch Sale Applauds as Maldonado Enters the Ring. . . . It was to be his final appearance at the annual Santa Gertrudis sale" (King Ranch Archives).

Beto spoke about his father's last three bedridden years: "My sister took care of him. The Ranch furnished the hospital bed, and the nurses and doctors, and a special therapist who came to the house. They would read the EKG by phone from the hospital—he wanted to be at home."

Catalina Maldonado described her grandfather after his stroke:

I remember when he had the stroke. He was paralyzed, couldn't talk, and refused to eat unless I fed him. I lived in town and would come out here and feed him on my lunch hour.

The bulls were his life. I remember the first auction after he was in bed, and he could hear the auctioneer. He sat in his room and cried the whole time because he could hear from his house—it was right there. I'm sure it just killed him that it was going on, and he wasn't there.

The Next Generation

. . . we had the first airborne auction on the way to Hawaii.
Alberto "Beto" Maldonado

Beto Maldonado worked with both King Ranch cattle and horses all his life, from the time he was a small boy tagging along after his father, to being hired to work at the Jersey barn. Most of his time, however, was spent working in various tasks related to cattle.

I went to work with the Santa Gertrudis cattle in the 1960s. King Ranch ran forty cows to the bull, and I kept records on them and looked after them. At weaning time, I found the calves by following the mother back from the water hole. The calves would be branded on the butt. I kept these records for twenty-six years.

When my brother, Plácido, went to World War II, I went to the veterinarian department and worked with Dr. Northway. He was a wonderful man and helped everybody. People would come to get the Santa Gertrudis bulls in pickup trucks—they were not used to them being so much bigger than Jerseys. Dr. Northway would send us to the garage to get railing for their trucks to keep the bulls from jumping out.

Those animals were very smart. When I had to draw blood, or do something else they didn't like, I would not say a word so they wouldn't know it was me. I wouldn't speak when I put the ring in the nose because they would recognize my voice. The voice is the main thing—not sight. . . . In the beginning, Santa Gertrudis bulls were selling for $100. Later, the two-year-old bulls brought

In 1985, Alberto "Beto" Maldonado Sr. took King Ranch's bull, Macho, to the Dallas, Texas, airport to "buy a ticket" to Hawaii as a promotion for the Santa Gertrudis Breeders' International (SGBI) first airborne auction. Beto learned his technique for handling bulls from his father, Librado Maldonado Sr., the expert King Ranch cattle showman.

> *between $4,000 and $16,000. The highest [price paid for a] bull at the Ranch was $52,000.*

Like his father, Beto was known for his gentle way with, and respect for, animals. In Beto's own words: "Macho and I were friends. I hated to put a ring in his nose, but that was the only way to control an animal that size. I had to do it. . . . I consider wildlife my pets. I don't do much hunting. . . . My father didn't hunt either."

After his father's death, Beto continued the family tradition of handling cattle. Just as his father had done before him, he became the top showman:

> *In 1985, we had the first airborne auction on the way to Hawaii. They asked me to take Macho to the Dallas airport and "buy him a ticket" to help [with] the publicity. We drove to Georgetown and spent the night there at a friend's ranch, then went on to Dallas where we spent the night at the airport. They had a special place set up for him. All the employees kept coming downstairs to see this bull.*

> *I learned from my father to take him off bran three days be-*
> *fore and off water the day before. I went over the path ahead of*
> *time. There were media there from all over. I walked to the ticket*
> *cabinet, and there were about 250 people there. Macho shined like*
> *glass and behaved like a gentleman. He weighed 2,800 pounds and*
> *stood there an hour because everybody wanted their picture made*
> *with him.*

Beto always refers to the cattle as this individual or that individual. He speaks with profound respect for these animals, as if they all have identity and importance. This near-reverence may be the key to the Maldonados' phenomenal success with cattle.

King Ranch Santa Cruz

By 1988, a new market segmentation had evolved, leading to the fourth phase of cattle breeding on King Ranch. The market created a need for earlier maturity and a demand for leaner beef. To meet the requirements of this niche, the Ranch began to develop a new breed, the King Ranch Santa Cruz. The composite breed is one-half Santa Gertrudis, one-fourth Gelbvieh, and one-fourth Red Angus. This combination is proving not only to be suitable for the South Texas climate, but is adaptable to other climates as well. The first calves were born in 1990, and the breed was officially introduced to the American ranching industry in 1994. According to Beto Maldonado, the Santa Cruz produce more meat and leaner meat than the Santa Gertrudis, because they reach maturity and ideal weight earlier. Santa Cruz calves weigh about 580 pounds, compared to 500 pounds for the Santa Gertrudis; the Santa Cruz cow weighs about 1,150 pounds, compared to the Santa Gertrudis' 1,250 pounds; and Santa Cruz bulls weigh about 1,800 pounds, compared to 1,600 pounds for the Santa Gertrudis bulls.

Tio Kleberg, vice president of agriculture for the Ranch, commented on the King Ranch Santa Cruz:

> We knew we could use hybrid vigor and increase fertility and
> feedyard performance of our cattle by bringing in other breeds.
> . . . But which breeds? We wanted to keep the red color, so we
> went with Gelbvieh and Red Angus. If we had found a breed
> that wasn't red but brought a lot more to the table, we would
> have used it. (Wolfshohl 1995, 44)

From the days of the first Longhorns to the new Santa Cruz breed, the use of cutting-edge technologies has enabled King Ranch to alter their cattle through breeding in order to meet market demands. During this process, stability and consistency in the day-to-day operation of the Ranch have been maintained because of the vaqueros. From the day a calf is born and recorded, it is fed, watered, doctored, and groomed by hands trained by generations of knowledge.

Horses

When Captain King turned his attention to horses, he again looked to northern Mexico for help. Just as he had bought his first cows from Pedro and Anselmo Flores, who lived in Tamaulipas, Mexico, he also bought a remuda of horses from them. As soon as word got out that King was buying horses, many people began to bring their horses to sell to him. He began by buying twenty-five mares and a stallion. In his memoirs, Victor Alvarado recalled that his grandmother's brother, Damón Ortíz, drove his horses to Captain King's new rancho on the Santa Gertrudis Creek. Captain King bought cheap mustang stock and immediately began upgrading the herd. As early as 1854, he bought a sorrel stud named Whirlpool for $600. Horses brought the first cash income for King only a year after he purchased his land. He sold horses and mules in two transactions, one for $23 and one for $1,000, in June 1854 (Denhardt 1970, 27).

But Captain King did not see himself as a horse trader. He wanted to develop the best possible Ranch horses, which he knew were necessary for working his cattle herds. He also knew that his safety and that of his men in the desert, who were still vulnerable to bandit raids, would depend on superior horses. First, he began moving out undesirables by selling, trading, or giving them away. This effort would continue for the next two generations on King Ranch. Victor Alvarado described the following instance:

> Then came bosses Luis Robles and Julian Cantu to catch the horses. They couldn't catch them all. Kleberg [Robert Sr.] needed to clean the pasture in order to use it, and he announced to everybody that wished that they could go and catch the horses they wanted in the pasture and he would give them [the horses] to them. Many men came and made temporary pens, and they roped until they caught them all.

King began paying top dollar for the best horse stock available and early on established King Ranch's reputation for excellent mounts.

One of the most interesting stories about King Ranch horses dates back to around 1884 (Lea 1957, 1:362). Martín Mendietta Jr. retold it:

> *These were the gray horses, and the legend is that Captain King offered a stranger lodging, and when the stranger left, he left his gray horse and told the vaquero to tell Captain King that Jesse James left him a horse. They called these horses the Comanches. The gray horses were kept at Norias. The grays are still on the Ranch.*

Robert Kleberg assumed the management role on King Ranch in January 1886 at the request of his future mother-in-law, and he continued to upbreed. Just as was his practice with cattle, he was determined to produce superior horse stock. He placed the best studs with a controlled group of mares, carefully selecting animals for uniformity of color and features. He continued to clear all non-breeding stock, disposing of them however he could, even driving them across the Rio Grande into Mexico. Julian Buentello recalled, "We killed out the wild horses and burros. If we caught them, we could have them or kill them. The wild horses caused a lot of trouble and scattered the other horses."

The Upgrade Accelerates

By the 1920s, Bob Kleberg Jr. had returned home from college to begin taking over supervision of the Ranch from his ailing father. His work over the next fifty-plus years was to greatly impact ranching worldwide. One of his major contributions to the industry was the creation of one of the four foundation families for the American Quarter Horse (Cypher 1995, 12).

Bob Kleberg's ideal horse for the Ranch was one that would have stamina, speed, cow sense, and a gentle nature. Finally, he located and purchased a foal he thought was the perfect animal for the building of his ideal horse family. Bob, who was only nineteen at the time, coaxed his cousin, Caesar Kleberg, into purchasing this particular stallion from George Clegg. This stallion, known as the Old Sorrel, became to the King Ranch Quarter Horse line what Monkey was to the Santa Gertrudis herd. The Old Sorrel was crossbred with Thoroughbreds, and eventually the sorrel King Ranch Quarter Horse was perfected.

Other King Ranch Quarter Horses, Mr. San Peppy and his son, Peppy San Badger (also called Little Peppy), became two of the most famous cutting horses in the world. Mr. San Peppy was the first cutting horse to win over $100,000, and he won the National Cutting Horse Association Open World Championship twice. By January 1995, Little Peppy's offspring had won in excess of $7 million (*Traveling Historic Texas,* 7).

Meanwhile, the effort to eradicate undesirable animals continued. The Kenedy and King Ranches could not afford for these animals to interfere with their carefully structured breeding programs. "The trick," said Jesus Gonzales of Kenedy Ranch, "was to control the lead stallion by getting him to follow tame horses. The other wild horses would follow, and they could be trapped in corrals. Sometimes thirty or forty wild horses could be trapped this way."

Critical Skills

. . . the vaquero in the center would rope his hind feet. Martín Mendietta Jr. (King Ranch)

While the Ranch owners conceptualized the direction the Ranches would take, the vaqueros executed the expert techniques necessary to accomplish these goals.

Julian Buentello married into one of the oldest Kineño families, the Quintanillas, and went to work with them at Laureles. He became one of the best at handling horses. Leonard Stiles rememberd how Julian knew all of the horses:

Each man would ride twelve to fifteen horses each. If you were out and couldn't find your horse, Julian would whistle in just a minute, and he had found the horse you were looking for. If you roped the wrong horse, Julian would tell you [that] you had someone else's horse.

He was the remuda boss, and he was expert at his job. When important people would come, Mr. Bob [Kleberg] or Mr. Dick [Kleberg Jr.] would ask Julian to choose the horse for them because he knew the horses so well.

No one rode Mr. Bob's horse but him, unless it was Julian. He would ask Julian to get the "kinks" out, and Julian would say "Why?" and Mr. Bob would say, "If someone is going to be bucked off, I want it to be you."

One time he told Mr. Bob to be careful of a particular horse because that horse did not like paper. While riding with the herd,

Mr. Bob was looking for certain bloodlines that he had written on paper, and he kept the paper tucked in his boot. He forgot one day, and pulled the paper out of his boot while he was still on the horse and nearly got bucked off.

Martín Mendietta Jr. is a fifth-generation vaquero on King Ranch who worked for years with the horse operation. His family members have been leaders in each generation: "My father, Martín Sr., came from Curida, Mexico, in the 1880s. He was a caporal at Santa Gertrudis. Javier Mendietta, his brother, was the next caporal, then my cousin Valentín Quintanilla Jr., then Sixto, another cousin, and I was caporal from 1963 to 1985. Alfredo 'Chito' Mendietta, my cousin, is a caporal today."

The Mendietta name on King Ranch is synonymous with expert knowledge of horses. Martín Jr., who worked on both the Kenedy and King Ranches, described his father's work:

Mr. Bob [Kleberg] sent the horses to the mare barn to be trained, and my father and his brothers trained them. They started by riding them bareback, then father trained them to the buggy. As a kid, I rode on the backs of the buggy horses to get them used to having somebody on them before they were broken to the saddle. This type mare was used to pull the carriage that took Mr. Bob's daughter, Helenita, to her wedding. These were Quarter Horses from the Ranch.

As an added detail, Miguel Muñiz recalled, "I drove the carriage of Helenita to her wedding. While I was taming that horse, I was kicked, and it broke my leg."

Martín, Jr., also had the uncanny ability to accurately identify horses through his almost perfect powers of observation and memory. This ability became invaluable, because accurate, intricate records were critical during the upbreeding period. According to Leonard Stiles:

Mr. Dick [Kleberg Jr.] could get his secretary to write down the descriptions of the mare and the type of markings and what stallion they were bred to. Martín could go out in the pasture and locate the colt. Every horse had a registration name and a nickname, and Martín knew both. Mr. Dick would say, "What horse is Chino [Gonzales] riding?" and Martín would tell him . . . what mare and stallion [had produced that horse].

He knows features and colors. Some people can remember and tell a man's son because he [the son] looks like him. Well, Martín could do that with horses.

Martín was an expert at breaking horses. He described the process vaqueros used when the numbers that needed to be broken escalated:

We would take the one-year-olds and halter break [them], lead [them], [and] pick up their feet to get them used to people. Then we branded them and took them off their mother. Next, we put them with old horses with bells on them—the males with an old male horse, and the females with an old female horse.

At two years old, we brought them back in. We had handled them a couple of times a year, trimming hooves and grooming, again to get them used to people. At three years old, we actually broke them. Many of the men already had their favorites by then.

We ran the horses in the corral for a few days, then mounted them. The old men would spread out in front and back, and we would trot, then lope the colts. The faster you got them to lope, the less chance of them bucking. We loped them from the corral to the bump gate—about a mile—and back. While they were winded, we stopped, started, got on and off. The next step was to work them a half day. We did this every spring about April.

Martín also described an earlier method of breaking horses:

We would have an old vaquero stand in the center of the corral with a rope. After the men had the horses used to the bridle, blanket, and saddle, they would put their horses in the corral, about five at a time. Upon signal from the vaquero in the center, who would say, "Riders Up," they would mount their horses and ride them in a circle around the corral with an older vaquero on a gentle horse in front and back. If a horse tried to buck, the vaquero in the center would rope his hind feet to distract him.

Vaqueros stopped breaking horses at about forty-five or fifty [years of age]. The old men always had respect and had the pick of the horse they wanted.

The vaqueros were highly skilled at gentling these animals, and each had his own special way of accomplishing the task. Enemorio Serna of the Kenedy Ranch described a slightly different method: "We would rope him, tie one foot up, pet him, lead him, and ride him. Then we would work him for a week in the pen and turn him loose. We used different bits. The Thoroughbreds were easier to train, more intelligent. But they were too skinny and tired too quickly."

No matter the method, breaking horses was a hazardous business. According to Villarreal, "Jesse Salazar remembers being dragged by a horse on two different occasions in his eight-year career. He escaped serious injury both times, but other vaqueros were not as lucky. Augustin Cavazos, who was working on the adjacent Armstrong Ranch, was kicked to death by a horse he was trying to break. . . . Augustin's death occurred even though he was working under controlled conditions. He was breaking a horse inside a corral while his father and several other vaqueros watched from the fence" (1972, 43).

In addition to his expert training and showmanship with cattle, Beto Maldonado also worked with King Ranch Quarter Horses. He worked as assistant to Dr. Northway, the veterinarian, and had extensive knowledge of the breeding program. Beto recalled:

> *I remember Old Sorrel very well. We were still hand-breeding him at the age of twenty-six. I still have a picture of Old Sorrel in my head. He was purchased in 1915 from George Clegg. He was the foundation of the Quarter Horse family here at the Ranch today. . . . Mr. Bob was a very smart, intelligent man, and had a good idea what a horse was going to be when he bought him. In 1941, Wimpy was the number one horse registered by the [American] Quarter Horse Association. He was the grandson of [the] Old Sorrel. In 1984, the two-millionth Quarter Horse was registered, and it was a filly from King Ranch, a descendant of Old Sorrel and Wimpy.*

Another famous King Ranch horse was Peppy. Beto was also attached to him.

> *I would ride Peppy before Dr. Northway was going to show him to people [in the 1940s]. It was like riding in a Cadillac. I can compare it to riding in the El Kineño, which was the family hunting car; one time Mr. Dick [Sr.] picked me up on the Ranch road and I rode in it. It was like riding Peppy, with the gentle rock and taking the bumps so easily.*
>
> *Dr. Northway would give Peppy peppermint sticks and when people knew this, they would send him peppermint sticks from all over. I always loved candy and would share with Peppy. He had a good disposition. He was broad, heavy, strong, powerful, turned on a dime and easy to rein.*
>
> *There was a twenty-five-pound flour sack that had the picture of Peppy on it.*

Beto was responsible for the daily, routine care of the these Quarter Horses:

I had three thousand Quarter Horses that I had to vaccinate, take care of, and keep records on. At first, they got four shots, one week apart. I vaccinated five hundred horses in one day. We ran them through the chute and vaccinated them with a 1 cc vial in a small syringe. I refilled it for each horse and used the same needle. I clipped the hair, used alcohol to clean the animal and the needle, refilled the syringe, picked up the hide, and drove the needle in. If it was a good vaccination, it would develop a nodule. I did the same thing with the mules at Santa Cruz—they were mean.

The horses were identified by the names of pens and pastures. When I first started identifying and vaccinating horses we had to vaccinate four times a year. When we got finished with the last group, it was time to start over again. Later they just got two a year. Now it's one.

I also helped with the auctions. At first the Quarter Horses would go for $500, and later the highest price paid for a stallion was $125,000.

Lolo Treviño of King Ranch recalled: "These horses were marked with the Running W brand, the Ranch division, year, [and] the sire and dam. The number was tattooed on the right leg. Mares were numbered on the right side of the neck—three numbers at the most."

To break horses, certain tools were necessary. Martín Mendietta Jr. described the rope and bits used: "I used a hair rope first without a bit. Then I used a snapping bit. Next I used a hard bit with a roller that allowed the horse to roll it around in his mouth. This kept him from throwing his head up." The bits were usually made on King Ranch.

Martín started working with his father at the mare barn at nine years of age. He was still working there when he got married, and paid a price for his expertise:

I was working with my father and was eighteen years old. Mr. Bob decided to send fifteen mares to Lexington, Kentucky. "Chorche" [George] Mayorga, Beto Maldonado, and I went. I got married on Sunday and left for Kentucky early Monday morning. They put us on the train with the mares, and we were gone a week before we came back to Kingsville. I spent my honeymoon by myself.

Like his father and grandfather before him, Martín passed his knowledge on to his sons.

I taught my nine sons, all but one—he didn't like horses. I said to them, "You stay here and watch me, then you take the calf from

*here to there." I took them after school and on the weekend so they
would learn. I gave them the old horses that knew what they were
doing. After you learn, you start making your own horses.*

Manuel Silva worked with horses for twenty-seven years. He had a
special motivation for making them his favorites:

*I took care of the small colts. They moved them to the race track,
then I tamed horses. It took a long time to make them mild and
tame. When they were like that, they took them away, brought
new wild ones, and we had to start all over again. Some were
tamed for sale. The tall reds were tamed for racing—they went to
Chicago, California, and New York. I took some horses to California for sale. The horses were taken to Hawaii. I preferred the horses
because I wanted to be one of the best lassoers.*

Manuel reached his goal. He was probably one of the best ropers ever to
work at King Ranch.

Manuel's brother, Rogerio Silva, is a caporal who has worked many
years on the Laureles Division's 256,000 acres. He estimated that he has
"ridden over 500,000 miles on a horse."

José Alvarado of King Ranch is a descendant of Francisco Alvarado
(born 1800), who died saving Captain King from Union soldiers during the American Civil War. The story is a familiar one to present-day
vaqueros:

As King was a Confederate, he was afraid that some day the Yankees might come to the Ranch and harm him because he belonged to the opposition party. It happened one day when he
was very peaceful with his family on the Ranch, thinking about
his business, then came before him a man, a friend of his, and
told him: "Captain, take care for I know well tonight a troop
of Yankees are coming to arrest you." King believed his friend
and prepared to leave. He notified his wife what was happening,
said he had to leave as soon as possible. He went to the house
where my grandfather [Francisco Alvarado] lived, because he
was one of the most trusted servants, and told him: "Francisco,
you go and sleep at my house and take care of my family. I
have to leave now, and I don't know when I can return." My
grandfather obeyed the orders of his boss. Very early he went
to the King house, and Mrs. King told him secretly what was
happening, and to be careful, to let her know if he saw anything.
Nightfall came, and Mrs. King placed a cot for him in the hall

Henrietta M. Chamberlain married Captain Richard King on December 10, 1854, in Brownsville, Texas, and moved with him to his Santa Gertrudis cow camp where they raised their family. After Captain King's death, Henrietta continued to transform the crude cow camp into one of the largest ranching establishments in the world. Courtesy of King Ranch Archives, King Ranch, Inc.

where my grandfather was to sleep. Very early, I don't know what time at night, the troop of Yankees appeared, and they surrounded the yard and house and began to fire at the house. My grandfather got up quickly to tell them not to fire on the house, that there was a family there, but as they saw the shadow of

This is the first family home that was built for Henrietta King by Captain King on the Santa Gertrudis Division. It was on this front porch that Francisco Alvarado was killed while protecting Mrs. King and her family from Union soldiers who were in pursuit of her husband, Captain King, during the American Civil War. Courtesy of King Ranch Archives, King Ranch, Inc.

my grandfather, they fired on him and there he fell dead on the porch of the house. When my grandmother and her sons learned of the tragedy that had happened, they hurried to lift the body. Among the troop of Yankees were some Mexicans, some of them were friends of the Alvarado family. They regretted very much what had happened by mistake. (Alvarado 1937, 11)

Generations later, Francisco's descendant José also worked with the King heirs. "We are in charge of the stables and carriages and saddle horses," added José.

Miguel Muñiz came to King Ranch around 1920, at about the same time Bob Kleberg returned home from college to begin managing it. Miguel spent his life in the Ranch's loyal service. He was in charge of the King Ranch Quarter Horses, including Peppy, Rey del Rancho, and Little Man. He was still riding a horse past the age of eighty. As the oldest vaquero, he would lead the funeral procession for his special friend, Bob Kleberg, in 1974. Miguel recalled: "Bob Kleberg was my good friend. I remember when he came back from college to take over the Ranch. Robert Kleberg [Sr.] was paralyzed at that point and had to be taken around by car."

The Thoroughbreds

I broke Assault. Lolo Treviño

In 1936, Bob Kleberg became fascinated with race horses during a visit to Kentucky. He was challenged, with what he saw in horse operations there, to become a breeder and a winner. He already owned a superior stallion named Chicaro. So, to create the ideal racing horse, he began purchasing top-rate mares for his Thoroughbred breeding program.

But Bob Kleberg wanted to race horses raised in Texas because he believed that they would be stronger. Even the colts that were foaled on the Kentucky property were shipped to the Ranch when weaned. A race track was constructed for them, along with fireproof stables. He implemented a highly regimented training program similar to the one that had worked so well for the Quarter Horses. Likewise, the hands-on work in this meticulously orchestrated program fell to the vaqueros.

First, the horses were gentled. By fourteen months of age they had been periodically bridled and saddled. They were then involved with "breezing," which means learning to run quickly and easily on the training track. By the time they were eighteen months old, they were working against a stopwatch (Lea 1957, 2:668). Throughout this process, the vaqueros gently cared for these future champions.

In 1938, Bob Kleberg made his ultimate purchase. He acquired the Kentucky Derby–winner Bold Venture, who was to sire Assault, the 1946 Triple Crown winner, and Middleground, the winner of the 1950 Kentucky Derby and Belmont Stakes. Martín Mendietta Jr. remembered when Bold Venture came: "They brought him on the train. I walked him from Caesar's Pens to Martín's [Mendietta Sr.] Barns, about ten miles, so we wouldn't injure him. He was very sturdy."

Beto Maldonado also worked with the Thoroughbreds, using the same gentle care he perfected with his bulls:

> *Assault was even better tempered than Bold Venture. He had a bad foot and was almost destroyed. I petted him all the time. A lot of stallions would try to nip you, but not Assault. He would just stand there and let you pet him.*
>
> *We [the Ranch] purchased Bold Venture for around $40,000 and everyone thought that was a "world of money," but he was worth it. Bold Venture was stout and looked like a Quarter Horse. He was very gentle. We hand-bred him to mares; we always hand-bred Thoroughbred mares.*

Martín Mendietta Jr. described his own experiences with Assault:

Dr. Northway thought Assault looked good. He was bred at King Ranch, and my father probably helped in breeding. Middleground and Assault were half-brothers by Bold Venture. They kept him [Assault] at King [Ranch] until he was two [years old] and broke him there. He stepped on a surveyor's stake. Juan Silva was the blacksmith, and he rebuilt the split hoof. We called him [Assault] "the slow-footed comet". . . . I was working cows at Laureles, branding calves. When the race came on, we gathered by the car radio. Everyone stopped, and Mr. Dick [Kleberg Sr.] said, "Let's listen to the race." We all listened to Assault win the Kentucky Derby! It was 1946.

When Assault moved into the winner's circle at the Kentucky Derby—the first race of the "Big 3" that he would win—and the blanket of roses was placed across his elegant shoulders, Bob Kleberg's ultimate dream became a reality. On that day, King Ranch was fully established as a major racehorse breeder. It would remain so for the next twenty years.

Beto's brother, Plácido, also worked with the King Ranch veterinary program before leaving for military service in 1942. He said: "I went to work in the vet department with Dr. Northway in 1937. I took care of the medicines and supplies. I was only fourteen years old, but I soon took over giving the injections."

José Garcia was the exercise jockey for Assault and the other Thoroughbreds. His wife, Nicolasa "Nico" Quintanilla Garcia, told of his adventures:

Lauro Cavazos saw him sweeping up the garage and noticed he was small and asked him if he would like to learn to ride. At first he was scared, but he learned to ride well. He went to New York every summer to train with Mr. Max Hirsch. The first time he went, he was only fourteen and he had to be sixteen, so they lied about his age.

We married on February 12, 1949, and in April Joe left for New York and stayed 'til November. He got morning sickness and was throwing up, and didn't know why. Then he got a letter telling him that I was expecting [a baby], and the men all teased him a lot.

He went every year until he had four sons, and he told them he didn't want to do that any more. So he worked full time on the Ranch with the horses. But one time Mr. Hirsch needed him because he had a horse that kept throwing the riders, and they

José Garcia riding Assault, the 1946 Triple Crown winner. Standing nearby is Max
Hirsch, the trainer. José was the exercise jockey for Assault and many other King Ranch
Thoroughbred racers.

> *needed Joe to come work with him. This was 1963. He took all of*
> *us, and we drove five days to get to New York and stayed there*
> *while he worked with the horse. Our son, Joe Jr., trains and races*
> *at the Santa Anita track in California now.*

After winning almost every major racing title in America, Assault
returned to King Ranch where he remained until he died in 1971. He had
a special run and stall, and was fed carrots by his visitors. A startling dis-
appointment for the Ranch was that the great champion, who should
have earned millions of dollars as a stud, proved to be sterile. Assault is
buried on the Santa Gertrudis Division.

"Joe [José] was crazy about Assault," said Nico. "The day they put
him to sleep and buried him, Joe was there and it was very sad for him."

Lolo Treviño is another in a long line of Treviño vaqueros. The Treviño family preceded Captain King at Santa Gertrudis; they are descendants of the de la Garza family, who named the Santa Gertrudis Creek
after their daughter's patron saint, Saint Gertrude. Lolo began exercising
and breaking horses when he was ten years old. He, too, worked with
Assault:

> *I broke Assault. When Assault was a colt his mother was in bad shape. We were told to kill both. Then Mr. Bob [Kleberg] came, and Assault was weaned, and we began to work to straighten out his bad foot. Dr. Northway and I took the loose stuff off his hoof, used ointment, and wrapped it with a thin cloth. He began to improve.*
>
> *Assault was desperate all the time, ready to go. He wouldn't stay still for anything. The race track was too wet, so I went to the barn to walk him. He started bucking and biting. He bit me! I walked him and then got on, and he settled down. I broke Thoroughbreds for eight years. My twin brother is really a better rider. My older brother was a jockey.*

Bob Kleberg's breeding program was an astounding success. The brown-and-cream silks of King Ranch Thoroughbreds have taken the winner's circle at three Belmont Stakes, two Kentucky Derbys, one Preakness, a Santa Anita Derby, and the Wood Memorial—and this is only a partial list. The list of victories includes, of course, Assault's Triple Crown. From 1946 to 1955, King Ranch Thoroughbreds earned purses totaling from $320,000 to $837,000 (*Traveling Historic Texas*, 6).

Owners Were Involved

> *. . . the owners presented the vaqueros a medallion.* Martín Mendietta Jr. (King Ranch)

Richard "Dick" Kleberg Jr. worked closely with the horse operation, side by side with the vaqueros. He was often quick to share with them his opinion about their work.

Martín Mendietta Jr. recalled that "Mr. Dick would say, 'You should have been riding without a bridle. I've always thought the horse had more sense than the rider. Take off the bridle, and let the horse work.'"

Valentín Quintanilla Sr. recollected that "when visitors came, Mr. Dick would ask for a horse that would pitch and put me on him and we would put on a show."

When Dick Kleberg Jr. died in 1979, the vaqueros were given the day off, and they were invited to come to the Main House at Santa Gertrudis, where the funeral took place outside. Kleberg's mare, saddled and riderless, was a poignant reminder of his role in the day-to-day operation of the Ranch. He had left orders for his funeral, which included cremation, no procession, and mementos for the vaqueros.

Martín Mendietta Jr. remembered the occasion:

> We had a big barbecue, and the corrida cooks came and helped fix the food. There was also a mariachi band. After the funeral, the family presented the vaqueros with a medallion that was struck by Lincoln Borglum [the son of Gutzon Borglum, the designer and architect of Mt. Rushmore]. One side had a picture of Pepino out of [by] Monkey, and the other side had Niño, a horse, on it. The medallion had been done early, and the horns on Pepino looked like a cucumber, which is English for pepino. On the edge it had "MLK-RMK."

Sheep and Goats

> . . . Can you find a goat for my Helenita? Catarino Moreno (King Ranch)

The cattle and horses were not the only livestock that brought profit to the Ranches. Sheep and goats also readily adapted to the terrain of these vast lands. Between 1870 and 1874, when the cattle market was soft, King "tided his Ranch over until the market grew firm" (Lea, "The Mighty Ranch of Richard King," 41). He had over twenty thousand head of sheep and eight thousand head of goats on his land (Lehman 1969, 105). Upon King's death in 1885, the *Corpus Christi Caller* described him as the largest wool producer. From this wool, King Ranch developed its famous cream-colored saddle blankets with the Running W brand. Their extraordinary thickness provided more protection and comfort for the horse than could be found elsewhere.

Catarino Moreno was a shepherd at Norias: "At first I had goats and lambs, but few, because Uncle Caesar [Kleberg] brought from Africa lambs with fat tails and black skin. They produced a lot. They grew up to be big and fat, and he was very pleased when he noticed that they were really producing a lot [of wool]."

Catarino said that, anytime Caesar Kleberg saw him, he used to greet Catarino like this:

> "What's up viejo?" [my old friend, or my old man]. "How are the chiquitos?" [referring to the goats, but mistakenly using the word for little babies, which sounds almost the same]. I said, "They're

looking pretty, they're fine. What about yours?" That was a joke already.

Uncle Caesar used to tease me a lot. He would come and ask me if I had seen his valentín *[nilgai], and when I told him that I saw one, he would tell his interpreter to ask me if I had seen an elephant or a camel.*

Mr. Roberto [Bob Kleberg], he was a good person, but I couldn't—I don't know how to say it—be myself with him. I felt embarrassed with him, or maybe less comfortable. I guess that is how it had to be. I met Helenita, Don Roberto [Jr.'s] daughter, because he used to ask me, "Can you find a goat for my Helenita?" So I would get her a small one that was black and white.

Wherever the prize King Ranch animals were shown anywhere in the world, knowledgeable, highly skilled vaqueros would be ever close at hand. The vaqueros never quite concealed the pride they took in their association with the finest. As María Luisa Montalvo Silva said, "I am a Kineño, and I am glad to be a Kineño."

Pride in being Kineños, King People, emerged from the long-term relationships between the King Ranch owners and the workers who stayed on the Ranch, often for generations. Similar relationships existed between the Kenedeños and the owners of the Kenedy Ranch. A mutual respect developed out of the workers' loyalty to the owners and the reliance of the owners on the vaqueros' expert knowledge in raising cattle and training horses (Graham 1994, 40). This knowledge was passed from father to son, from mother to daughter, and afforded the Ranches the stable work force that was vital to their success.

Note

1. During her interview, Norma Martinez recounted her conversations with some of the old vaqueros, one of which was Valentín Quintanilla, a family member. They told her that their ancestors came from a village called Cruias (Cruillas), which was located in northern Mexico at the foot of the Sierra Madre mountain range, southeast from Monterrey four to six hours. While doing research, Martinez said that she found the name, Cruias, on a map made in the 1930s or 1940s.

Porfirio Alvarado (1861–1933) was the grandson of Francisco Alvarado, the Kineño who died helping to save Henrietta King from Union troops when they raided Santa Gertrudis hoping to capture Captain King during the American Civil War. Porfirio also worked as a caporal for Captain King.

Macario Alegría and his wife Manuela are the parents of José Alegría. José was the cook for the Main House at the Santa Gertrudis Division and was famous for his small biscuits.

Antonia Gaytan worked for Henrietta King, as did Antonia's mother, Virginia Cavazos, and daughter, Manuela Mayorga. They would spend hours preparing enchiladas for Mrs. King and her guests. Photograph by Toni Frizzell, courtesy of King Ranch Archives, King Ranch, Inc.

Manuela G. Mayorga is the daughter of Antonia Gaytan. Manuela often missed her school recess so she could go home to help grind fresh corn for Henrietta King's enchiladas. Manuela was married to George "Chorche" Mayorga, who was a vaquero at the Santa Gertrudis Division of King Ranch, as was his father, Macario Mayorga.

From left: Librado Maldonado Sr., George "Chorche" Mayorga, and Miguel Muñiz. All were famous vaqueros on King Ranch. Librado was the master showman, George was an excellent roper, and Miguel was in charge of the Quarter Horses. Miguel also became a master braider in later years.

Librado Maldonado Sr. (second from left) is showing off El Carlos, a King Ranch Quarter Horse stallion, to his famous visitors, Bing and Kathy Crosby during their visit to King Ranch in the 1940s. Standing next to the Crosbys is Major Thomas R. Armstrong, who was married to Henrietta Kleberg Larkin Armstrong.

Xavier Quintanilla with his wife, Teresa. They are Valentín P. Quintanilla's parents. The Quintanilla family probably came to the Ranch from the Mexican village, Cruias (Cruillas), with Captain King. The Quintanilla family has worked with the King family for more than 140 years.

Plácido Maldonado III worked with the Quarter Horses and Thoroughbreds in the Veterinarian Department of King Ranch at the Santa Gertrudis Division. He also earned a Bronze Star in World War II.

Manuel Silva Sr. has been called one of the most skillful men with a rope on King Ranch. Before his retirement, he was also in charge of gentling and handling the Thoroughbreds on the Santa Gertrudis Division. Photograph by Toni Frizzell, courtesy of King Ranch Archives, King Ranch, Inc.

From left: Roberto Mendietta, Julian Buentello, Valentín Quintanilla Jr., and George Mayorga. Pictured here on King Ranch in 1980, these four vaqueros served together for forty-eight years.

Juan Guevara Sr. is a third-generation vaquero on the Kenedy Ranch, and he has worked all aspects of the Ranch. He is married to Stella Guevara and is the father of Juan Guevara Jr.

Stephen J. "Tio" Kleberg presents each of these King Ranch vaqueros with an award for their contributions to the South Texas Ranching tradition. The awards were presented in 1993 by the Ranching Heritage Festival during the annual gala that is held each February on the Texas A&M University–Kingsville campus. From left: Valentín P. Quintanilla Jr., Jamie Quintanilla, Julian Buentello, Manuel Silva, Kleberg, Rogerio Silva, and King Ranch retiree Leonard Stiles.

Growing Up on the Wild Horse Desert

"*Levántate.*" "Time to get up," his mother said gently. It was 5:00 A.M., and time for the boy's day to begin. Alberto "Beto" Maldonado, age seven, put his feet on the hard plank floor and dragged himself out of a deep sleep born of a combination of fresh air and fourteen-hour work-days. Pulling on the clothes he had worn yesterday, he trotted twenty-five yards to the outside toilet, then quickly walked the quarter-mile to the barn with his father and brothers to his first jobs of the morning— milking the family cow and feeding the calves. His father, Librado Mal-donado Sr., was in charge of the dairy operation, so Beto's boy jobs be-gan in the dairy barn.

With the cow milked, Beto then turned his attention to his job of teaching calves ready to be weaned from their mothers how to drink milk from a bucket, a job that was no small task, even for an adult. Coaxing the calf to the bucket, Beto stuck his fingers into the bucket of warm milk. He rubbed it across the soft, velvety lips of the baby calf, moved his hand to the nostrils to let the calf smell, then back to the lips, enticing the calf to suck the milk from his fingers. He repeated the process. After some practice, the calf finally bypassed the fingers and learned to drink directly from the bucket, a very important transition for maximum growth in minimum time.

Every morning Beto and his brother, Lee [Librado Jr.], worked with their calves, moving them from mother to bucket. The $5 a month Beto was paid for this work was big money for a boy his age. The dairy oper-ation was a precise, no-nonsense business to their father, but Beto and Lee could hardly resist roping these calves, for they offered the perfect targets for lasso practice. The boys would be in trouble with their father, though; roping one of "his" famed King Ranch Jersey herd was strictly forbidden.

By 6:30 A.M., Beto was back home to change for school into his clean, handsewn pants and shirt, which were usually white or khaki. He carefully removed them from his clothes box. He had two sets of clothes, and today his mother would wash the set he wore yesterday, remove the wrinkles with the iron heated on the stove, and place these clean clothes in his box for him to wear tomorrow. He scrubbed his hands up to his elbows, washed his face, and neatly arranged his straight black hair. Finally dressed, he ate his breakfast of eggs, potatoes, and fresh flour tortillas prepared by his mother. He picked up his lunch of fried veal wrapped in tortillas and reached for the reader he had struggled with last night. He had secretly hoped for a lunch, purchased from the Commissary, of potted meat (three cents) and crackers (five cents), but this rare treat cost money and would have to wait until a special occasion. Today, he would eat the lunch his mother had prepared. There was no candy or fruit, but, unlike most of the other children, his lunch did include a special treat. His mother was very good at baking yeast-based sweet rolls and breads in the wood stove, a rare talent among the ranch women, and so he would be the envy of his friends. His drink, as usual, would be water from the faucet at school.

Beto set off for the mile walk to school. Later he would have a Shetland pony to ride, but today he walked. Some of his luckier classmates, who lived four miles away from the school, would arrive on horseback.

At the Santa Gertrudis School in 1937, classes lasted from 8:00 in the morning to 3:00 in the afternoon, with both a morning and afternoon recess. After he gobbled down his lunch, Beto and the other children raced off to play games such as baseball or marbles during the hour allotted for lunch. On chilly days, part of their lunch hour would be spent splitting and hauling the wood in a wheelbarrow for the school's wood-burning stove. But today, they would be able to enjoy the freedom to play.

"I was not fluent in English when I started," Beto explained, an expression of anxiety, from days long gone, returning to his face. "There was no Spanish taught or spoken in school. It was very difficult."

While at play, Beto spoke to his friends in Spanish, quickly and on the sly. He reverted to his native language for convenience and in defiance of the seemingly cruel rule and its teacher enforcer.

Beto entered the wood-framed school and reluctantly went into one of the three classrooms. One classroom held grades 1 through 3, another held grades 4 through 6, and the third held grades 7 and 8. Each classroom had one teacher. Beto's desk was made of wood and was attached, with metal feet on wooden boards, to other desks in a row; the back of his seat became the front of the desk behind him. The seat was hinged and could be raised up in order to remove dirt tracked in from the playground. Along the top of his desk there was an indention a half-inch wide to corral pencils and sometimes fountain pens. Just below this indention was a break where the desktop was hinged, so that the lid could be raised to reveal space for books and supplies he would not use until later.

Beto labored over the strange-sounding English words. Next, he and his classmates studied mathematics. Beto took his turn working at the blackboard, adding and subtracting sets of numbers with chalk and eraser in hand. After that, he wrote spelling words in his "Big Chief" tablet as his teacher called the words out. In first grade he had difficulty scrawling ABCs in this same sort of tablet, his fingers laboriously bent around shiny, yellow, no. 2 pencils. By fifth grade, geography would be added to the curriculum, and studying maps of the world would excite Beto. But he could not have dreamed that, one day, he would travel across those unfamiliar regions of the world to Morocco, as the foremost cattle showman of the world-famous King Ranch. There he would proudly help his father, Librado, introduce the first American cattle breed—the Santa Gertrudis—to the King of Morocco and to the African continent.

After school Beto usually was not able to resist a quick game of marbles, but on this day he played hurriedly. There would be much work waiting for him back at the Ranch.

After trotting home, Beto chopped wood and carefully stacked it on the pile so it would be ready for fires in the cook stove, which doubled as a heater in winter. Next he went to the dairy barn and began raking stalls and preparing feed. He worked under his father's direction until 6:00 or 7:00 at night. He never wondered why the job was necessary, and there was no discussion as to whether he would do it. It was expected, and, like the other vaquero children, he did what he was told.

The family then gathered for the evening meal. Fresh tortillas, beans, and sometimes rice made up the menu. There was always plenty of whole milk from the family cow. The thick cream rose to the top and had to be mixed before drinking. After supper, Beto's boy jobs would continue. Next, his mother and brothers would try to help him a little with English, and he would finally be in bed by 9:00 or 10:00. But not before the nightly ritual, the bath. The big no. 3 galvanized tub was situated so that it could be filled with water from the outside faucet. The water would feel cold and refreshing to Beto after the long, hot, dusty day. Taking a rag salvaged from some worn-out garment and the soap made of lye and tallow by his mother, he would systematically remove from his body the dirt of the Wild Horse Desert. Like every other child of vaquero families, this was his nightly ritual, every night, hot or cold, summer or winter. At this time of year he was just glad the water needed no heating, because, if it did, after his bath he would have to build a fire under another tub so that hot water would be available for his family. Tonight he could just slip into his bed.

Two generations ago, in the early 1900s, the sons and daughters of Mexican vaqueros growing up on the King and Kenedy Ranches in South Texas knew only one way of life: prairie stretching to the horizon, prickly mesquite, panoramic sky, world-class horses and cattle, a small amount of playtime with family and friends, and lots of hard work. They took for granted a stable, secure family structure that included strict discipline, even if they were orphaned and raised by relatives. Their world was uncluttered by such present-day intrusions as newspapers, magazines, television, movies, or books. School was peripheral. The boys and girls of these South Texas ranching families knew from the very beginning what their life's work would be, and they began preparing for it almost as soon as they could walk.

First They Played

Children on the Kenedy and King Ranches, when they played, engaged in play common to most young children. Forms of play were remarkably similar from generation to generation. "Make a house" was no doubt masterminded by the vaquero daughters, but the boys joined in. Stella Guevara recalls this type of play from her own childhood at the Kenedy Ranch during the 1940s:

> *We would go out on the prairie and make a house. This we did by drawing with a sharp stick a house outline in the dirt. It had all the rooms of our real house: a kitchen and two bedrooms. We made tortillas of mud and water. Then we made tamales from those large leaves and mud and served them on those Mason jar lid plates. The boys would ride their stick horses off to be vaqueros.*

Stella's son, Juan Guevara Jr., recalls playing the same way as his mother. Stella's mother, Teresa Mayorga Cuellar, who was born in 1915, also played the same way as a child, except that the boys actually killed small animals, built fires, and cooked their prey.

The stick horse was a young boy's favorite and most constant toy.

Even before the future vaquero began playing with homemade toys tooled from discarded household articles, he was already riding horses—stick horses. He might use a discarded or confiscated broom, or he might ride a straight stick he found on the prairie. One thing is sure: he learned to walk, then he began riding a stick horse, and alternated this with a few other forms of play.

> *I played in the dirt, and we raced our stick horses. We didn't play much.* Miguel Muñiz (born 1896)

> *As a child we played tops, marbles, and baseball.* Antonio Salinas (born 1913)

> *We played with stick horses. Mother lost her broom. We played with horny toads. Played tag and hide-and-go seek. Made cars from thread spools. The girls had dolls.* Enemorio Serna (born 1931)

> *We had sling shots. Girls made corn husk dolls.* Juan Guevara Sr. (born 1937)

> *We didn't have anything to play with. My mother didn't work. Played jump rope, jacks, hopscotch. A lot of time was spent on chores.* Dora Maldonado Garcia (born 1949)

It was not uncommon for the sons and daughters of vaqueros to play with the children of caporals (the bosses of the cow operation), or with those of the owners. The owners' children were taught Spanish before school age, so communication with their Hispanic playmates was very comfortable early on. Though the children were aware of their different backgrounds, it did not affect the many hours they spent playing together. Manuel Silva (born 1905) remembered coming home after school and playing with Richard Lee King, the son of Richard King III and Pierpont Heaney: "I learned to shoot when I was twelve. I was always with Don Ricardo. When I got home from school I used to go into the stables with him, and he would shoot pennies that I threw in the air."

María Luisa Montalvo Silva grew up on the Laureles Division of King Ranch. Her first house was in the Chiltipin Pasture. Her second house was near the Laureles Main House, because her family had exchanged houses with her grandfather, since his house was closer to the school. She remembered: "I was friends with Mary Burwell. Her father was the caporal of Laureles. My Grandpa, Pedro Montalvo, taught us both to ride. We would ride every afternoon after school. He would have the horses ready and he would ride with us." Perhaps María Luisa had an idea even then that she would one day become one of the few women ever to work as a vaquera on King Ranch.

The children of the Wild Horse Desert often imitated life with play. They played the time-honored childhood games of hide-and-seek and chase, but they would always return to their imitative play. As they grew up, the vaquero children began their boy and girl jobs, and before long, the distinction between play and work blurred.

Their Lives Were Not Always Carefree

When she died, my sister and I made candy to sell at the Ranch to make money. Juan Guevara Sr. (Kenedy Ranch)

The stable, secure lifestyle of the Ranches could not always shield children from family tragedy. Nicolas Rodríguez lived on the isolated Norias Division of King Ranch in a lonely jacal (a hut made of straw, and sometimes mud or adobe), with his widowed mother, Manuela Flores Rodríguez. He was baptized during one of the priest's infrequent visits to that remote part of the Ranch. As his godfather, Nicolas had a Texas Ranger named Paulino Coy. Nicolas's father died when Nicolas was only six months old.

"When my father died," said Nicolas, "they made my mother the caretaker of the entrance door [gate] to the Ranch and built her a house there. She had to make sure the door was always closed. They gave us rations of food each week: four pounds of sugar, twenty pounds of rice, four pounds of coffee. We had five or six milk cows and plenty of meat."

This arrangement secured the family a livelihood. For keeping the gate always closed, Manuela was paid five pesos. After Nicolas was old enough, he also needed to work to help buy such necessary items as cloth, from which his mother would sew the family's clothing, and shoes for his younger brother, Manuel, and sister, Marcela. School was out of the question. When asked about school, Nicolas said: "No school. I went only one month to El Monte." His first paying job at age eleven was hauling water: "In 1909 I worked at Norias. I worked with Señor Lopez. I carried water from the well to El Hotel [the residence of Caesar Kleberg]. I used big barrels and donkeys to carry them. I was paid three pesos each time."

The family was able to survive, but then one day in 1915, everything changed. Nicolas went to the field as usual, only to be interrupted by the sounds of bandit guns:

*I was working in the field and, when it was almost sunset, I could
hear the guns shooting. It sounded more like an old boiler or cal-
dron. It was at the house of Caesar, at the big house which they
called El Hotel. One of the bandits tried to come into the house, but
he first put in the rifle carbine through the door, and everyone got
scared and jumped under the bed. When the gunshots died down,
we got back to the Ranch to find that our mother had been killed.*

One story related that a stray bullet hit Nicolas's mother and that his
brother Manuel lived only because the bullet hit his belt. The bandits
stayed until dark, kidnapping Manuel as they left. By Nicolas's account:
"My brother Manuel was taken by one of them who had received orders
of taking my brother on the horse with him. When the other bandits
were ahead and my brother and the man who had him stayed behind,
my brother just fell off the horse and hid in the grass. That is how he
got back."

Manuel hid in the pitch-black night until all seemed calm; he then
walked back toward the Ranch until around 2 A.M. He was finally joined
by Nicolas, who had hidden out during the attack in the field located,
according to Nicolas, "in the middle of Armstrong and Norias, next to
the lake."

The next day a carload of Texas Rangers under the command of
Captain Tom Tate arrived by train to protect the Ranch. Orders were
given for everyone to stay inside. Nicolas remembered his mother's funeral: "Nobody came. It was only us, the children. It was dangerous at
that time because of the bandits. Everyone was scared and, therefore, nobody came to the funeral for fear that the bandits would come back.
There were like fifty rangers in the hotel, and nobody could go out. It
was 1915, and I was seventeen years old."

One of the young defenders of the Ranch that day was Lauro F.
Cavazos Sr. He had come to work for Henrietta King as a young cowboy
in 1912. Cavazos was a descendant of José Narciso Cavazos, who in 1781
received the San Juan de Carricitos grant from the Spanish crown. Lauro
Cavazos killed the bandit leader's horse and stopped the advance; Nicolas Rodríguez remembered that Cavazos fired from behind a large roll of
wire. Later Cavazos served in World War I and returned to work on the
Ranch in 1921. In 1926, he was made foreman of the Santa Gertrudis Division, replacing Sam Ragland (Lea 1957, 2:585, 638).

It was, and still is, common for children to be raised by an extended
family when their primary family experiences difficulties. When Juan
Guevara Sr. was a young boy, his mother became terminally ill with tu-

Young Librado Maldonado (left) with his grandfather, Plácido Maldonado Sr., around 1908. Librado, born April 3, 1898, was raised by his grandfather on Lasater Ranch and began working at King Ranch in 1925. He would become the Ranch's master showman of both Jersey and Santa Gertrudis cattle.

berculosis. He and his sister helped her with the household chores and attended to her needs as well as they could: "We gave her anise tea to help with her cough," said Juan. "When she died, my sister and I made candy to sell at the Ranch to make money. We would heat one quart of Pet milk and two cups of sugar and boil it. We stirred and stirred and poured it into a pan, and it would set. Then we would slice it and sell it for one cent a piece." Juan and his sister lived with an aunt after their mother's death.

Librado Maldonado was born in 1898 at the Lasater Ranch. He was raised at the ranch by his grandfather, Plácido Maldonado Sr., who was exacting of his grandson. Librado Sr. would someday become the foremost showman of King Ranch cattle. His son, Alberto "Beto" Maldonado Sr. recounted a story his father once told him: "As a teenager my father [Librado Sr.] would sometimes stay out until 2:00 in the morning and hope to sneak in the house undetected. His grandfather [Plácido Sr.] would never say a word, but would have him up at the regular time at 4:00 and would work him hard all day long."

Dora Maldonado, Beto's wife, was raised by an aunt and uncle in Kingsville and Corpus Christi after her mother's death.

My aunt raised me. My father's sister, Helvita Alvarez, raised me in Corpus. My father [uncle] passed away when I was nine years old, so we had to move to Corpus. When my father [uncle] passed away she had to go to work. She had a baby, and we stayed with a neighbor, and I watched the baby, 'cause we didn't have any light or gas or anything.

When asked what games she played as a child, she replied:

I'm gonna tell you the truth. When I have to go to school, I go to the school, the bell rings, I come home. I clean up the house and washing and everything. I did housework.

After my uncle got real sick, my real father came and picked us up and took us to Riviera and my uncle passed away in Riviera. He died at home. When he passed away we were real poor.

Dora came to King Ranch when she married Beto Maldonado and has lived there since that time.

Sometimes young children were raised by an extended family because their fathers worked away from home for long periods of time.

Teresa Mayorga grew up on the Norias Division of King Ranch during the 1920s. Her father was the famous vaquero Macario Mayorga of the Kenedy, King, and East Ranches. He was a highly skilled, competitive rider who represented the Ranches in rodeos all over Texas and Mexico. He was gone most of the time, and Teresa, whose mother was dead, was raised by her aunts and uncles. A twinkle returned to Teresa's eyes as she remembered: "My father would return home bringing clothes for me wrapped in his yellow slicker on the back of his horse. He brought presents. He brought his check for the past months to help pay my way [food and clothing]."

Teresa related another story about her father's childhood: "Mrs. Tate at Norias took my father candy because his mother died, and he had no mother. She was Tom Tate's wife. My father lived with his aunt. The aunt gave candy to her children, but not to him. So Mrs. Tate took him candy. His aunt's name was Lupe Rivera Mayorga."

Sometimes mothers were the sole parent for weeks or months at a time while the men were in the *corrida*. While the father was the undisputed head of the family, the mother was a strong presence, commanded great respect, and had no difficulty assuming her husband's role in his absence. By the time her children were grown, she was granted the status of matriarch. Manuela Mayorga remembered being teased about her absent father:

Miguel Muñiz was our neighbor, and he would go back and forth to the camp. I would ask how my father was, and he would say, "He has another little girl out there and gives her lots of candy." I would sit on the steps and cry and cry. Then I would go in and put on a dress and sit on the fence and sing to him [Miguel Muñiz] to make him mad.

The Boys Learned to Rope

One day in 1953 ... I roped a Mexican eagle and caught it in flight.
Enemorio Serna (Kenedy Ranch)

The rope was the single most important tool of the vaquero, for his ability to use it would likely determine his livelihood and that of his family. Roping was the first skill a young boy learned. He began by learning to tie a knot. His task was to bring one end of the rope back against itself, then around and under it, and thus make the knot. Even though a boy would have seen his dad make the knot many times, at age five he sometimes did not yet have the manual dexterity to perform the same task. After sufficient practice, the knot finally held. Now he would be able to pull the other end of the rope through the small opening to form the loop. He learned to pull it tight to make the loop smaller and to loosen it to make the loop larger.

The fledgling vaqueros' targets were many and varied, though all were stationary at first. The weathered gray mesquite fence posts were just the right height, and there were plenty of them. He formed his loop and practiced, first with a large loop. As he became more confident and proficient, he adjusted the loop to a smaller size. The object was to rope the target using the smallest loop possible.

Beto Maldonado remembered that "Javier Mendietta was one of the best vaqueros. He could throw a rope loop just big enough to go over the neck."

This skill was necessary for holding a calf for branding—a calf that was looking for any loophole to make its getaway. By the time a boy was six or seven years old, he had graduated to moving targets and became the scourge of chickens, pigs, turkeys, rabbits, and dogs. They were his first moving targets, and they did not escape his loop for long. Manuel Silva said, "I began by roping chickens, rabbits ... anything that moved."

Martín Medietta Jr. remembered that "Mr. Bob [Kleberg] sent nine ropes to my house to give to my nine boys and then sent goats to the house so the boys could learn to rope."

After mastering moving targets in the ranch yard, the young vaqueros moved up to lassoing calves, first on foot and finally from a horse. Next he tried wild donkeys and javelinas or collared peccaries, which were apt to charge with a fierceness driven by their survival instinct. But even these animals did not escape Manuel Silva's rope. His constant practice paid off. He explained: "By age fifteen I was an expert roper. I started working cattle. My team of three could brand a hundred cattle an hour."

Seferino Gutierrez of Kenedy Ranch was another highly skilled roper. He began learning these skills as a young boy and perfected them throughout his life on the Ranch. At age eighty-four, with dignity born of self-knowledge, he described his personal style: "I used a manila hemp rope and a turnover loop. I threw the rope overhanded instead of windup, and I was the head roper, the best, no competition. I roped between one hundred and two hundred cows a day."

Pride in Seferino's expertise was obviously shared by his family during this interview. At one point his young grandson suddenly ran to the back porch and brought back his grandfather's favorite rope. Seferino set about showing the proper way to hold the rope and then demonstrated his skill, not by roping a cow on the range, but a worn wooden chair there in his kitchen. His amazing skill and considerable agility from his vaquero days were still evident.

Enemorio Serna eventually turned his roping skill to more unusual targets: "I roped jack rabbits. One day in 1953 or 1954 I roped a Mexican eagle and caught it in flight."

Some budding vaqueros learned to rope at a later age. Julian Buentello was one of these: "I was twelve when I learned to rope."

Catarino Moreno was born in Mexico, where he grew up tending cows, bulls, and then sheep. In 1929, at age twenty-five, he came to King Ranch to get a job. He first tended about eight hundred sheep, which furnished wool for the famous King Ranch saddle blankets. The sheep also furnished food for the families. When sheep were no longer on the Ranch, Catarino learned to work in the *corrida:* "I did a lot. I learned how to rope. I did not envy any other good roper."

Every young boy growing up on the Ranches learned to rope. Competition was keen. Each young vaquero would try to out rope his friends to prove that he was the superior roper. As teenagers, some would engage in contests on a regular basis to test their skill. Skill meant money. Julian Buentello learned this firsthand: "I broke horses at fifteen or sixteen. I helped at first, and they paid me $10. When I got older, they paid me more."

Boys generally wanted to stay and work on the Ranch land, which was the only home or even geographic location familiar to them. Relatives and other vaqueros had some influence and provided boys with important information, but a boy's father—the undisputed head of his household—was the teacher of this way of life and the primary role model. The father's role as teacher created the stability necessary for the quality work force that has existed on the Ranches for generations. Boys learned literally everything they knew by tagging after and imitating their fathers.

"My father taught me what I know," said Enemorio Serna. "I started going with him at age seven. I started breaking horses at eleven." Julian Buentello echoed this sentiment: "I followed my father. The old people taught him."

Next Came Learning to Ride

I would grab him, take him to the house, pull up a chair, and get on. Enemorio Serna (Kenedy Ranch)

Of all skills required of a vaquero, roping and riding were the most basic. After roping, the next skill a young boy learned was horsemanship. The horse was the basic means of transportation on the ranches, as well as the means by which the working chores were accomplished. Skill in handling and riding horses was a basic necessity. Most young boys were already fairly adept at forming and using a lasso by the time they began learning to ride.

"I learned to ride by riding calves," said Enemorio Serna. "Then I rode ponies bareback." Enemorio remembered getting in big trouble when his dad caught him, because riding calves was forbidden. But the calves were just too tempting. Every day Enemorio watched the vaqueros ride the sleek, shiny Quarter Horses, and he longed for the day when he, too, would sit atop the finest horses. But he had to begin somewhere, and the calves, though forbidden, were his only alternative. At age seven he knew how to throw the loop and confine the calf, pull him to the fence, climb on, and hang on as long as possible. The calf, of course, was not always cooperative, and the game was to see how long he could stay on.

With no saddle, Enemorio's task was challenging. Time after time, he climbed on until he finally got the hang of matching the swaying and stopping motion of the calf. He learned to stay on, no matter what. This ability endured as he progressed to riding a horse, and it earned him his nickname. "Teco is my nickname—Tequito [Little Tick]," he explained. "When I was little, I would grab onto a horse and wouldn't let go. He couldn't shake me loose."

Enemorio Serna, a vaquero on the Kenedy Ranch. His nickname is "Tequito" (little tick), because of his childhood ability to grab onto a horse and not let go.

Perhaps Enemorio inherited his horsemanship skills from his grand-father, who was a *capitan* with Pancho Villa's Mexican rebels from 1915 to 1920. Anyway, Enemorio felt genuine elation at his success riding calves. Then one day his dad caught him. The strict rule of "no riding the calves" was enforced in the traditional manner: his father inflicted a whipping. Little was said, for Enemorio knew the rule, and he knew his father would enforce it. Enemorio understood the strict, universal, va-quero family code of parental authority, and to test or even question it was unthinkable. Next time, he would be more careful. In his words: "I made sure not to get caught riding the calves next time."

But soon, Enemorio had access to a pony, and the calves became passé. He was on his way to becoming an expert rider, and he used his skill both on and off the Kenedy Ranch: "I rode in rodeos for money. I got $5.00 for riding a horse, $10.00 for a bull. I could make $35.00 a night. My father made $.75 a day. One time a carnival kicked me out be-cause I wouldn't fall."

Getting up on a pony was the first challenge for a young would-be rider. Manuel Silva said: "I would grab him, take him to the house, pull up a chair, and get on."

Likewise, Enemorio would coax one of the ponies into just the right position at the fence line or at the end of the porch, lift himself up, and jump on. He rode bareback at first, or fell off, and when this often treacherous yet exciting skill was mastered, his father began training him in the saddle. Between the ages of twelve and fifteen, he began rid-ing with his father and learning to work cattle.

The first day a boy rode with his father was a rite of passage on the Ranches. The youngster had prepared for this day all his life, since the time he began riding his stick horse. A boy's growing pride and expecta-tion were soon mixed with a good deal of apprehension. If he passed, if he had properly prepared himself and had acceptable skills as a roper and rider, he knew that by age sixteen he might be allowed to participate in the summer roundups and go on the payroll. If he failed . . . but that was unthinkable. Rogerio Silva described his first day:

My brother-in-law, Venuseriano "Niño" Quintanilla, was the boss, and he made sure I got a fully trained horse from the remuda. He knew that King Ranch Quarter Horses would do most of the work for the rider. When I made a mistake, Niño called me aside for fur-ther instruction so as not to embarrass me in front of the other men. Then he said, "Watch me," and demonstrated the proper way to cut the cow, rope the calf, or whatever skill he was showing me.

Martín Mendietta Jr. described how budding vaqueros were trained:

> *You call them to you and tell them they did something wrong, and*
> *to stay here in the back and watch the boys who know what they*
> *are doing and learn. You say, "You go to the back of the line like in*
> *school, and we'll let you try again." I would say, "You stay there*
> *and watch me—then you take the calf from here to there."*

Vaqueras

I loved horses from the very first and learned to ride at about nine
years old. María Luisa Montalvo Silva (King Ranch)

In only a few instances did women on the Ranches work in the same
capacity as vaqueros. The traditional woman's role was centered around
home and family, and for a woman to work in the *corrida* was most unusual. There were a few exceptions, however, and Josefina Robles Adrián
of King Ranch was one of them. Josefina, who was born in 1923, is the
granddaughter of Luis Robles, one of the first vaqueros on King Ranch.
Luis is listed as Captain Richard King's bodyguard, thus documenting
the Robles family as vaqueros at the beginning of the Ranch (Account
Book of Employee Wages, October 1, 1889–October 1, 1892, King Ranch
Archives). Josefina's father was Ramón Robles (Luis's son) of the Caesar
Pen area on the Santa Gertrudis Division. He was a caporal in charge of
livestock.

There are two interesting versions of what happened to Luis Robles,
according to Josefina and her grandson, Oscar Cortez Jr., who represents the fifth generation of the Robles family on the Ranch.

> *Luis was charged with murder for killing Red Fred. There is a let-*
> *ter written from a lawyer asking for payment for defending Robles.*
> *The story is that King didn't pay the fine, and he [Luis] was hung.*
> *The other story is that he [Luis] was kidnapped and taken across*
> *the border, and King was contacted to pay a ransom. He refused to*
> *pay the ransom, and Robles was hung.*

Josefina recounted how she learned to work like the vaqueros. Although she was not a vaquera for King Ranch, she learned the skills and
helped her father on the *ranchito*, but she was not allowed to work in the
ranch roundups:

I was trained as a vaquera by my father. Maybe it's because he did not have too many children, but I did all my brother did, and my father taught me. I started riding at seven. My daddy taught me to ride. I would bring the cattle in from the brush with him, and then he would let me do it by myself under his direction. I wore a brush jacket, khakis, men's boots, and used chaps in the pen. My sister, Carolina, also rode and worked the ranchito, *while my other sister, Aurora, did not. I also rode the fences.*

I was taught to rope, and my father taught me. I started at about seven and began by roping posts, then hogs, then turkeys. I would also rope calves away from the dairy cows. Each afternoon, I would help to bring the calves and cows in, and I would have to separate the calves from their mothers, and sometimes I would have to rope them.

The rope I used was a big one. I did not start with a little rope. I helped them brand, too, by getting the irons hot and handing them the irons.

María Luisa Montalvo Silva and her sister, Lupe, who both grew up on the Laureles Division of King Ranch, also learned to ride and work cattle. María Luisa related: "I loved horses from the very first and learned to ride at about nine years old. I would help my father bring in the cows and separate the cows from the calves. We would do this about 3:00 or 4:00 in the afternoon."

These are the only recorded accounts of vaqueras working on the Ranches. Traditionally, women worked in the home, though sometimes they worked at an outside job on or off the Ranches later on. Both Josefina and María Luisa stopped working as vaqueras when they married and later worked at outside jobs.

Boy Jobs

Learn all the jobs you can—then you will always have a job.
Manuel Silva (King Ranch)

Jobs on the Kenedy and King Ranches could be divided into two categories: those performed on horseback and those that required working on foot. Rounding up and branding cattle and moving them from place to place were the fundamental tasks of the vaquero on horseback.

Tick eradication and inoculation against disease were usually part of this work. The worker on foot tended to dozens of other jobs necessary to the operation of the Ranches. Some of these jobs included working with the cattle and horse breeding programs, tending windmills, building and mending fences, helping with brush control, working in building construction, cooking, working with the veterinarian, driving trucks, and assisting owners with hunts and the entertainment of guests. It was important for the workers to learn as many jobs as possible early in life.

Before boys reached adolescence, they began a long training period during which they performed certain tasks daily. At about seven or eight years of age, these future vaqueros were assigned boy jobs. These jobs marked the beginning of their formal apprenticeship, of learning responsibility and skills necessary to carry on the vaquero tradition and enter the adult world of work. Common boy jobs were chopping wood, milking cows, and feeding animals. All boy jobs contributed directly to the family or to the ranch; boy jobs were not busy work. Leonard Stiles, a former foreman at the Santa Gertrudis Division, and, since his retirement, with the Visitors Management Department, said: "Kids did more work than their fathers. Kids were running here and there, fetching this and that. The kids followed their dads."

Learning respect for authority was indelibly woven into the boys' training. Miguel Muñiz described the respect boys learned early: "I carried water for a boy job. I would fold my arms while waiting for the men to drink to show respect. Then I would take the cup back. I would kiss my mother and father's hands to show respect. I always took off my hat to show respect."

After mastering typical boy jobs, Martín Mendietta Jr.'s next job was throwing calves. He learned to throw about three hundred in a day.

Jesus Gonzales began his boy jobs on Kenedy Ranch as a cook's helper: "I hitched up the wagons and helped with the water at first. I also washed dishes. I used bar soap for dishes, boiled the water. We used kerosene oil to start the fire, and I gathered firewood."

Manuel Silva's first boy job was working with the tamed oxen, but he also had other jobs: "I helped with fence building and repair, cut grass, shaped trees, and worked at any task I could because my father taught me, 'Always learn all the jobs you can—then you will always have a job.'"

Boy jobs might also include working at the Main House at the Ranch headquarters, as Beto Maldonado did: "I would clean the yard at the Big House. I was dishwasher at the Big House."

Sometimes tending goats at King Ranch was a boy job; as many as twenty-five head were milked, furnishing as much as fifty liters a day for

Alberto "Beto" Maldonado Sr. (left) and his brother Librado Jr. "Lee" at the November 1940 Kleberg County Fair. Beto's calf won first place, and Beto believes that it was the first award won by the new Santa Gertrudis breed.

the use of the vaqueros' families if they wanted it. Catarino Moreno recalled: "I worked with goats and lambs since I was six years old."

Budding vaqueros like Beto and Lee Maldonado were required to sweep the dairy barn. Their dad, Librado, was in charge of the dairy operation, including the Jersey herd. Beto said: "We helped our dad with the Jersey cattle in any way we could . . . my kids did the same thing."

One of the proudest days of Beto's life was when he and his younger brother, Lee, brought their calves for entry into the Kleberg County Fair. Under the careful, expert eye of their father, they had tended the calves from the very beginning, and this would be the day for all the world to see the results: their efforts would be rewarded with a blue ribbon for Beto's calf. Beto remembered: "The calf won first place, and I believe this was the first win for the new Santa Gertrudis breed. I was so proud of that blue ribbon that I took it home and put it in the stall in the barn and was disappointed to find when I turned around that the calf had liked it, too, and had eaten it."

Once boy jobs were mastered and had become a part of a boy's daily routine, he might begin going out with his dad, first in a wagon, watching, learning, waiting to prove himself, and then grabbing the first opportunity to graduate to a horse, the only legitimate means of transportation for a "son of the brush." Only then could he begin learning what he really needed to know. After he graduated to the range, a boy might begin his cow camp work by learning how to throw a calf for branding under the watchful eye of an expert vaquero roper.

Girl Jobs

. . . at recess I didn't get to play. Manuela Mayorga (King Ranch)

Girls followed after their mothers and learned from them in much the same way as boys learned boy jobs from their fathers. In the early 1900s, a young Manuela Mayorga, with her mother, Antonia, and her grandmother, Virginia, prepared special meals for guests at the Main House on King Ranch:

> *Ms. Alice [East] and Mr. Tom East would send out and have rabbits killed for mother to make tamales. The recipe came through the family. The chauffeur would skin the jack rabbits and cut them up. Then we would boil them and grind them up and spice the meat. We would fix* masa *up with shortening, salt, and soup broth left over from cooking the meat. Mr. Robert Kleberg Jr.'s mother liked for mother to boil the fresh corn and use an antique hand grinder to make the tortillas.*
>
> *We also made enchiladas for Mrs. King. We would fix big wash tubs full of both for the Big House. We made two kinds of tortillas: plain and, for the ones to be used in enchiladas, we used chili powder in them. To make enchiladas, we made gravy with flour, chili powder, salt, ground yellow cheese from town, and onions. We soaked the tortillas in gravy 'til soft, rolled while hot with cheese, onions, and meat. We always used King Ranch beef.*
>
> *I helped my mother, and since the school was across the street from our house, at recess I didn't get to play. I went home and helped mother grind corn.*
>
> *I started working at seven years old. I helped wash. I helped Mom fix breakfast by 5:00 in the morning. I made beds and made the fire. I chopped wood for it. For breakfast we had tortillas with sausage, egg, or potato, and egg or tortillas with chocolate. We drank chocolate or coffee. We didn't have [drink] milk. After breakfast we washed.*

Sometimes the women worked outside the home to supplement income, and often the young girls helped their mothers with this work. Manuela described working in one of the households on the Ranch:

Mother did housework for the Larry Cavazos [Sr.] family. We washed and ironed their clothes. We washed the clothes outside in tubs. We had water faucets outside. We hung the clothes on the line to dry. We ironed outside on the porch; sometimes we would iron 'til midnight. Mr. Cavazos had five children so we did wash for seven and were paid $6 a month. The irons we heated on the fire, and I still remember all the pleats and ruffles.

Manuela also added to the family income by helping her father:

When it was cotton picking time, I helped pick cotton. I would leave at 4:00 in the morning with my dad. We walked toward Bishop along the railroad tracks to the cotton fields. I was very fast. I would pick two hundred pounds of cotton by 5:00 in the afternoon. I was paid $1.25 for every one hundred pounds. I went every day with my dad.

In the 1930s, Nicolasa Quintanilla Garcia worked in the Main House at King Ranch with her uncle, José Alegría, the cook. She remembered: "I would help when they had a lot of company. I would serve the table. My uncle was a wonderful cook. They particularly liked his small biscuits."

When they were older, girls also sometimes worked on their own outside the home. "I went to work at the age of fifteen for Mrs. Burwell," said Ofelia Longória. "I kept house. I was paid $10 a month. I also worked for Dick Mosely and was paid $15 a month."

Similarly, Nicolasa remembered that, in 1944, she "went to work for Mr. Bob Kleberg and Miss Helen."

On the King and Kenedy Ranches, all the members of the vaquero families worked. They handled the dozens of jobs that have made the Ranches work like well-oiled machines for the past five generations.

Training for Work

I am a Kineño and I am glad to be a Kineño. María Luisa Montalvo Silva

Pride in being Kineños, King People, emerged from the long-term relationships between the King Ranch owners and the workers who stayed on the Ranch, often for generations. Similar relationships existed between the Kenedeños and the owners of Kenedy Ranch. A mutual respect developed out of the workers' loyalty to the owners and the reliance of the owners on the vaqueros' expert knowledge of raising cattle and training horses (Graham 1994, 40). This knowledge was passed from father to son and afforded the Ranches the stable workforce that was vital to their success.

The first task of a budding vaquero, who had some proficiency as a rider and roper, might be learning to separate calves from their mothers and delivering the calves to the desired destination. Often this would be a location where tame oxen were positioned, since for some reason the calves were content to stay with the oxen while the working of the cattle continued. For this job, a boy might be paid with a little money or a gift.

Antonio Salinas of Kenedy Ranch remembered: "I was twelve when I began riding with John Kenedy. He paid me with a pair of boots. I later made $25 a month. I worked from 7:00 A.M. to 6:00 P.M."

Plácido Maldonado III grew up on King Ranch during the 1920s and 1930s. He said: "I first remember being with Dad at ten. I went to the barn with him and would sweep and do other jobs. My first payroll job was at thirteen or fourteen. I raised calves."

The apprenticeship progressed. It included training in rounding up cattle from the brush, cutting cattle for branding or penning, roping and tying three legs of a calf for branding, rounding up and breaking horses, and later showing to the rest of the world the prize cattle and horses that symbolized King Ranch. Most were accomplished cowboys by their late teens and were already well into their life's work. Miguel Muñiz is a prime example: "My parents came to the United States in 1907 from Mexico. I began learning and was a good cowboy by age twenty."

In addition to jobs directly connected to working cattle, a wide array of other tasks, all vital to ranch operations, beckoned vaqueros who had special skills or interests. These jobs, not directly related to working cattle, were also for older workers or those with health conditions that prohibited their participation in the demanding, physically strenuous lifestyle of the cow camps. It was not unusual for a vaquero to live to be well into his eighties or even nineties.

In earlier days, no vaquero ever completely retired if his health was sound. With a strong work ethic and pride in his job, work was usually a defining force in a vaquero's life. Nicolasa Quintanilla Garcia's father was an example: "My father was the *corrida* boss until he developed diabetes and had to come to the stables and work."

Working with the fences was one of the less-demanding jobs, but one of the most lonely. The more than 825,000 acres of King Ranch and the 400,000 acres of the Kenedy Ranch constantly require fencing upkeep. On King Ranch alone, more than 2,000 miles of net-wire fencing mark the exterior boundaries and form the individual pastures. This is enough wire to reach from Kingsville, Texas, to Boston, Massachusetts (Broyles 1980, 161). Ranch hands were in charge of fences and gates and rode long days along the net-wire fence lines to keep them in first-class repair. Felipe Garcia remembered: "I checked the fences with my dad. I started on the back of dad's saddle, then rode my own horse."

Sometimes There Were Celebrations

We had gifts at home, but they were small because we didn't have any money. Manuela Mayorga (King Ranch)

Holidays among vaquero families on the Ranches were few, but celebrations typically included all family members. The most common celebrations were related to the church. Christmas, weddings, and the baptisms of babies were most often the occasions for special festivities and gatherings of family and friends. Sometimes plays with religious themes were produced during the Christmas season and were usually presented in the school building. Entertainment sometimes included dances, which often lasted from dusk until dawn. There were no birthday parties. In some families, birthdays were at least noted. Beto Maldonado described the customs of his family: "We had no gifts and no party for birthdays. We would have a cake with cocoa, and people would congratulate us. We did not celebrate birthdays."

The Christmas season was the most memorable for youngsters. It was a time for joyous celebrations and usually included the only gifts they would receive all year. The holiday was even more special because at this time their dads, the vaqueros, had their only vacation time, which was from Christmas until after New Year's Day. Families gathered, cooked special foods, and visited. Parents made or otherwise provided whatever they could as gifts so that their children would have a happy Christmas. Friends were also an important part of this season, and they gathered for dances, plays, and to share special foods. Some celebrations also involved the ranch owners.

"The oak tree at the Big House was the Christmas tree," said Antonio Salinas. "We would all gather there, and [John Gregory] Kenedy [Sr.] would come and bring fruit, candies, gifts."

Manuela Mayorga shared the following reminiscences about the Christmas celebrations:

Martín Mendietta Jr. with his wife and their nine sons at the annual King Ranch Christmas party. Each boy received a toy truck as a gift. Eight of these boys grew up to become vaqueros like their father and grandfather, Martín Mendietta Sr.

> *There was a big celebration at 4:00 on Christmas Eve. All employ-ees with their families would pass by at the Commissary. The school was too small. There was candy for the children, sweaters for children and women, coats for the men. There was a big dance afterwards at the school. At first, Mrs. King had an orchestra. Later, she had accordions. Everyone came, including the children, and stayed 'til 1:00 or 3:00 in the morning.*

On Christmas Day, we had lots of tamales. We had gifts at home, but they were little because we didn't have any money. Gifts were made sometimes.

On New Year's we made buñuelos—big tortillas—and took them to our friends as gifts. We put a little sugar in the flour, and 1/2 tsp. baking powder, and mixed [it] with warm water. We used no shortening. We mixed this and rolled [it] into balls. Using wax paper, we rolled them out like tortillas. Then we melted shortening in the skillet, fried them, poked [them] with a fork when they bubbled up, and turned them over to lightly brown. We took them out and sprinkled brown sugar and cinnamon [on them]. We took them to our neighbors on a plate as a gift of good will. The men were off from December 22 until New Year's.

Librado Maldonado Sr. had another talent, in addition to his expert ability to handle cattle. His son, Beto, described the Christmas ritual at King Ranch when he was young:

My dad was the Santa Claus for the longest time on the Ranch. The children would go to the Christmas tree, and Dad would pass out the presents to each child. He was dressed up like Santa. Children did not know who he was. We would celebrate Christmas on December 24. We would get together at the schoolhouse; before that, it was the Commissary.

Mr. Dick [Jr.], Mr. Bob, and Larry Cavazos [Sr.] were there. Everybody got gifts. Wives [got] blankets, pillow cases, sheets. Men got gloves, jackets. Kids got a present and a bag of fruit, candy, and nuts.

Other vaqueros shared their recollections of holiday celebrations on King Ranch:

At Christmas we had a dance—killed two cows to feed everyone. We did not celebrate birthdays. Manuel Silva

We had a Christmas play, Las Pastorelas. It was a play about a shepherd [and] a devil who visit the baby Jesus. It lasted from 6:00 p.m. Christmas Eve to 1:00 or 2:00 a.m. There were twelve shepherds, three devils, an angel, La Aile, Bartolo, and a chorus. Plácido Maldonado III

At Christmas, we would go house to house visiting. We had dances. Miguel Muñiz

We had Christmas celebrations at home. We would get a branch or something to decorate. We used paper and put out our socks. Our gifts were dress shoes, or something beneficial. Mother put it in a big box to make it look like something.

Special food was tamales—beef and pork—buñuelos, fried sweet bread. *We had our socks filled with pecans, fruit, candy. We hung them up.* Julian Buentello

Usually the families remained on the Ranches for the Christmas holidays. Though they were free to come and go at will, logistics and economic considerations made travel difficult. Without public transportation, and in most cases without an automobile, travel was necessarily limited. But some families did travel to other locations to be with their families. Enemoria Serna was one of these: "We went to Rio Grande to celebrate. Stayed a couple of days, or three or four. We went to church. There were no gifts. Special foods were tamales and candies. We went by car—1930 Chevrolet—and everybody in it. We did not celebrate birthdays."

Schooling on the Ranches

There was no Spanish at school . . . Alberto "Beto" Maldonado (King Ranch)

As early as the 1860s, King Ranch built a one-room school for vaquero children, probably at the instigation of Henrietta King, who was from a family that championed education, even for girls (Cheeseman 1993, 69). However, schooling was sporadic and peripheral to the work on the Ranches. Motivating children was usually a challenge because many of the youngsters knew only the life of the Ranch and intended to spend their lives there. Even in Anglo schools, reading and mathematics were often considered irrelevant to farming and ranching skills, until the 1930s, when education began to be viewed as a way to escape failing farms during the Great Depression. King Ranch remained strong and provided constant, stable jobs at a time when there were very few jobs in South Texas, so education was usually not considered a priority. To a great extent, attendance at school depended on the needs of the Ranch. When Ranch requirements demanded it, children were kept out of school to work. Attendance also depended on the value the vaquero parents placed on education. Sometimes families moved from remote areas of the Ranch so that their children could attend school, as in the case of Ofelia M. Longória:

We moved into the main camp at Laureles when I was seven, so we could go to school. Sofia Davila was my teacher. The school had one room, small windows, two doors, a wooden desk. There were thirty to forty students, all grades in one room, and it went from beginning to the seventh grade. The older students went from 8:00 to 3:00 and the younger ones from 8:00 to 2:00. We played baseball at recess, and had one recess in the morning.

I worked there [Norias Division of King Ranch] until I figured out that my children were not learning much in school. I had to make time for them. I had to go and see them at school, and I had to help them some more. There was a school here [Norias], but they did not learn much. I don't know why. Catarino Moreno

Usually, a teacher would teach approximately twenty students at several grade levels in one room. Students might begin school at age six or seven, or maybe not until age twelve, or maybe not at all. Attendance was affected by the location of the family and the value the family placed on education. The practice generally was that, if children lived near Ranch headquarters, they went to school, at least for a while. If they lived in remote areas of the Ranches, they were less likely to attend. In either case, attendance was irregular, as is evident in the following reminiscences of these vaqueros and their wives:

I went to school 'til fifth grade. Had to quit to help my father. Manuel Silva

I didn't start to school until I was twelve years old. I went through the fifth grade. I remember a book, This Is Will. I spent two or three years on it. We had no desks. Just a table with long benches on each side. We talked a lot. Manuela Mayorga

I went to school at Norias. I went on a van or bus. One teacher taught us in one room, grades 1–5. Mother fixed lunch of beans, tortillas. We drank water at school. I was home by 4:00 P.M. Felipe Garcia

I started school at six or seven. I went on the Ranch. It was limited. I had to work to help out. Most dropped out. Plácido Maldonado III

We had a wood-frame school. It was divided into classes and opened up for dances. We had grades 1–3 with one teacher, 4–5

with one teacher, and 6–8 together. Later we had our own Shetland pony to ride to school.

We had recess in the morning and lunch from 12:00 to 1:00. We had recess in the afternoon and got out about 3:00. We ate lunch on the south side of the garage, and ate in small houses being built for the Ranch. Then we played baseball. After school sometimes we would play marbles. We had outdoor restrooms. We had a heated stove and had to carry wood in a wheelbarrow and sometimes cut the wood. I remember [José] Cantú [the caporal] helped me cover my first book. It was Spot and the Cat. *We studied math, spelling, and geography.* Beto Maldonado

The school was located in the Old Colony and went from grades 1–7. I finished the seventh grade. The school was large and [had] one room that could be broken into six to eight rooms for school and opened up for dances and celebrations. There were two grades per room. Nicolasa Quintanilla Garcia

Our schools had grades 1–7 and one teacher. We went to school from 8:00 to 3:30. We went home for lunch of rice, beans, and tortillas. María Luisa Montalvo Silva

Interviewees who were born around 1900, such as Miguel Muñiz, did not mention going to school: "I had no school and did not go to school. I can read a little Spanish, but very little. Everyone spoke Spanish so I didn't need an education. The Ranch provided everything I needed."

Students attended elementary grades at schools established in the early 1900s on King Ranch and on the Kenedy Ranch at La Parra and Sarita. A few students went on to high school. The students at Santa Gertrudis attended high school in Kingsville, the Laureles students went to Corpus Christi and Kingsville, and those on Norias attended high school in nearby communities.

Both boys and girls were likely to drop out of school by age thirteen or fourteen. They already knew that they would spend their lives on the Ranches, either as vaqueros or as wives and mothers of vaqueros. They had been training for this type of work since their early childhood. School was simply irrelevant. The decision to drop out was usually no cause for regret, but there were exceptions. Beto Maldonado, a ninth-grade dropout, was one of these:

I went through the eighth grade at the Ranch. At fourteen I went to one year of school in town and quit. I now think my dad should

This picture was taken on the day that the nuns visited the school on the Norias Division of King Ranch. Photograph by Toni Frizzell, courtesy of King Ranch Archives, King Ranch, Inc.

have given me a good spanking and sent me back. He was real mad, but he let me quit.

I missed school so much that I would dream of being back there again. When they offered the GED classes I went back to school and got my GED. I passed everything the first time except English. I had to take it a second time. This is what happened. One of the children had graduated and had a cap and gown. I wore the cap and gown and got gifts. My mother was still alive and was so proud. We had a big party, and everybody was real happy. It was ten years ago that I did it.

School was in session from September until May. Children walked to school or rode a horse if they lived far from the school. Yellow school buses began crawling along the hard-surfaced roads that were built after oil wells were drilled on the Ranches in the 1930s. They quickly replaced the horse as the primary means of transportation to school.

Antonio Salinas remembered his school days:

> *We sang songs in school. Miss Laura and Miss Jackson were the teachers. I attended the first grade at La Parra [Kenedy Ranch headquarters] with about eight children, then transferred to Sarita for grades 2–6. School went through eighth grade in Sarita, 9–12 at Riviera. We were in school all day. We had recess, went home to eat. We learned ABCs, had Big Chief tablets, pencils, and a blackboard. I studied geography. I came to school in the bus.*

On school days, boys and girls would have to get up before daylight to do their chores before going to school. After school, more chores awaited them. The evening meal, a few minutes of homework, and a bath completed their day by 9:00 or 10:00 at night. Enemorio Serna described his schedules for work and school:

> *We came to the big Ranch to school, and it was about four miles. Three of us rode on one horse. I went to school until I was thirteen years old, and I quit. I went in one room with one teacher. We had about twenty in the class. We went from September 'til May. We went from 8:00 to 3:00. I would often get up at 4:00 in the morning to do chores and wouldn't get home 'til after dark, maybe 8:00. When the boss needed me, they took me out.*

The language barrier was formidable for vaquero children because only English was allowed in school. Most of them knew little, if any, English, and the teachers often spoke no Spanish. The students were fortunate if their parents had learned some English on the Ranch, or if they had older brothers or sisters who could help them to learn English. Anglo children attended the same schools as the vaquero children and often fared better since they knew both languages by school age. They conversed with the vaquero children in Spanish. Spanish was spoken almost universally in the vaqueros' homes, so there was limited opportunity for youngsters to practice their new, required language.

Beto described this unfortunate language barrier:

> *There was no Spanish at school—taught or spoken. I was not fluent in English when I started. We had no television, radio, or papers, so we did not know the language.*

> *The teachers spoke no Spanish. It was very difficult. We were*
> *not supposed to speak Spanish at recess or anytime at school, but,*
> *of course, we did. My dad spoke English even though he did not go*
> *to school. My mother went to school, probably to the fifth grade.*
> *My older brothers and sisters helped me, and mother sometimes.*
> *I lived ten miles from school so I didn't go. I was killing frogs*
> *with a slingshot instead.* Julian Buentello (King Ranch)

To be confined in a school setting all day was tedious; it was a difficult experience for youngsters who were accustomed to spending their
days working and playing on the open range. To be confronted simulta-
neously with a new language made the situation doubly challenging.

The children of the Wild Horse Desert grew up with a strict code stem-
ming from a proud tradition. Generation after generation these children
have developed into the dedicated, highly specialized, loyal work force
that has enabled the Ranches to operate with a minimum of disruption,
ever since the late 1850s and 1860s when Captain Richard King and his
friend, Captain Mifflin Kenedy, began their great ranching ventures.

The Vaquero Family

The family tradition continues to be valued above all else in vaquero culture. This tradition involves both the immediate vaquero family and the extended family, which includes the Ranch owners. Vaquero family structure has always been stable, dependable, predictable, and secure. Even when children were orphaned, members of the extended family unfailingly cared for them as their own. There has also been an interdependence between the families and their employers. The Ranch owners have furnished shelter, food, and medical care, and, if a vaquero works, he has the security of knowing that the basic needs of his family will always be supplied. In return, vaquero families have provided the stable, skilled work force without which the Ranches could not function, much less prosper.

During the years from 1910 to 1930, Mexicans fleeing the Mexican Revolution were desperate for jobs and were no doubt glad to find employment on the King and Kenedy Ranches. From 1930 to 1940 during the Great Depression, when unemployment was rampant throughout Texas and the nation, workers would not have risked leaving a secure job. Only during and following World War II did job opportunities begin opening up elsewhere. Still, many of the family members remained on the Ranches. The vaquero families were also dependent on each other.

The families are very close—they support each other. When one hurts, all hurt. In Kenedy Ranch we have friendship, security, and unity. Olga Serna

The families are like a big family. My grandmother [Antonia Cavazos] was a widow, and her brother, [José Gonzales], brought her here because she had five children to raise. Antonia lived with José. She did housework for Larry Cavazos [Sr.]. Manuela Mayorga

Laureles was beautiful, and the family was close, and there were only about forty houses with the school nearby and the Commissary. All the people were supported by each other. María Luisa Montalvo Silva

The social order of vaquero families on the Ranches was structured by clearly defined roles. Each family member functioned with a clear understanding of what was expected of him or her by the family and by the employers.

Family Structure

He's the boss, and he's been the boss . . . Dora Maldonado

The father was undisputed head of the family and, as such, was the provider, disciplinarian, and business manager. He usually did all the shopping, drove the car if there was one, and made any other business transaction or decision necessary for the family. His wife stayed much closer to home and was in command of the household. Plácido Maldonado explained: "Authority rested with the parents, husbands, and males. Sometimes the oldest son had authority over mom. My mother did not know how to shop for groceries. Her husband did it. She never paid a bill." This was the case in Ofelia M. Longória's family also: "We would go to town in a wagon, and my father did all the shopping."

The same was true in most families. "Women had no social life and didn't go out," said Enemorio Serna. Manuela Mayorga said that her grandmother "stayed home." Catalina Maldonado said, "Mom would always stay home. My grandmother—nobody ever knew her outside the house. She always stayed home. She never traveled with him."

Dora Maldonado has had the same experience herself:

I've been here forty-six years, and I went to the Commissary once. Beto did the shopping. He's the boss, and he's been the boss, and he buys. He does everything. He pays the bills. I don't know about anything. I don't drive. If I need something, I just tell Beto. Or I say how can I do this? He's the boss.

I had five kids at home, and I have to stay home 'til he comes back 'cause I don't drive. He didn't come back for two or three weeks—I was there just waiting for him to come. My sister-in-law was there, but she didn't drive. It was different when she learned to drive. We didn't have phones or anything.

When Beto was gone, he would leave everything I needed. Plá-cido [III, Beto's brother] helped if I needed help with children, if they were sick. Beto was real nice to me all those years, and I'm the one's been sick, and I tell him, "Well I hope God will help you never get sick, 'cause I'm gonna take care of you. I know you're gonna take care of me." He's been real nice, real, real nice.

While his wife worked at home, the vaquero's life was dominated by extended hours of backbreaking work outside the home. He usually had part of Saturday and Sunday off, and from December 22 to after New Year's Day. He spent the rest of his time on the job. Each member of the family was attuned to this strict work ethic.

My dad would leave at 2:00 A.M. because he was in charge of the huge milking operation. There were six kids, and everyone would work. Beto Maldonado

My day started at 4:00 A.M. and ended at 8:00 P.M. Enemorio Serna

We worked in threes, in case one wanted to rest. We worked until you couldn't see because of the dark. We stopped working when the cold started and came back when it warmed up. Manuel Silva

We went to bed at 9:00. Too tired to do anything else. . . . We would come in Saturday noon and go back [to the corrida*] at 5:00 or 6:00 Sunday.* Jesus Gonzales

We got up at 4:00, ate, saddled, and rode. Worked 'til dark with no breaks. Ate in relays during roundup. Two or three would eat at a time. Seferino Gutierrez

Nicolas Rodríguez described how hard the vaqueros worked:

In those days, everything was work. We were given only one or two days to rest every month or two. During roundup, the workers in the corrida *woke up at 3:00 A.M. to start working, and we came back to the camp at night. We almost never saw the camp during the day, only at night.*

We were gone for a long time. Sometimes we were close to the Ranch, so maybe we would come [home] at night to change our clothes. But if a man asked permission to come change his clothes, the boss would not give him permission because there was too much work.

I was in charge of all the animal houses [barns], mostly the horses. I used to paint all the water holes for the animals all the

*way from San José to La Laguna [pastures]. I worked very hard in
those days, and for many years.*

*My father-in law [Manuel Garcia] was very strict with
people. He was very good with everyone and everything, but he did
not give anyone a chance to rest. He worked very hard. Even if he
was tired he did not stop. For example, there were times when we
were like one or two miles away from the corral while driving the
cattle, and he would start talking to me. He sometimes said things
like, "Look at that cow's tongue," or other things that for me were
unimportant at that time. I just wanted to get home and rest. He
was also tired, but he was always active and happy.*

*We worked from sunrise to sunset. We rested for a little while
during lunch time. We stayed up very late at night and woke up
before sunrise. We worked very, very hard in that time. One worked
all day. After sunset, around 8:00 or 9:00, they brought the cattle.*

The work was arduous, and some vaqueros would just walk away.
Limited opportunities elsewhere sometimes brought them back, or sometimes they moved from ranch to ranch, like Juan Guevara Sr.'s grandfather: "My grandfather Gumb [Gutierrez] worked at Laureles [King],
then Kenedy, then King, then Kenedy."

Catarino Moreno was one of the vaqueros who walked away:

*With the years I got tired of working. There were times when I
would just leave. There was one time when I left to go to San Antonio, and I left all the dogs from the house and all the hens which
were mine. I came like a month later, and they said they had no
job for me since I had left. Then they came looking for me and
telling me that they needed me to help them. I accepted.*

The Role of Women

The women deserved much credit. Enemorio Serna

The unsung heroes of the cowboy era are the women. In general,
women understood and accepted the male-dominated social structure,
and, by all accounts, they were content to relegate to men the role of un-
questioned head of the family. A woman likewise accepted her own role
in the family and became the great silent partner of the husband-wife
partnership. She did not question, but, rather, she conformed to what
was expected of her. Without her, the work of the vaquero would have

suffered. The stability of both the vaquero family unit and of the ranch owners' families—and the meshing of the two—contributed directly to the orderly, uninterrupted development of the ranching industry in the Southwest.

A woman structured and was very much in control of her household. Certain aspects of life were almost exclusively her domain. Though she was perfectly capable of assuming her husband's family role in his absence, she found satisfaction in her own jobs and apparently had no desire to take over his role. Her jobs included the family's day-to-day needs in regard to bed and board, health and medicinal remedies, religious training, celebrations, birthings, and funerals. As Manuela Mayorga said, "Mother did everything." A woman's tasks were endless. In addition, she shared with her husband the responsibility of disciplining the children. And she commanded respect.

> *I chopped wood and moved it inside for cooking in the morning. I washed my face, and then went to my mother every morning and said, "Good Morning." And I would bring her wildflowers.* Lolo Treviño

> *My parents were strict. I also raised my children with the customs of my parents. I have never had any problems with them.* Manuel Silva

> *Mom raised the family. She chopped wood, milked cows, fed chickens, turkeys, and did the garden. Mom also whipped.* Rogerio Silva

> *Father had strong discipline. Mother was strong, too. Boys fought a lot. We shot a basket down with tortillas in it. I still remember my father's whipping.* Enemorio Serna

> *He [Dora's grandfather, Librado Maldonado Sr.] was good at giving advice, at telling us right from wrong. He got on to us if we did something wrong, but never in a harsh manner, never raised his voice. Never. I never remember a day when he used a harsh word.* Dora Maldonado Garcia

> *My children were spanked if they didn't mind. I did not wait for Beto. I had it on the kitchen door. A belt.* Dora Maldonado

Though a woman may have performed work duties in the home of a caporal or owner at times, her first responsibility was to take care of her own household and raise the children. Children were not only valued for themselves, but they were also necessary to get the work done and continue the vaquero tradition. In Enemorio Serna's opinion, "The women deserved much credit."

The range of a woman's responsibilities differed somewhat depending on her husband's job. A few fathers were home every night, for their jobs were at headquarters working with the Jerseys in the cattle breeding program, or with the Quarter Horse and Thoroughbred enterprises. Some, like Plácido Maldonado III, assisted Dr. J. K. Northway, the nationally respected King Ranch veterinarian. These men, who had jobs close to home, could share at least some of the tasks of home and child care, specifically disciplining the children.

But most fathers worked as cowhands on the range. They left for the *corrida* Sunday night or before dawn on Monday morning, and returned home Friday night or Saturday at noon, only to leave again for the range two days later. But, because of the size of the Ranches, some of the men stayed out for fifteen days at a time; then they would come home for two days, rest before returning to the pastures, and the work cycle began again. Then there were those vaqueros who were gone much longer. Beto Maldonado was gone two or three months at a time working with the show cattle of King Ranch and traveling with them as far away as Morocco. Other vaqueros traveled to Australia and South America.

"When I was born," said Nicolas Rodríguez, "my father did not see me until I was one month old. My mother had to have both of us—because I have a twin brother—all by herself. He was not there. . . . men were gone for a long time." Ofelia Longória said that her dad "was in the *corrida* and sometimes was gone for a month at a time."

According to María Luisa Montalvo Silva, "The women were very supportive of each other while the men were gone, many times a month at a time. They would bring each other food and fix them a plate if they were sick." María Luisa further described the ways in which women passed the time together:

> We did a lot of handwork. We made quilts. We created our own designs and dyed the material. We used Rit dye to get the colors we needed. We also made presents for others on special occasions. We made little blankets and booties for newborn babies, and for brides, and for other occasions we did handwork with colored thread on pillowcases, sheets, and doilies.

During the long weeks or months that their husbands were gone, wives would have total responsibility for performing or supervising all household chores: cutting wood, building fires, milking cows, churning

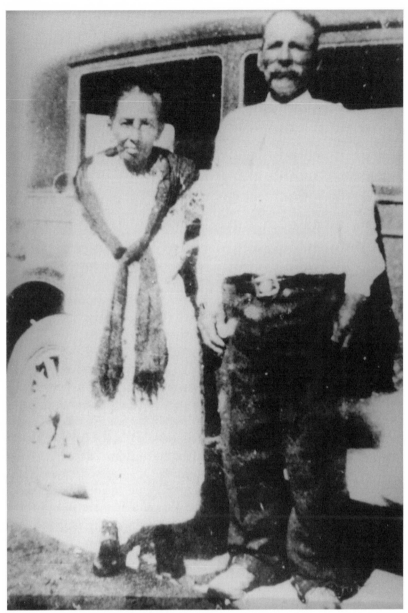

Valentín Quintanilla Sr. with his wife, Elesa Pérez. A major hurricane hit King Ranch while Valentín was out "tying down" the windmills. Elesa barely got their children out of the house before it was blown away.

butter, and feeding chickens. They were also responsible for the children, for their safety—for everything. In the absence of the father, the mother maintained strict discipline, carried on the work of the family, worked at jobs for the owners, and coped with challenges as they arose.

For instance, when Valentín Quintanilla Jr. was ten years old, his father, Valentín Sr., was out "tying down" windmills to prevent their destruction during an approaching storm. This task required Valentín Sr. to secure the "long arm" (the tail) to the wheel to create one stationary unit for more strength. Valentín Jr.'s mother, Elesa, looked up and saw the storm coming. She hurried the seven children to safety, and, when they were less than one hundred yards away from their house, they watched in disbelief as the house was totally destroyed. The roof was also blown off the barn, leaving only the supports curving like huge metal half-bracelets into the air and back to the earth again. Fighting a drowning rain, the ranch hands tugged and strained to pull huge tarpaulins across the naked supports. From 1:00 P.M. until 6:00 A.M., Elesa huddled with her children and the ranch hands under the tarps and rode out the storm, not knowing if her husband was dead or alive. All of them survived. The Quintanilla family was soon reunited and relocated elsewhere on the Ranch. The ability to relocate at the expense of the Ranch after losing everything may be an example of why workers were content to remain on the Ranches.

The women coped with all kinds of perilous situations as they arose. Nicolas Rodríguez related the following instance: "My brother came running to tell my mother that there was an armadillo in the cactus. He did that so many times that finally my mother went to see and found that it was not an armadillo, but a snake. The black snake [blue indigo] was eating the rattlesnake."

Enemorio Serna remembered that his mother "was a good shot. She used the gun to shoot snakes. I am not a good shot and don't like to shoot."

Safety was a concern while American Indians still roamed the Wild Horse Desert around the turn of the century. Nicolas Rodríguez told this story:

> *The Indians took one of my mother's aunts with them. She was pregnant, and she lived in a small house. The Indians were both women and men, and they were all riding horses. They had also with them a young man who spoke Spanish, who took care of the Indians' horses and whom they had raised. One day, the Indians left the boy in charge of my aunt, and they all left. The young man*

took two of the best horses and told my aunt that they were going to escape. They both went all the way to the Rio Grande—I am not sure how far away that was—and crossed the river. They crossed the river on horses. The Indians were all on the other side and could not do anything about their escape. The Indians almost caught them because my aunt and the young man had just crossed the river when the Indians showed up on the Texas side of it.

In 1910, my mother went to Brownsville by train because her aunt got real sick. When she got there, she saw her aunt and stayed with her. This was like ten years after the incident. This was when her aunt told her the story about the Indians.

I think they were the same Indians that moved to the territory in Oklahoma, the ones that the government helped by giving them food and clothing.

Aside from such hazards, simply performing routine tasks necessary for the family required organization, long hours, and hard work. A wife rose before her husband, long before dawn, and was the last to lay her head on the pillow at night. Life was not easy.

Cleanliness was as much a part of a family's routine as eating. Men and women labored, often in sweltering heat. The men worked on the land, where hot, dry winds swept grit and dirt into every crevice of their faces, eyes, noses, and ears. Children played in the dirt, and a bath every night for everybody was a necessity.

Enemorio Serna remembered how hard his mother worked to keep her family clean:

My mother believed you were somebody if you were clean, and so we were scrubbed every day using the same soap made from tallow and lye used for the clothes. It was made from a recipe handed down from her mother. There were nine children, and it took until midnight to bathe and put us all to bed. Then she was up again before daylight to begin cooking the day's food. You wonder when the lady slept. Mother was a patient woman and would work until midnight to get us all taken care of and bathed.

The House

. . . I lived in Norias in a house made of hay. Nicolas Rodríguez (King Ranch)

The jacal (straw and wood hut) was a typical kind of house that newlywed Henrietta King would have seen on the Wild Horse Desert when she married Captain King in 1854. Many of the early inhabitants of the Wild Horse Desert lived in these houses during the nineteenth century.

Much of a woman's time was spent in and around her house, which made the house an important aspect of her life. When Captain King first brought the Kineños from Mexico in 1854, the families lived in one-room jacales. A King Ranch ledger book indicates that Francisco "Pancho" Alvarado and his son, Ramón, built the first jacales on the Ranch and were paid $20 for a month's service in 1854 (Young 1992, 5). The first structures were small and crudely constructed of mud and grass. They had dirt floors and thatched roofs supported by four corner posts forked at the top and buried in the ground. The horizontal post running the length of the roof was likewise supported by posts in the ground. This room served as living room and bedroom. The roofless kitchen was located a short distance from the house as a fire safety precaution and was made of corn stalks or grass. An eating area sometimes was located nearby. The furniture was made by the vaquero and usually consisted of a bed, a few chairs, and a table (Graham 1994, 25).

As time passed, the jacal was improved to be a more livable dwelling. The posts were installed in pairs so that mesquite logs could be fitted between them horizontally, forming the walls of the house. The crevices were then filled with a mixture of clay, lime, and grass, which was usually *sacahuiste* (a type of grass) cut in short pieces. The foot-thick walls served as such good insulation that the outside temperature could vary as much as thirty degrees without a noticeable difference inside the house.

The Kenedy Ranch provided wood-frame houses for the vaqueros. They were about the same size as the rural Mexican homes, usually ten by fourteen feet, and were occupied by two families using a common fireplace with an opening on either side. They also had dirt floors. Temperature control was not as efficient as that of the jacal, since the walls were thin and poorly insulated (Villarreal 1972, 52).

Housing on the sprawling King Ranch varied on each of the four divisions. On all of them, family members lived close together, often next door. Nicolas Rodríguez described the early housing he remembered on the Ranch:

> *When I first got here, I lived at Norias in a house made of hay. That was in 1909. Later on they built better houses. Now they moved us to the "forty," the ranch they call El Saltillo.*
>
> *I do not remember when they made the house that is in the old Ranch. The house that I do remember is the house where "Hall" lives. It is wooden, and it was constructed in 1911. I worked there with the administrator. They had a little kid. The administrator had just started the job, and he used to sleep at the* corrida. *I stayed at his house with his wife and helped her take care of the baby. The baby gave lots of trouble, so we would both take care of him. He was the first child they had.*

Other residents of King Ranch also provided details about housing:

> *We had wood floors. We went to the bathroom outside, not too far from the house. You could see it from the house. [The bathroom] was made of wood. It had a board and one hole, and a wood floor.*
>
> *I cleaned the floors [of the house] with soap and a little brush by hand. Scrubbed, then rinsed. Then I had to mop it. I washed the floor twice or more a week—went by how dirty it looked. I used soap and water to clean the windows. I got hot water when I moved to my mother-in-law's in 1949.* Dora Maldonado
>
> *This house was built in 1939. They built twenty-one houses. I worked building those houses. We had to carry the materials.* Catarino Moreno

Plácido Maldonado III with his sisters in about 1939 in front of their home in the Old Colony, a housing settlement that was provided for the workers on the Santa Gertrudis Division of King Ranch.

I had six brothers, four sisters, and four died. I was sixth in line. Our house was east of the schoolhouse. It had four rooms. It had an inside kitchen—wood stove. We had an outside bathroom. Rogerio Silva

Our houses were fourteen by twenty-four feet. There were two rooms, one family in each room. It was a frame house, had dirt floors and separate kitchens. Each family had a twelve-by-fourteen-foot room. It was a dual chimney, one side for each family. In 1918, wood-burning stoves came in. Plácido Maldonado III

I remember two houses. My grandparents and great-[grand]parent lived in one house, and my family lived in the other. I lived there in 1931, when I was five years old, and had no electricity and no in-door bathrooms. We cooked with wood in a stove and used kerosene lanterns. I remember my grandmother's house, which was a big house. It is the camp house now. Ofelia Longória

The men made benches and tables for their houses. The houses had four rooms. The boys were in one room, girls in one, parents in one, and the kitchen. Sometimes the kitchen was outside. We used fireplaces for warmth. We also made fires outside, made coals, brought them in big tubs for heat, and used them for bed warmers. Enemorio Serna

The women made bed linens from white, 100 percent cotton fabric purchased at the Commissary. Bed frames were built of wood by the vaqueros. According to Dora Maldonado, "The mattresses were stuffed with cotton."

She Prepared All the Food for the Family

She was always in the kitchen with that apron on. Dora Maldonado Garcia

Preparing the food was the first and most important task of the day for the woman of the house. Three hearty meals every day were a must to enable family members to complete the strenuous work that was expected of them.

Most families ate a hearty diet of beans, meat, tortillas, eggs, milk, and homemade cheese. Potatoes and eggs were typical breakfast fare, and some meat was available. There was always plenty of strong, steaming, black coffee.

As the following recollections illustrate, the preparation of particular foods might last from one day to the next. Large pots of beans would sometimes simmer overnight in order to be ready for lunch or supper the next day, and it was not uncommon for meat to be cooked all night. All these meals were prepared without even the most basic household conveniences, such as indoor running water and electricity.

She got up first. She put on a pot of beans — she cooked on a wood stove. Then she put on corn, and it would cook for one hour. Then she ground the corn and made tortillas. At night, she would put meat on, and it would cook all night. Used it all day in meals and lunch. She made flour tortillas, too. She fixed breakfast and lunches to take. We took taquitos *of eggs and meat and sauce, beans, or any combination.* Enemorio Serna

We cooked with firewood. The only place with electricity was the Hotel where Mr. Caesar [Kleberg] lived at the Old Ranch. They had seventy batteries of water, and they ran some light bulbs off of it. Nicolas Rodríguez

My father would get up at 3:00 or 4:00 to milk the cows. I was raised on milk from a cow called La Corona, meaning "The Crown," because the horns came around its head. My mother got up at 3:00 or 4:00, also. She cooked breakfast of bacon and eggs, and she made both corn and flour tortillas.

We had no electricity, no indoor bathrooms. She cooked on a wood stove and used kerosene lanterns [for light]. Ofelia M. Longória

There was always barbecue, rice, beans, and tortillas — flour. She [Ella Maldonado] was always in the kitchen with that apron on. She would fix lunch for him [Librado Sr.]. She would have supper ready for him. Dora Maldonado Garcia

The men would often take food with them to the *corrida* or would come home for lunch if they were working close enough. The children always took their lunches to school unless they lived nearby and could come home at noon. There was no school cafeteria. "We went home for lunch for rice, beans, and tortillas," said María Luisa Montalvo Silva.

At least there was always an adequate supply of food, though it was lacking in variety by present-day standards. Until the late 1970s, the Ranches provided weekly rations of food allocated according to the size of the family. This practice was almost nonexistent among Anglo work-

Table 1. Food Inventory, 1889–1892

Item	Price $	Price $
Allspice	.15	
Butter	.50	2.00
Beans (qt.)	.25	1.00
Bacon (lb.)	.25	.85
Clams	.15	
Cornmeal	.35	
Coffee	.25	1.00
Corn (bbl.)	.50	.75
Flour (lb. - .03)	.25	6.50
Crackers (Crax)	.15	.30
Meat	.25	3.97
Oats (82 lbs.)	1.15	
Rice	.10	.50
Soup	.25	
Soda	.10	
Spices	.50	.75
Salt	.25	
Sugar (lb. - .08)	.20	2.00
Tomatoes	1.50	
Lemons	.45	.50
Honey (5 gal.)	5.00	

Source: Journal of the King Ranch, 1889–1892. Printed from Andrew Herbert Young, "Life and Labor on the King Ranch: 1853–1900," Texas A&I University, 1992, 71.
Note: Columns 2 and 3 list the most common prices of the various items stocked in the King Ranch Commissary.

ers on Texas ranches. The families had chickens, and thus eggs. Items not furnished by King Ranch could be purchased in the Commissary, which served both owners and workers. Table 1 shows a list of foods available in the Commissary, some of which were not part of the rations.

A few of the families tended gardens. Enemorio Serna said his family had a garden in which they grew beans, corn, and squash, "when we could," meaning when there was adequate time and water. Their long work hours did not leave much time for gardening. Families were also free to hunt certain small wild game for food.

Each family got a milk ration. If [the family had] four or five kids, [they] got a gallon a day. Made butter and cream from it. We got rations from the Commissary: lard, beans, rice, flour, and baking powder. Some meat was provided in the late '40's and '50's. When the corrida *would butcher, they brought leftovers in, and if a cow got hurt, we got it.*

We went to Kingsville for some groceries. Dad had a car, and $15 would fill the car. Plácido Maldonado III

[My mother] would boil milk, make white cheese. Water was put in milk to make clabber. Rogerio Silva

My mother made cottage cheese each day by skimming cream off sour milk. This would become clabber. It was then placed in a sack and hung up on the porch to drain. Julian Buentello

They gave us rations. Rice and potatoes and flour and like that. Got about ten pounds of meat. The meat was cut and wrapped. It was steak or roast or whatever. We had a refrigerator. Ella [Maldonado] had chickens, eggs. Dora Maldonado

We always had enough to eat because my father was a cowboy. We also raised chickens, so we had eggs. Manuela Mayorga

Our family had a cow. We used block ice in an icebox to keep milk cool. We made butter for the Ranch. Used a crank churn. Vegetables were furnished from gardens at the Big House. I worked cabbage and onions. Antonio Salinas

We ate rabbits, armadillo, and wild duck. Daddy loved armadillo. We cleaned and washed it. Rubbed it with chili powder, covered with foil, baked slow two or three hours. Used chili powder to kill the taste of javelina. We steamed it. Stella Guevara

Then There Was Always the Laundry

First, a fire was built outside . . . Alberto "Beto" Maldonado

Families usually had few clothes, so washing almost every day that the weather permitted was a necessity. The clothes were washed outside in large tubs. Beto Maldonado detailed the clothes washing procedure:

My mother washed in a size no. 3 galvanized metal tub using a rub board. First, a fire was built outside and water heated to boiling so the clothes would come clean. Soap, made of lye and tallow by my

mother, would be added to the tub. Then the clothes were rinsed in clean, clear water and hung on a fence or clothesline to dry. The clothes were ironed the next day. There were no wash-and-wear fabrics, only cotton. Irons were heated on the wood stove or on the fire. I can remember when my father bought my mother her first gasoline iron.

Beto's wife, Dora, remembered a similar procedure used by her family:

We washed in a tub with a rub board and yellow soap. Then put some water to boil and boiled the white clothes. We took it out, rinsed it, and hung it. The colored clothes, you just use the board and rinse and hang. Soap was used for stains. Lye soap. We cooked the starch, had to iron everything. I couldn't go to bed until I finished.

Beto and Dora's daughter, Dora Maldonado Garcia, added: "My grandmother [Ella Maldonado] had these bushes at the end of the sidewalk that she would get a little limb, and she would pass the iron over that, and it made [the iron] go smooth. Looked like a little Christmas tree. I was good at ironing and am 'til this day."

Enemorio Serna said that his mother "used one day to wash, one to mend, and one to iron."

By the 1940s, the method of washing in some of the homes had progressed from tubs of boiling water over open fires to washing machines that stood on four legs. The washing and the two rinsing tubs were filled with water from indoor faucets and had a wringer. Refrigerators made it possible to postpone ironing part of the dampened clothes until another day, as Dora Maldonado Garcia described:

I remember when my mother would take out the old, wringer washing machine, and she washed only on Mondays. She separated the colored and the white. She rinsed, then put that bluing in the white clothes rinse water. Then she'd throw out that water and get some clean. I think she ironed once a week, and I helped her. She cooked the starch and dipped those blue jeans in there and hung them on the clothesline, and they would be stiff. She dampened 'em and put 'em in a plastic bag. If she didn't get through, she put 'em in the refrigerator. She ironed everything—my dad's T-shirts, underwear, pillowcases, handkerchiefs—everything. My mother always set the ironing board up in the living room. It was an all day thing. Now just throw it in the dryer—right quick.

And She Made the Clothes

My mother used flour sacks with patterns on them . . . Josefina
Robles Adrián (King Ranch)

Up until 1935, virtually all of the clothing worn by vaquero families
was made by the women. Only shoes or boots, belts, and hats were
bought. These items were usually purchased in the Commissary on the
Ranch, but sometimes they were purchased in Kingsville. Fabric was
generally purchased by the yard at the Commissary, but some shirts and
dresses were also made of flour sacks. Clothing, tablecloths, curtains,
and bedding were usually made of calico, imperial, or manta. Linen was
seldom used because it was the most expensive fabric. Manta was a coarse
cotton and the least expensive. Much of the fabric was khaki or white,
but calico was sometimes designed with bright colors. There was more
than one price for some of the items, indicating a difference in quality.
Table 2 lists prices of clothing goods available in the Commissary.

Nicolas Rodríguez remembered his mother making the family's
clothing:

> *The women sewed all the men's clothes and also the children's and
> their own. There was a white material that men used for the pants
> which was like linen.*
>
> *Mother handmade all clothes—there were nine of us. She
> made all clothes by hand until she got a sewing machine in 1926. I
> still have that sewing machine at home.*
>
> *We bought boots, belts, and shoes in town. Before that, we had
> to send somebody to buy them. They had to go all the way to
> Brownsville.*

And in answer to a question about visits from traveling salesmen,
Nicolas said: "Yes, there was one, but I do not remember because I was
too young. He came in a wagon pulled by three donkeys. He came only
once in a while."

Other members of vaquero families remembered mothers and
grandmothers sewing clothing from scratch:

> *My mother used flour sacks with patterns on them and made our
> clothes from that.* Josefina Robles Adrián
>
> *All the clothes were sewed by hand, and we used the mantilla cloth
> for clothes.* Ofelia M. Longória

Table 2. Commissary Clothing, 1889–1892

Item	Price $	Price $	Price $
Bandana	.50		
Blanket (pr.)	2.75	3.50	4.50
Boots	2.00	3.25	5.00
Calico	.20	.75	2.50
Chivarros	6.00		
Coats	3.00	3.50	4.50
Coats (duck)	1.50	1.75	2.00
Domestic (cloth)	.50	1.00	2.00
Drawers	.40	.75	1.00
Gloves	.50	.75	
Handkerchiefs	.10	.25	.50
Hats	1.25	3.50	6.00
Hose	.20		
Imperial	.50	.60	1.00
Jeans	1.50		
Manta	.10	.60	1.50
Overalls	1.00	1.25	1.50
Pants	.75	1.25	1.75
Sacks (white)	.40	.50	
Sacks (wool)	.40	.50	
Sash	.50		
Shirt	.25	1.75	3.50
Shirt	.50	1.00	
Shirting (cloth)	.65	1.00	
Shoes	1.00	4.50	5.00
Slicker	2.25	2.75	3.00
Slippers	.75		
Socks (sox)	.10	.20	.25
Socks (wool)	.20	1.00	
Stockings	.25	.50	.90
Suits	4.00	8.50	10.00
Suit clothes	7.00	11.00	15.00
Suspenders	.50	.60	
Thread	.10	.25	
Towels	.20	.40	.50
Vest	.75	1.25	2.00

Source: Journal of the King Ranch, 1889–1892. Printed from Andrew Herbert Young, "Life and Labor on the King Ranch: 1853–1900," Texas A&I University, 1992, 72.

Note: Columns 2–4 list the most common prices of the various items stocked in the King Ranch Commissary.

I went barefoot a lot and used Acme boots from the store. Our mother made our shirts and dresses from cloth bought by the bolt from the Commissary—there were nine of us. One time she forgot to put a fly in a pair of my pants, and I had to hurry and cut a hole with a knife—it was funny. Enemorio Serna

My grandmother [Ella Maldonado] was short, stout, and very light complexioned, hair always pulled back in a bun. Dressed as simple as you could get. She made her dresses with buttons down the front, with belts. She would cover the buckles. She never wore anything bright, only light blue—pale colors. Dora Maldonado Garcia

She Was the Source of Spiritual Guidance

I did the rosary every night . . . Gavina Mendietta

The church touched the lives of vaquero families on certain momentous occasions—at baptisms following the birth of a new family member, at weddings, and at burials. The role of the women included daily training of the children in church teachings and rituals. She also prepared for religious observances.

The Kenedy Ranch vaquero families attended church in the chapel on La Parra or in Sarita. On King Ranch on the Laureles Division, part of the Main House area was used for church services at first, then the school was used, and finally a chapel in the early 1980s, when the original manager's home was remodeled for this purpose. On Norias, the school, built in the 1940s, doubled as a chapel. The permanent chapel, built in memory of Helen Campbell Kleberg, was completed in 1971. On Santa Gertrudis, vaquero families attended church in Kingsville; then, in 1980, a building was moved into the New Colony for use as a chapel. Often the families waited for an itinerant priest to come to the Ranches to perform wedding ceremonies and baptisms and to celebrate mass. During the remainder of the year, in the absence of a priest, it was considered the woman's role to teach her children religious doctrine and to lead the family in prayer before the altar in the home (Graham 1994, 25). Vaquero children were not only scrubbed clean before going to bed, they usually recited prayers with their mother. On the rare occasions when the priest was expected, preparation would begin days in advance by cooking special foods, washing and ironing linens, and decorating the altar.

Every home, regardless of how humble, had an *altarcito*, a small altar that boasted a picture of the Virgen de Guadalupe or another saint, surrounded by paper flowers or candles. Some altars were larger and more complex, with small statues, paintings, and decorations. Around this place of honor that she had specially designed, the mother taught her children the various Catholic prayers and rites (Graham 1994, 25).

Gavina Mendietta's altar could be considered typical. It included a cloth, handmade candles, a picture of the Virgin Mary, a statue of St. Guadalupe, a cross, and handmade crepe-paper flowers in hues of brilliant orange, red, yellow, green, and pink. "I said the rosary every night before the altar with [my] children kneeling," said Gavina. "At Christmas, I put moon and stars above the altar. My mother had a small cradle with baby Jesus on the altar at Christmas."

Many vaquero family members attended mass, either in town or on the Ranch:

> The priest usually came about once a month. I did the rosary every day. The rosary takes about an hour and forty-five minutes. My grandmother's altar had a cross with Christ on it, the Virgin Mary statue, the Sacred Heart of Jesus, and candles. Ofelia M. Longória

> [The priest] came from the river by Brownsville on a horse. He came to each little ranch in Corpus. In each ranch there would be like one or two families, and the same in a ranch farther away. When word was given that the priest would come to visit, a number of families would get together in a ranch. The priest would then give mass or would pray the rosary. He would also marry couples. He came like three or four times a year. He would then go back the same way he came and would do the same thing. He would also baptize babies. Nicolas Rodríguez

> We had a church on the Ranch. The Kenedys all went to church on Sunday. It lasted an hour. Antonio Salinas

> We went to church in town, but not every Sunday. We usually went with our mother. Beto Maldonado

> There was no church on the Ranch. Had to go to Sarita. Enemorio Serna

> My grandmother might go to town on Saturday, but on Sunday for sure, to go to church every Sunday. Because we didn't have a church out here. My Aunt Alicia [Maldonado], Dad's sister—we would all go to church with her. When I was older, I can remember

my grandmother would go to town on Sunday for 6:00 mass. We used to have a place called Burger Chef, twenty-five-cent hamburgers, fix your own burger, and that was her thing, to go eat there on Sunday before she went to church. This was her treat for herself. Catalina Maldonado

I remember we used to get a church calendar, and they had every day for a saint, and a lot of people were named for a saint. One of the names would be biblical. Chito Mendietta

We went to Kingsville to church. Sometimes the priest would come to the school auditorium for communion. My grandfather would take us, but that didn't last very long. We went into Kingsville. My parents were never church-going people; they're still not. Then we went to St. Martín's, and I would always go with my grandmother. I was the oldest, so my mother always sent me. My aunt took my grandmother and me. Dora Maldonado Garcia

We go to church on Good Friday, and we have a big fish fry. Mass is held mostly in the morning for saints, and there's work or school. I can't always go. Sonia Maldonado Garcia

She Coordinated Celebrations

The two sets of parents set the date . . . Plácido Maldonado III

The universal celebrations among the families were church-related, and the women planned and coordinated these events. Christmas, baptisms, and weddings were occasions for visiting over special foods prepared for the extended family and for friends. The *quinceañeras* celebrated the approach of womanhood for girls when they reached their fifteenth birthday. Music and dancing were usually part of the festivities. Dances were also held at other times during the year. Today, Thanksgiving and Easter are celebrated in some families, and even birthdays have become occasions for parties.

CHRISTMAS

Christmas celebrations today include some changes since earlier days, but some traditions have remained unchanged. Dora Maldonado described Christmas during her adult years on King Ranch.

Christmas was at my mother-in-law's—Ella's. And Christmas was at the school. Father-in-law [Librado Sr.] was Santa Claus. At first, gifts were given at the Big House, then at the school. Then gifts were delivered to the houses in trucks. They brought blankets, towels, sheets, and things like that. Toys for the kids—dolls, play guns for the boys. I still have some. They brought candy, oranges, fruit. The men got coats. Everybody got the same gifts. They delivered on December 24.

Later on, when we had the little church, we would go to church, go caroling and stop, and they were waiting for us with some cake and some chocolate. We didn't buy children anything because they were going to get things from the Ranch.

Dora was not so fortunate as a child living in Corpus Christi before coming to King Ranch. She said: "I don't remember going to church. It was not near the house—too far. Did not celebrate holidays, no birthday, or Christmas. Had same thing to eat on holidays. Meat or chicken. No room for garden. It was a little house and two rooms."

Christmas celebrations at King Ranch have generally been festive. Only Nicolas Rodríguez said, "We did not celebrate Christmas. We did not know anything about it."

At Christmas we would go house to house visiting. We had dances. Miguel Muñiz

At Christmas we decorated a branch with candles. We had no lights. We made decorations out of paper and made cutouts to hang on the limbs. Our gifts were shoes, clothes, dresses—things that we needed. We put out socks for stockings for Santa Claus, and he brought peanuts, walnuts, fruit, and candy. Antonia Quintanilla

I celebrated a Saint Reyes [Los Reyes] Catholic celebration [Day of the Three Kings—the day the three kings brought gifts to the Christ child] held each January 6th with my family. We went to church, then came home and had chocolates, buñuelos, and wedding cookies. Manuela Mayorga

Celebrations were Christmas at Laureles. Kids got toys, and adults got necessities like sheets and blankets, and it was a peaceful time. We got a week off. We had dances at Laureles, and we had an accordion for music. At Christmas, we ate tamales and turkey and wedding cookies. Ofelia M. Longória

The main holiday we celebrate now is Christmas—sometimes Christmas Eve, sometimes Christmas Day, whatever we agree on. We have lots of food—ham, smoked turkey, tamales, pan de polvo *[Mexican wedding cakes], sugar cookies, oatmeal cookies, relish trays, and salads—potato and fruit. We sit all over the place and eat. Then we clean up. My uncle from San Antonio spreads the presents out—Albert Maldonado Jr.—and gives out the presents, the youngest to the oldest child. One person opens all his presents, then the next person. Then the grandparents open theirs, then the other adults. My uncle taught me not to have temper tantrums when I was no longer the youngest, because I was spoiled. Takes two to three hours to open the gifts.* Sonia Maldonado Garcia

Similar customs for celebrating Christmas were observed on the Kenedy Ranch.

We went to dances in houses. We had accordion music. The grownups went. Antonio Salinas

Sarita East was very nice. At Christmas, she sent gifts to the houses. Everybody in the family got a gift. The ladies got linens, towels, and the kids, toys; the men got a bonus. Nuts and candy were sent to the house. Sarita did this. Stella Guevara

On December 24th, we went to the Big House. We were given gifts of blankets, shirts, and coats. Then we had a dance—had an accordion or guitar. We danced 'til midnight at the school. At New Year's we had buñuelos. Enemorio Serna

Only occasionally did families celebrate other holdiays, such as Easter. Enemorio said: "At Easter, we went to the bay, twenty miles from here. We had barbecue and a swim at the beach. We fished for drum, redfish, speckled trout, flounder, mullet, and shrimp. Caught whatever we could. There was a dock down there. We fished off that."

Today, in addition to the traditional celebrations of generations past, families are adding Easter, Thanksgiving, and birthdays as days for special family gatherings, as Sonia Maldonado Garcia described:

We celebrate Thanksgiving. At Easter we have a big barbecue, egg hunt, egg toss, softball, water balloon toss. Normally we all get together down at Ricardo, south of town at one of my grandfather's sister's little ranch. All their family and our family get together and have one big party all day long. . . . I was born February 16, 1974.

This one I had to work. Normally, we go out to eat on my birthday.
I had big parties when I was smaller. When I was eighteen, they
had a big party for me.

BAPTISMS AND GODPARENTS

Baptisms were significant occasions in the lives of family members.
Godparents were selected for baptisms, confirmations, and first com-
munions; frequently, different individuals were selected for each event.
Godparents helped to create the bond that united Mexican families. Not
only was the godparent to godchild relationship important, but even
more important was the relationship between a father and the godfather
of his child, or between a mother and the godmother of her child. When
a godparent was not already kin, the relationship created a *comadre* (co-
mother) or a *compadre* (co-father), who were as close or closer to the
godchild than cousins. More prosperous members of the community
were often chosen to be godparents, since the cost of giving gifts or raising a child could be very expensive.

I was baptized in Laico. The priest came to the Ranch and bap-
tized me there. He had to come to give the rosary. My godfather
was American—he was a ranger. His name was Paulino Coy.
Nicolas Rodríguez

My twin brother and I had godparents, one for baptism and one
for communion. They switched. I was close to my godparents. They
came to the Ranch and taught lessons like Sunday School.
    I went to church every Sunday before marriage. I have a lot of
godchildren. I have the obligation to teach them to obey their par-
ents and give thanks to God. If it's too hot or too dark, I tell them to
always invite God. The things you can't do, God will take care of.
I get cards from my godchildren. Lolo Treviño

We had a big celebration for a baptism. Godparents were usually
family members or some couple very close to you. I can remember
that [parents] picked a couple that, if something happened to
them, the couple would step in and raise the child. Big responsi-
bility. My godparents were my mother's sister and her husband.
For my confirmation it was my mother's aunt. I also had one for
communion.
    My children were born in Kingsville. My real sister was one of
the godparents. Beto's brother . . . and Beto's aunt [were god-

parents]. And my sister-in-law, Alicia, Beto's sister. Not hard to choose. We took them to church and baptized. My children were baptized while babies. They wore white dresses bought in Kingsville. I made a little dinner for the family.

Confirmation was when [children were] little back then. I was very young when I had my confirmation, [and I had] communion in the second or third grade. Had different godparents for every one. Now children have to be older. My oldest daughter was confirmed when she was in the tenth grade. Went every week to learn all the things they have to learn. Veronica was in the fifth grade. Samantha had confirmation and communion on the same day when she was in the second grade. Churches and priests had different rules. Dora Maldonado

David's [Maldonado] father is one of my godparents. If your parents died or something, your godfather saw that you were taken care of. They would see that you got through school. A cousin was another one. I had one set for baptism and one set for confirmation. My first cousin on my mother's side is my confirmation godparent. His name is José Quintanilla. My godparent didn't work in the same part [of the Ranch], but when he would see me, he would come over and see if I needed anything and give me fifty cents. Chito Mendietta

My padrino *[Eugenio Quintanilla] and I worked together in the Vet. Department for many years. There was always that special respect.* David Maldonado

DANCES

Dances were important social events among some Mexican families. Some dances, according to Manuela Mayorga, were held to raise money. Often they were the occasions during which young men and women met and got to know each other. Without these occasions, there would have been less opportunity for young people to meet and socialize and thereby begin the foundation for future families. Some of the interviewees attended dances regularly, and some only occasionally, if at all.

There was a lady in Sarita who gave a celebration every month. There were violins and guitars, ice cream, coffee, and beef and pork tamales. We danced the schottische 'til midnight. Seferino Gutierrez

I like to square dance. My father [Macario Mayorga] taught his daughters to dance. He played the accordion, too. He wore a claw of a mountain lion to hold his handkerchief. George Mayorga

Dances started Saturday evening and lasted 'til Sunday morning. Music was accordion, guitar, flute, violin. The dances were waltzes, polkas, paso doble, cuadrillas, dansa loches, *and* el ocho. Plácido Maldonado III

In 1945, I married Chon—Encarnación Silva, who was a vaquero and was left-handed and a good roper. He loved to dance, and we would have a dance once a week usually. He started them. We used a record player and used Ranch music or polkas. Sometimes we would have an accordion, and we danced from 9:00 until 12:00 or 1:00 or more. María Luisa Montalvo Silva

THE QUINCEAÑERAS

The *quinceañera* was a party given in celebration of a girl's coming of age and was held on her fifteenth birthday. Once a minor church function, this celebration became more prominent during the 1940s when economic conditions improved. Today it is even more elaborate, giving parents the opportunity to show off their daughters, and sometimes the family's prosperity. Sonia Maldonado Garcia described a typical *quinceañera:*

The girl gets fourteen bridesmaids, or attendants, and escorts and goes to church, and there is mass for them. The girls all wear the same [type of] dresses. Men wear tuxedos or jeans with white shirts. The symbolism is getting into the woman-age, and the father [priest] wants to bless you and let you know you're still pure and all that. Because from there you start hitting the woman-hood years.

   There is a reception, and they serve cake and punch and pan de polvo, *sometimes after a dinner, sometimes not. About 8:00 or 9:00 they have the presentation—all the bridesmaids and the honoree of the* quinceañera. *The dress is white, usually, with a hoop—not a wedding dress; it has no tail [veil and train]. It is like a ball gown. She wears a crown on her head made with rhine-stones—a small one. They usually hire a master of ceremonies. It is held at a dance hall. The dance is from 9:00 until 1:00. There are lots of guests and they give gifts, mostly money, so she'll buy what* *she wants. The usual amount is $10 to $20. The number can vary from two hundred to five hundred people. Most of the time it gets filled up with just relatives. It is still a custom. The bridesmaids are my same age, some younger, like little cousins.*

I did not want to do this. I was in several of them. One was a western *quinceañera; I wore a denim skirt with western blouse. That was my type.*

Weddings

Marriage has been cause for elaborate preparation and celebration in vaquero families for four generations. In the past, the courtship, proposal, and acceptance followed prescribed procedures and customs. An intermediary was almost always involved. Once the date was set, preparations were begun involving the immediate and extended families, and, in many cases, the ranch owners. Memories of their weddings invariably brought expressions of joy to the faces of interviewees. Following the wedding ceremony, the couple customarily lived with one set of parents until they received housing of their own.

THE COURTSHIP

Manuela Mayorga described the courtship customs that she has observed:

Couples would meet at a dance. The young man would decide he wanted to marry and told his father. The father arranged for a postadores *to pay a visit to the girl's family. Sometimes a respected member of the family would do this duty. The girl's family usually didn't know the suitor until the* postadores *told them. The* postadores *made two visits. He asked for the girl's hand in marriage on the first visit. The girl's family would tell the* postadores *to come back in fifteen days for an answer, if the answer was to be affirmative. If the answer was negative, the* postadores *was told to come back in eight days. Fifteen days meant yes; eight days meant no.*

The two sets of parents set the date and ironed out the details, usually one month before the wedding. The parents did it all. The couple married on Sunday morning at mass. Afterwards there was wedding chocolate and cake at a reception. Then at noon, there was a large meal with several guests. That evening, supper was served before the dance. It started Saturday evening and lasted 'til Sunday morning. The music was accordion, guitar, flute, violin. The dances were waltzes, polkas, paso doble, cuadrillas, dansa loches, el ocho. Before 1900, the dance would last several days.

Manuela then discussed her own daughter's courtship:

My daughter Enriqueta's husband was from Mexico—sixteen in the family. She was our only daughter. It was hard to convince us. The postadores *came and talked to us. Her father said come back in fifteen days. Enriqueta counted the days. We said nothing to her about it. She was eating supper on the fifteenth day and her father said, "I've sent and they are to wait fifteen days more." She told her father, "You'd better think it over because with your approval or not, I'm going to marry him." Then he went with another man to [talk with] her [future] in-laws and told them it was okay.*

She had to wait 'til the in-laws came to visit. When they came, her mother-in-law and I made the arrangements and set the date. They [the bride and groom] had nothing to say about it.

On May 10 was the first visit. The wedding date was set for September 20. She couldn't talk to him. She had to sneak around at church. She would take flowers to the trash to sneak out and talk to him. There was no dating except to sneak out.

Other interviewees related their courtship stories:

My husband and I dated a little over a year. His name was Reynaldo S. Longória. I was eighteen when I married, and Reynaldo was twenty. After we were married, we lived with my parents. Ofelia M. Longória

I met my husband at the theater. [Dora laughs.] He was my uncle's friend, Beto was. I was seventeen. I knew him a year before we were married. We've been married forty-five years, and I'm enjoying where I am.

When we wanted to get married, his father went to talk with my grandmother. And then my father had got married again and lived in Riviera. So my father came to see my grandmother, and my grandmother told him that Beto's father came to talk about Beto getting married with me. My grandmother said it was okay. I was nervous. But those days were not like today. Today they make their plans and that's it.

They gave Beto coffee. I was in the other room hiding. My

father came the next day. He got married again, and I never lived with him. Dora Maldonado

I met my husband in school, [in] junior high. He was a year or two ahead of me. He's from out here also. Then he went off to the service, and I was still in school when he left. He went to Germany. He returned and got a job. I was already working at the Ranch. He came back in September of 1969, and we married July 11 of 1970. When he was overseas, his parents took me to Corpus Christi, and I picked out the engagement ring and his wedding band. This was a couple of months after he left. They liked me.

Joe was the only son. He had a sister six or seven years older. He was spoiled. We waited a while.

When we decided to get married, Joe talked to my dad and told him we wanted to get married. After that, his parents came to my house and talked to my parents. This was after he came back. Being engaged didn't necessarily mean that we would marry, so they wanted to know if it was okay. If they'd said no, there wouldn't have been a wedding. Not then anyway.

Joe's parents were older. Their tradition was that when they came and asked for the daughter, from that day forward they had to provide for her as far as food and what she needed, if they consented to the wedding. This was his mother's tradition. If my parents had been poor, they would have provided food or clothes. Of course, it never happened. When my parents accepted, Joe's mother went out and bought me a set of luggage and bought me this and that. Not because she had to, but she wanted to. I still have the luggage. When Joe was overseas, they would come every weekend and take me here and take me there. Dora Maldonado Garcia

We decided we wanted to get married. Her father died the same year my father died. She's four years younger than I am. In those days, you had to have somebody to ask her parents for me to get married to their daughter—somebody older related to you who would speak for you. My uncle did that. I don't know which one. Two men, or a couple, would go. I would tell my wife-to-be they were coming, and her family would have to approve for them to come for the visit. If they don't like me, they don't let them come. Then we would have to elope. I had been hurt by a horse that day and had to be at the hospital. I didn't even remember that that was the day they were going to ask.

I couldn't go visit my wife for so many days. Two or three

*weeks. I couldn't see her—I guess to prove my love for her. Then
you set a date to get married.*

*We dated unescorted for two or three years. My mother-in-
law liked me a lot and she trusted me.* Chito Mendietta

THE WEDDING CEREMONY AND RECEPTION

The wedding took place in a church and included a mass. The time
of day varied from early in the morning to sometime in the evening.
Family members, friends, and sometimes the Ranch owners attended.
The celebration lasted from one to two days and customarily included
generous amounts of food, music, and dancing. The Ranch owners often gave gifts—sometimes money—and furnished the meat for the barbecue at more elaborate weddings. The couple wore traditional wedding
clothes, the bride in a long white dress and the groom in a suit. The vaquero's boots might even be replaced by shoes for the event. The two
families shared the expenses of the wedding celebration.

Vaqueros and their wives were often involved in the weddings of the
owner families.

*I drove the carriage for Helenita Kleberg's wedding. I drove the
carriage from the Main House to the church, then back to the
Main House.* Miguel Muñiz

*Lucia Gonzales raised Helenita Kleberg. She rode with her to her
wedding. [Lucia's] uncle, Miguel [Muñiz] brought [Helenita] to
town in the stagecoach, and Lucia rode with her. She married in
the afternoon at 4:00. Lucia was her second mother. She had a
mother, but Lucia was the one who raised her. Helenita bought
[Lucia] clothes to wear to the wedding. Helenita asked her if she
wanted her to marry. Lucia said yes because she [Lucia] was getting old. She went to the reception in the Big House and had barbecue and drinks.* Manuela Mayorga

Manuela then described her own wedding and reception:

*I got married at 3:00 in the afternoon on April 27, 1929, at St.
Martín's [Church] in Kingsville. The musicians were coming as we
left to get married. My mother [Antonia Cavazos] was not at the
wedding. She died in 1928. My husband's father was there. There
was a reception. My uncle [José Angeles] took me to the church to
get married. We came back to the Ranch for the reception. We had
supper. They gave us a whole cow because he [George Mayorga]*

was a vaquero. They barbecued meat; we had gravy. After the dance, we ate cake and cookies. After we came back from church, a man who worked for Mrs. Kleberg brought me an envelope. She [Alice Gertrudis Kleberg] had sent me $50. She sent me a cake, too, decorated like Easter lilies. It was very special. Both were special. I knew Miss Alice. Our whole family would pass by at Christmas time. Miss Alice liked me especially. She knew my mother real well, and I was the oldest child.

We had a big tent and tables in the yard. We ate outside. There was music. We danced at the school that night. We danced 'til 5:00 in the morning. People went to the house to eat and drink during the dance. There was some liquor. No one left 'til morning. In the morning, we had cake, cookies, and homemade chocolate — the Mexican kind. My aunt made it.

We lived with his mother in her house after we married. There were three bedrooms.

Manuela also described her daughter Enriqueta's wedding in 1968.

She wanted a big wedding. She was married at 6:00 A.M. at St. Martín's [Church] in Kingsville on September 20, 1968. We had two dances. We had them at the Ranch. One was given by the bridesmaids and one by the parents. We danced 'til 1:00. We had baked ham, wedding cookies, and cakes. We had a tent near house #27 in the colony. The cook from the cow camp, Manuel López, cooked. There was music at the house. There was breakfast, lunch, and supper. We stayed dressed 'til night in time for the dance. It rained during the dance at the school.

They lived with us. Her husband worked with Caterpillars [tractors] under [Bobby] Cavazos [Sr.]. She has a son on the Ranch now. Raul [fourth generation] does welding. Raul's son, Christopher [fifth generation], is six years old. He goes to school on the Ranch.

Other King Ranch vaquero family members described their weddings and receptions:

I married at twenty years old. I rode horseback to the church in town. Josefina Robles Adrián

The wedding was at 6:30 in the morning on a Saturday. I got up at 5:00 and wore a white dress. The attendants were José Muñiz and his wife, and Martín Mendietta and his wife. The mass was over at

Nicolasa Quintanilla Garcia and José Garcia at their wedding on February 12, 1949.

8:00. Mr. and Mrs. John Armstrong and their young son, Charlie, came, and Charlie called out to me from the back. Mrs. Armstrong [Henrietta "Etta" Larkin Armstrong] gave me a cedar chest. After the wedding we all went to my house, and I changed into a beige suit — a casual suit — and had punch, coffee, and cookies. They served lunch, which was carne asada *[barbecue] and potato salad and* cabrito *[goat] for about a hundred people. The Ranch gave us the meat. Then there was a dance at 7:00, and it lasted until 12:00. The wedding date was February 12, 1949. We went to the Ricardo Hotel in town for our honeymoon night. Our presents were dishes, sheets, bowls, and things like that. We lived with my mother.*
Nicolasa Quintanilla Garcia

My uncle and I got married the same day. I married at 6:00, and he got married at 7:00 A.M. Johnny [the uncle] was Beto's good friend. Johnny married Helena Carerra. We both married at the St. Martín's Church. The family was there. We had a reception at my grandmother's house. We went to my parents' house, and then we came to Beto's parents', and they cooked over here at the Ranch. White cake and chocolate were served.

I wore a long white dress with a short veil. It was a silk dress. Beto wore a suit and shoes — no boots. At Beto's parents' they barbecued and had lots of food. It was on Sunday, and the barbecue was at noon. The bridesmaids were my sister — she was my half-sister — and my cousin, just two. They wore long pink dresses. The wedding was on February 6, 1949. It was not too cold, but rainy. We lived with Beto's parents. It was not hard. They were real nice to me all my life. They treated me like I was their daughter. We lived with them a year, and then we moved to our house, a new house. They made a house next door, and we lived there next door — houses #1 and #2.

Beto and I made plans for the wedding. The families helped pay for the wedding. We got gifts of towels, dishes, or what we needed for the house. They bought what they wanted; you did not tell them [did not register patterns]. I still have some of the towels from when I got married. They are forty-five years old.

Beto's parents gave us the living room and dining room furniture. I still have it. I have some dishes that my father, who raised me, gave me when I was four years old, and my aunt gave me a little set of dishes when I was six years old, and I still have them in a little cabinet. Dora Maldonado

Our parents went half-and-half on everything for the wedding. Joe paid for my dress and everything. My parents and his parents halved the rest. We also had padrinos *who furnished things. There are four, usually two from each side. I chose mine, and he chose from his side. Their obligations are the cake on one side, the other the kneeler* (cojines) *at the wedding and the lasso, like a rosary, half for the bride and half for the groom. In the middle of the mass, they lasso, or tie, the two together. We got the lasso in Mexico. It had teardrops made of wax, like a rosary. It was exactly like my bouquet. My bouquet was artificial, and the boutonnieres and lasso all matched; they were bought in Reynosa. The fourth was an* arras—*a little container with ten little dimes signifying that you would never be poor.*

We were married at St. Martín's around 6:30 in the afternoon. Then we had the reception at the Crimson Palace, a big dance hall. We had a dance, had cake and cookies—traditional wedding cookies. A week before we had a barbecue. Back then, you had for the rehearsal dinner a big barbecue for the wedding party and family and friends. We had it at Kleberg Park. About 150 came. Both sets of parents pay for this.

I had a maid of honor and four bridesmaids, two from my side and two from his side. Our wedding trip was a week to Houston.
Dora Maldonado Garcia

My wife set the date. We married in Alice [Texas] twenty-eight years ago. It's time for a change. [He laughs.] We married in the church. The reception was at the dance hall. Spanish music by a live band, had a little beer—not too much drinking. The dance was from 8:00 to 12:00. We had cake. On the honeymoon we went to Laredo [Texas] and over to Mexico. There was Spanish dancing and music.

We had a family reunion last year, and we found out that my mother and my father were first cousins. We did a family tree. My son and a daughter of Michael's [a cousin] got it together. I'm a cousin to Martín [Medietta]—we always thought that we were cousins on the Mendietta side. We found out at the family reunion that his grandmother and my grandmother were sisters on my mother's side. Her maiden name was Quintanilla. That's how it all started: Maldonados, Quintanillas, Mendiettas, and Silvas— that's all there was on King Ranch. Some way or another everybody had to be related. They had to marry their same cousins.
Chito Mendietta

She Was Both Nurse and Doctor

If you had a headache, sometimes she would wait for an apple to rot and mix it with shortening. Nicolas Rodríguez (King Ranch)

No doctors or nurses lived on the Ranches. Only in cases of critical illness or injury to workers or owners were doctors called to the Ranch or patients taken into town to visit a doctor. The Kenedy and King Ranches assumed responsibility for this infrequent medical care. Most of the medical treatment was provided by women using medicinal herb cures handed down through generations.

A woman's medical responsibilities encompassed two general categories. One of these was to treat the everyday maladies of colds, flu, fever, chills, headaches, upset stomachs, and minor infections. These treatments almost always included the use of herbs native to the Ranches. The other responsibility was to assist in the birthing of babies.

BIRTHING

Most babies were delivered by *parteras*, midwives. Manuela Mayorga was the only interviewee who related an instance of a birth involving a doctor, and, even then, the doctor was assisted by his wife: "Bobby Shelton's father [Dr. Shelton] delivered [my daughter]. With my daughter, it took from Friday 'til Saturday at 3:00. Mrs. Shelton helped Dr. Shelton. I would not go to Kingsville."

All the other accounts of deliveries involve women acting as midwives.

All the children were born at home in Laico in the house. There were no doctors, only ladies called parteras. Nicolas Rodríguez

My grandmother delivered my two sisters. Ofelia M. Longória

The women served as midwives. My grandmother, Manuela, delivered Concepción as a midwife. This was my sister. She boiled the water 'til it was clear. She prepared and washed all the linens so that they were clean and made the bed up fresh so it was clean. The babies were born in the bed, and the men were told to leave. The mother was washed with soap and water. We believe you could tell the sex before the child came out, because the girls were born with their heads up and the boys with the head tucked. The mother would hold on to the sheet, and they cut the cord as soon as the baby got there, and they wrapped [the baby] in the freshly pre-pared sheets. They kept the mother in bed about a week. María Luisa Montalvo Silva

Children were born at home with a midwife. They were breast-fed for one year to fifteen months. At about four months, we fed babies mashed potatoes. Enemorio Serna

Medicine

Women administered herbal medicines, usually in the form of teas. Some of their home remedies were also laced with superstition. Whatever the malady, the women were usually expected to take care of healing.

If you had a headache, sometimes she would wait for an apple to rot and mix it with shortening. She would wash the shortening well first and then smashed it with the apple. Then one put a little bit of that on one's head or forehead.

They would cut your skin to make it bleed so that the poison would come out [snakebite remedy].

We cured ourselves at home, but not in the field. We did not take anything with us to the field.

We had an herb that was called the comanche, *which was used for fevers. The herb was cut, smashed, and put in clean water. The water would turn purple, and then a cup or two would be given to the babies or the one who had fever. That would be enough to cut the fever.*

There was an herb called el negro *[the black]. It was very good for the cough. It grew around lakes [creeks].* Nicolas Rodríguez

As a child, there were no doctors nearby. We were treated with herb teas. They boiled the peel of amarosa *for stomach distress. Kero-sene oil was used for snakebite. They cut a hole in the bite, stuck a dagger plant around the bite, and poured in kerosene oil. Spider bites were rubbed with the head of a match. Spider webs were used to stop bleeding on a cut. Sarita [Kenedy] took the men to the doc-tor when they got hurt on the Ranch.* Seferino Gutierrez

Mint and honey, or honey and cinnamon, were used for coughing. Manuela Mayorga

My mother-in-law had TB [tuberculosis]. We used a plant, cenizo, for the cough. We boiled the leaves for tea, and she would drink it for the cough.

We used yerbaníz. *When you were scared or wanted to lose weight, you made crosses out of it and wore them. It was placed under the bed sometimes. We still use it as a tea.*

Toronjil *tea was for nerves.* Estefrate *was a tea for colic.* Manzanilla *was for stomachaches. For snakebites, a tourniquet was used, cut "XX" on the bite, sucked it, and spit it out.* Stella Guevara

The staffeleto *plant was used for cuts. Kerosene oil was used. We made a cross on the forehead and bottom of the foot with the kerosene and then took three drops of kerosene with a spoonful of sugar for colds. [At this point, Raffela went to the yard and brought in a plant; then she took a bottle of Pepto Bismol from the cabinet to show the interpreter and interviewers that they were for the same use.]* Raffela and Jesus Gonzales

An herb, cenizo, was for coughs. Mixed it with honey. Nuda *was used for the stomach.* Viverierda *was used for a stomachache cure.* Rogerio Silva

We used purple sage for coughs. Midwives treated most illnesses unless they were serious. María Luisa Montalvo Silva

When there was a snakebite, we cut the leg and tied it. We used kerosene to clean it. Cowboys didn't usually get bitten.

We used cinnamon tea for medicine. We used orange tree leaves for nerves—it would settle you down. It would relax [you] and was good at night. Rosemary was good for colic for babies and coughs. A bitter plant named amarosa *was boiled for stomachaches.* Enemorio Serna

On occasion, injuries or illnesses were too severe to be properly treated on the Ranch, and the patients were transported into Kingsville to a doctor or to the hospital. Catarino Moreno described two injuries he received that required a doctor's care:

We used herbs, but when the accident with the valentíns *butted me, they gave me ampicillin.*

These animals [nilgai antelope] were not domestic at all. One had to be very careful because they could hit you and hurt you. I was raising this sancho *[pet] once, and he butted me. Whenever I saw him coming, I would hide from him. There was one time when I was not paying attention, and he butted me with his horns. With one horn he hit me next to the spinal cord and with the other one right here [he shows the interviewer the place]. I fell down imme-*

diately. When I fell down, I thought, "Am I going to die? But they might need me to sign some papers." This was my immediate thought. Can you believe it?

I then went to Cecilia's [Cecilia Garcia Dern]. She asked me what I had, and I told her I did not have anything. I was not going to tell her so that she did not worry. When I asked why she was asking, she said because my shirt was all muddy and dirty. I then just asked her if she had a grapefruit. She brought me two, so I cut one, started eating it, and left. At noon, when I went to feed the pigs, I tried to lift a sack. The sack was a hundred pounds, and, when I picked it up, my back just cracked. I heard this cracking sound. I then saw blood dripping on my shoe, so I just grabbed some sand and dirt and threw it on the wound. Then this guy named Pedro asked me if the valentín *had butted me. He asked me what I had put on the wound, and I answered, "Dirt." He said, "Are you crazy!? Come on, get in the truck, let's go." He took me to the hospital, and the doctor gave me a shot and sent me to bed for nine days. After the nine days, they sent for me. I went again later, and they took the stitches out from both wounds. After this, they stopped having* valentíns *because they figured out that nothing tames them and that they were too dangerous.*

There was another time when I got run over by a vagón *[wagon]. It happened in 1952. It was the time when Juan Bena-vides was there. He was the one whose goats died all the time. They told me to work with the* vagón. *It had rubber tires just like a trailer. I had to carry food for the cattle, carry garbage, and other things. There was one time when the door was almost closed, and I thought I could jump on it, but I fell. I could have left the horses alone and let them take the* vagón, *but I did not because somebody else had ruined it once, and I did not want to do it again. When I tried to get the reins again, the horses ran scared and knocked me over. When I fell, the first tire passed over my chest and the second one on my ribs. I just heard a big pop, and my neck hurt terribly. They gave me medicine.* Catarino Moreno

Today, emergency medical care is much more accessible on the Ranches because of advanced communication systems and an increase in the availability of medical services. Chito Mendietta pointed out the potential for accidents on the Ranch and described the accident in which his dad died:

When somebody gets hurt now, we call 911, and they come from Riviera or wherever is closer. It's about twenty miles there. Sometimes a horse stumbles, and you get hurt. I take other guys in for a checkup if they get hurt. I stayed ten days in the hospital because a horse fell on my leg.

My dad died in a fire explosion on the Laureles Division. They used to drive cattle trucks, and Laureles is about thirty miles [from where we lived], so they would just camp over there. They got up early in the morning, and the cook wasn't there yet, and they were building the fire, and they had a can of gasoline. He thought it was kerosene. It burned 90 percent of his body.

Funerals

. . . they put cotton in her ears and nose. Stella Guevara (Kenedy Ranch)

In the early days, family members died at home and were prepared for burial by the women, usually in a place out back of the house. The funeral was held the next day, and, if the weather was warm, ice was placed under the table that held the body. Similar funeral customs were observed among the vaquero and owner families on the Ranches. The women in the family wore solid black in mourning for a year or longer.

Richard Kleberg's [Sr.] father had a heart attack. [Robert Justus Kleberg Sr. died in 1932 following the last of several strokes.] His mother [Alice Gertrudis King Kleberg] and Mrs. Kleberg [his wife, Mamie] died at home. Tom East [Sr.] died at King Ranch. In my family, my grandmother, Virginia Cavazos, died at the Ranch.

When Mrs. King died [March 25, 1925], they did not take her to the hospital. She died at home. There was a small creek in front of the Big House, and before she died, at about 4:00 P.M. [each day], two nurses would walk with her from the Big House to the creek. When she died, they sent riders from the Ranch to let the vaqueros know she had died and they should respect her death and keep quiet.

They told everyone to come and pay respects. Her body was in the living room, and they passed by. I went. Mrs. King was dressed in lilac pink. She was a small lady. She was very well-liked because she helped the people on the Ranch. Manuela Mayorga

When Petra [Teresa Mayorga Cuellar's maternal grandmother] died, they put cotton in her ears and nose. They laid her on a table. There were candles all around. They put ice under the bed. They sat up all night. Stella Guevara

When my aunt died, they laid her out at the house and stayed up with her all night. My grandmother gave the rosary. The priest came for the burial. Ofelia M. Longória

When somebody died, they bought the box [coffin]. They held the funeral the next day. The body was kept at home. Everyone came and brought food. The women wore black from head to toe, including the veil. Some wore it a year. My aunt, for the rest of her life. Enemorio Serna

When Mrs. Alice Kleberg died in 1944, they took the body to the mortuary and brought it back to the Big House. They laid her out in the first room in a coffin. Everyone came. They stayed up all night with the body. They took all the furniture out of the room and had the coffin and chairs there. Coffee and sweet breads were served in the kitchen. Neighbors brought food. The family stayed up all night. The funeral was [the] next day at the church in town and [at the] cemetery. Everybody had the day off. Manuela Mayorga

An early funeral home was established in Kingsville about 1953 and was located in the Allen Furniture Store, which had been established in 1926. The funeral home served both Anglos and Mexicans. Clyde M. Allen Jr., owner of Allen Furniture Store, shared information about this arrangement that began after his father established the store:

Mr. C. Bernard Kennedy worked for my father, Mr. Clyde M. Allen Sr., who owned the furniture store. Mr. Kennedy was interested in the mortuary business. He serviced that side of the business, as well as being a furniture salesman. He got his embalming license, as did my father. A chapel and an embalming room were located in the furniture store, and they also sold caskets and burial supplies. They had a hearse in the 1920s that was drawn by four white horses. Later they had motor hearses that were kept in the garage next door. The people who worked in the furniture store also dug the graves and drove the hearse. During World War II, they ran the ambulance service out of the furniture store, too. They sold the funeral side of the business in 1945, after the war, to the Cage-Piper Funeral Home.

Working Women

I did a little bit of everything. Catalina Maldonado (King Ranch)

Some women worked in the homes of the owners or the caporals, in the Commissary, in the Saddle Shop, or at the annual summer camp conducted on King Ranch for descendants of the owners. This work provided extra income.

Dora Maldonado Garcia worked at the Ranch while she was engaged, and her fiancée was in the service. He returned in 1969, and they were married in 1970.

Nicolasa Quintanilla Garcia worked for the Klebergs so long that they gave her the house she lives in, which she had moved to Kingsville. As a young woman, Nico worked in the Main House with her uncle, José Alegría, the cook. She served the tables when there were many guests. "In 1944, I worked for Mr. Bob and Miss Helen [Kleberg]," she explained. "I married in 1949. In 1960, I worked for Mr. Dick Kleberg [Jr.]. I still work for Mrs. Dick Kleberg [Jr.]. I cook for her."

A number of other women described their work experiences outside of their own homes:

Lillie worked at the Commissary. We married before I went to the military. She wouldn't let me go 'til we married. She didn't work after we were married. Plácido Maldonado III

When I was fifteen, I worked for Mr. [Charlie] Burwell and was paid $10 a month. I also worked for Dick Mosely for $15 a month. I married when I was eighteen.

I later worked at the Saddle Shop, which was a wooden two-story building behind the Main House. It was destroyed in the 1970s. I did this after my children were grown. I would wash the leather and dry it out, and, when they made the saddle blankets, I would help put the leather trim on them. Ofelia M. Longória

I babysat for Jack Turcotte. I went to Colorado with them for three months. Stella Guevara

[Enriqueta's] two daughters, Sylvia and Elvia [Manuela's grand-daughters], worked at the summer camp. Manuela Mayorga

In the 1970s at King Ranch, Janell Kleberg (the wife of Stephen J. "Tio" Kleberg) was instrumental in instituting the practice of hiring Kineños' children who were students in vocational programs in public school. Trained as a teacher and with a continuing interest in education, Janell helped to expand opportunities for the employment of women, as well as men. Catalina Maldonado was one of the students hired at King Ranch.

> *When I was seventeen, I started working here. I did a little bit of everything. It was supposed to be a summer job. Tio's wife, Janell, decided that they ought to start hiring King Ranch employees' children who were Vocational Office Education (VOE) students. So they interviewed three of us in alphabetical order. They hired me, and the other [applicants] gave me a hard time. But I started working in 1974 and graduated in 1975. I went to school half-a-day and worked half-a-day. Then they offered me a full-time job. I made $1.05 during the program. I was a student, and that was twenty years ago. I still have the stub from my first paycheck. I don't remember the dollar amount, but it sounded so wonderful. . . .*

The strong family tradition among the workers on the King and Kenedy Ranches has added undeniable strength to the workers' lives. This strength has carried the vaqueros through their day-to-day journey with unbridled success for four generations. Though their lives have been modified by the accessibility of modern conveniences and changes in work force trends, this essential strength still exists at the center of their lives today.

Into the Twenty-first Century

The program reads: "1994 La Posada de Kingsville. Friday–Sunday, November 18–20. *Tales of the Wild Horse Desert,* A Musical Play." They come on stage in authentic costumes—boots, chaps, hats, ropes, and bandannas—in Jones Auditorium on the Texas A&M-Kingsville campus. Two hundred peformers, at least half of whom are from King Ranch, sing and dance and tell the story. Their performance is a re-enactment of King Ranch's history, beginning with Captain King's relocation of the inhabitants and cattle of an entire village from the state of Tamaulipas, Mexico, to his new land purchased on the Santa Gertrudis Creek. Third-, fourth-, and fifth-generation vaqueros and their offspring—the emerging sixth generation—fill the stage at Thanksgiving time. While performing, the more seasoned vaqueros recall the old days and remember—and the new generation learns the stories.

The original play was written by Janell Kleberg, the wife of Stephen Justus "Tio" Kleberg, and produced by the Drama Department of Texas A&M University–Kingsville in cooperation with King Ranch. The 1994 production of the play was sold out for three performances. The musical play, with tickets at $8, is one of the newest attractions in a series of events geared toward the tourist industry. These events take place every year in Kingsville from November through mid-December and are part of the city's annual La Posada de Kingsville celebration. Events include a Ranch Hand Breakfast, Children's Day, Parade of Lights, Fiesta Market of Arts and Crafts, Ranch Country Downtown Marketplace, 5K Jingle Bell Run/Walk, and a Christmas Tree Forest. Tourism is becoming a viable industry in Kingsville and on King Ranch. This is only one of the many changes the Ranch is experiencing as it moves into the twenty-first century.

The Work Today

Sweeping changes are occurring in every phase of American ranch management, including management of the King and Kenedy Ranches. They range all the way from the way the *corrida* is organized, to the way cattle are handled, sold, and transported. Today's "Information Society" has introduced new methods of corporate management all across America, even in Ranch headquarters.

MANAGEMENT ON KING RANCH

We each have our own statistical base . . . Lin Becerra

Changes in management philosophy are occurring in all major industries in the country. At King Ranch, these changes are directly affecting the work of the vaqueros.

Today there are thirteen units and four area cattle managers in charge of the total operation. Since fewer people are doing the same tasks, the men in the units rotate between the divisions to help each other during busy times. Lin Becerra, a former employee who was a King Ranch unit boss at the time of his interview, provided an example involving another unit boss, Chito Mendietta: "Chito's cattle don't work like mine do. He'll come over and help me, and when he comes, I'm the boss, and when I help him, he's the boss. Whatever he says, we do. Everybody works together. It works perfectly. It's the best thing that ever happened because we're undermanned."

Lin Becerra has a degree from Texas A&I (now Texas A&M University–Kingsville) in agricultural education, with a minor in animal science. He was born in Brownsville, Texas, into a ranching family. For forty years, his grandfather was a foreman at a spread adjoining King Ranch. Lin had been with King Ranch for six years.

> *I am in charge of the elite herd. I'm the only one who breeds Santa Gertrudis bulls to Santa Gertrudis cows. The elite herd is about forty-five hundred mama cows—the best King Ranch has. We're breeding them multiple sire—more than one bull in a pasture— not single sire any more. We use one bull to twenty-five cows. I haul and keep up with what bulls go to what pastures. They are numbered on the ear and hip. My truck is my office; complete records are kept.*

Lin discussed further some of the changes on the Ranch. Here again, the old and new intermingle as the metamorphosis of King Ranch continues.

> *We each have our own statistical base, our own budget. The results are there in black and white. There is total credibility and account-ability. Changes are the only way we could have made it and be competitive with everybody else.*
>
> *There has to be a combination of education, working together, new ideas—mostly teamwork. Everybody has his own input. We brainstorm a lot. We have management meetings several times a year. Everybody brings his own ideas. Total Quality Management is practiced on King Ranch. Management teams go all the way to Tio Kleberg [Stephen J. Kleberg, vice president of agribusiness]. Everybody puts in their own word. He [Tio Kleberg] might ask how our cattle are doing, how the feeding operation's going, are your pastures holding up, how much rain, how are the cattle do-ing. He asks for suggestions. There are many educated people now working for King Ranch. We're one big team.*
>
> *We still use ropes and work calves the old way in my unit— dragging, branding, working with horses. This is cow work on horseback. Not all units do this. Some squeeze calves in the chute. Working with horses, the calves don't get bruised like in the chute. Three or four of us look at the cattle to see which will go and which will stay. The manager gets the last word.*
>
> *Another unit boss, Alfredo "Chito" Mendietta, was born on King Ranch and is fourth generation. Among the changes he has seen is the use of helicopters to round up cattle.*

Chito Mendietta described the changes brought about by helicopters:

> *I am a unit boss. My main job is taking care of sixty thousand acres—working cows, taking care of fences, water troughs— everything we need to keep the cattle coming. I work with cattle. I was born here on Santa Gertrudis; my father was born here on the Laureles Division. I started as a twelve-year-old boy in the sum-mers. I went to school on the Ranch and then at Kingsville.*
>
> *Ranching has changed a lot since I started working. We gather the cattle with helicopters. At least fifteen years we've been doing that. This came about because there was a fever tick in the middle or late 1970s, and we had to gather all the cattle in fourteen days*

and dip them. We couldn't do it on horseback, so we got the helicopters. It's a lot faster. We began contracting with helicopter companies.

Before helicopters, it took about fifteen cowboys a week to gather a pasture of three or four hundred cows. We would ride horses from one end to the other, gather them in groups, then start penning them in smaller traps 'til we had them gathered. With three helicopters we can gather a six-thousand-acre pasture in about three hours and get the same number of cattle. We get them in a pen one morning, work in the afternoon separating them, then work them—brand calves or palpate the cows—and the following day by late afternoon, they're in the pasture. All in two days. Tomorrow we gather steers in the Concho Pasture.

CONTRACTING

A contract guy breaks all the horses . . . Chito Mendietta

Until recently, all tasks were performed by employees of the Ranches. Ranch operations have been by nature labor intensive, but this is beginning to change. While once hundreds of cowboys were needed to operate King Ranch, now only about sixty oversee sixty thousand head of cattle and three hundred head of horses (Myers 1996, 33). Chito described the changes that contracting out work has brought to King Ranch:

Another change: We do with fewer people. I do not cut brush. Other people do that. If a vehicle runs over a fence, we fix it, but we contract out new fences. Contracting is a change—it used to be people from the Ranch.

We contract with trucks outside to take the cattle to market. We see how many [head of cattle] we have and order so many trailers to come pick them up. They take them to either San Antonio or Mercedes. We don't send any to the feedlot on trucks [outside buyers]—the buyers decide whether to put them on a feedlot or take them directly to market.

We used to get two-year-old horses, and everybody broke his own horses, and you kept them until you retired them or yourself. Not anymore. A contract guy breaks all the horses for sixty rides, then he gives it to whoever needs it. Everybody has his own judgment about what horse he wants. . . . All horses are registered [Quarter Horses], most from Mr. San Peppy, but other sires are used.

I ride maybe 50 percent of the time, more than typical. I pick my horse from ones broken by a contractor—I don't have time to break my own horse. Each cowboy has five or six horses. These are the best Quarter Horses in the world.

CATTLE SALES

There's a cattle market video channel . . . Chito Mendietta

When Librado Maldonado Sr. presided over cattle sales in a huge auction barn with buyers from around the world, he could not have even dreamed of the turn this activity would take in the 1990s. Very often now, the cattle are videotaped, and the buyer makes his purchase without ever having actually seen the live animals. Lin Becerra described the videotaping process:

When we work the cattle, we pull out the ones we want to keep. It's done when we work the cattle. Superior Helicopter Company does the videos.

Chito gathers the cattle with the sirens and feeders. Then you let them be around the feeder, at least fifty or sixty at a time. What you want is an atmosphere that is quiet, and the cattle are not riled up, and the cattle are eating and they look gentle, not hot and bothered. You bait 'em, but don't feed 'em because they'll stack up. Just video them right there. Cool, late in the afternoon is best.

Chito described buying and selling cattle by video:

Several companies do videoing of cattle. They have satellites just like a dish for HBO. There's a cattle market video channel, Channel 21, with national exposure. We have a big buyer who has nine or ten feedlots located from the Panhandle [of Texas] to southern Kansas. He buys to feed out.

What we sell under the video is sold—it's a contract. Some people don't like to buy by video, but will place an order for calves that weigh anywhere from 500 to 550 pounds. They want a certain number, and we agree on a price.

I already have my cattle sold—Red Angus crosses. They'll be ready between the 15th and 25th of April [1994]. They were sold in the pen. It's a done deal. Every calf I leave behind I lose money on.

If we can get them up to 580 [pounds] we get more money. There's a sliding scale, though. If they weigh over 525 [pounds], they might slide 'em down. The price can slide down as weight goes higher by as much as ten cents.

Alfredo "Chito" Mendietta is one of a long line of caporals from the Mendietta and Quintanilla families on King Ranch. Today he is a unit manager on the Santa Gertrudis Division and is in charge of 120,000 acres.

FEEDING

They can hear sirens . . . a mile away. Chito Mendietta

Feeding cattle is becoming more technical and more scientific. As a result, South Texas ranches are much better prepared to deal with droughts now. The cattle are gathered for feeding using sirens. Chito described the diet and feeding of the cattle on King Ranch today.

The cattle are fed mostly on grass supplemented with blocks of minerals. Mas carote *[cubes of cattle feed] are made on the premises at the Ranch feed yard. One type is used for pregnant cows and another for calves. We have feeders where the water troughs are, and, when they go to water, they grab a bite, especially during dry spells. Big trucks drop the [mineral] blocks on the main road, and we put the siren on and they come when they hear it. They can hear sirens probably a mile away. Once they get used to it, they come when they hear it.*

Chito chuckled as he related another story.

We had an accident before Christmas. We had some schoolboys helping us, and we were putting out mineral blocks in this pasture right over here, and a boy was standing on top of the blocks. The blocks slipped, and he fell and hit his head and was out for a good while. So I had to call the ambulance. The ambulance came in with the siren on. The cows heard it, of course. He came to where we were; we gathered the boy in the ambulance. I told the man in the ambulance, "Let me go with you because I assure you there will be a lot of cows in the way." He said, "No, we didn't see any." "Did you have your siren on?" [Chito asked]. "Yeah." "Okay," I said, You're gonna have some cows in the way." We got up there, and there were about three hundred cows on the road! So I had to go in front and put my siren on so they would follow me and let the ambulance by.

Into History

By 1995, the routine feeding of the men by cooks in the *corrida* and in the cow camp houses had ceased. The aroma of fresh beef, *pan de campo,* and steaming black coffee over open fires had wafted into history. The camp houses were closed. The men now either take their lunches or go into town to eat. Pickup trucks take them wherever they decide to go. Some of the chuck wagons are already museum pieces to be brought out only on special occasions.

Some things have not changed, however. Innovative leadership in the industry by the ranch-owning family, and the skill and dedication of the vaqueros, still survive after five generations. Ranch management has changed to meet the demands of a technological society, but between the owners and the vaqueros there remains a strong partnership dedicated to delivering an excellent product.

Roundup Today: The Authors at Roundup

Arriving at the cow camp house several miles out from Santa Gertrudis, we were eager to interview Alfredo Chito Mendietta, a fourth-generation vaquero on the Ranch, and Lin Becerra. They were two of the thirteen unit managers in 1994, and our anticipation was that they would give invaluable insights into the way roundups operate today. Chito, Lin, and our escort, David Maldonado, wore roper boots— not cowboy boots with the traditional higher heels. A crew was working in a set of cattle pens behind the camp house. They were palpating cattle—examining them to see if they were pregnant, and if so, how far along they were.

Today we were also to observe an actual roundup. We moved to the location where cattle were being gathered. There were three vaqueros wearing brush jackets manufactured by Carhardt; these jackets were unlined and made of coarse, heavy, brown cotton fabric, with a collar, pockets, and cuffs trimmed in the same color corduroy. The four bradded metal buttons down the front were not needed today, for it was March, and the weather was mild and clear. The seams of the jackets were double-stitched. Made to withstand the wear and tear of brush country, these jackets looked as if they would last a lifetime. The vaqueros wore leather chaps and an interesting array of shirts that were not of typical cowboy style. They were plaid or knit—just plain shirts—worn outside the jeans, not tucked in. Theirs was a contrast in dress, half the old way, half modern.

Likewise, the demeanor of the vaqueros presented a notable contrast. They were playing with ropes, laughing and jostling with each other. We heard a remark that this would not have been allowed with guests in the old days. As we approached, the vaqueros were respectful and friendly, and they gladly posed for pictures, expressing interest in

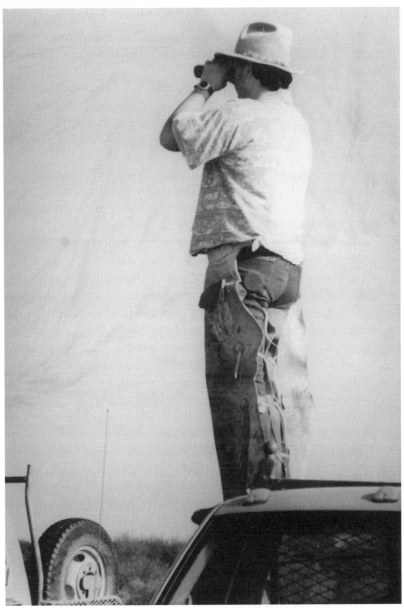

A present-day vaquero on the Santa Gertrudis Division of King Ranch stands on top of his pickup truck looking for the helicopter that will help to round up cattle.

our quest for their story. The vaqueros seemed to epitomize the meta-morphosis taking place in the workings of King Ranch, and, indeed, in the whole ranching industry. The old ways are changing.

We saw a windmill on the horizon. There was a hush, then the faint sound of an engine. A helicopter appeared on the horizon, looking like a mosquito. Still some distance away, it looked almost as near to the earth as the windmill. Another helicopter appeared from the left. There would be three in all.

A Kineño, in an alert stance on the truck bed, gazed intently through binoculars, observing the helicopters working. Nearby, long gooseneck trailers held horses—three in one trailer, two in the other—saddled and ready to go. They could have been show horses. But they were some of the sleek, cinnamon-colored Quarter Horses for which King Ranch is famous, the only working horses used on the Ranch.

No cattle were in sight. All that could be seen were low, very green bushy mesquite trees, which looked almost feathery, the sky, and three helicopters. Coming closer now, the helicopters circled the horizon, presenting a contrast to the saddled horses and even to the white Chevrolet Silverado that had brought us on location.

Just then, the helicopters brought two stray head of cattle into our immediate area. The vaqueros sprang into action like a well-greased ma-chine with moving parts. The calves had no chance. Each one was roped and loaded into the gooseneck within moments.

As we boarded the helicopter, we were quickly instructed as to the use of the headphones and the light-dimmer switch-type button on the floor. With this button, we could signal for verbal communication with the pilot. As we climbed above the trees, we saw only soft green stretch-ing to the horizon, with one or two windmills standing like exclamation points against a sky of clear, pure blue. The pilot, whose company is un-der contract for cattle roundups, estimated we could see as far as thirty-five to fifty miles in the distance.

The helicopter swayed, bumped, and whirled as it began to clear the calves from beneath the trees. The pilot maneuvered the aircraft pre-cisely, knowing just how far to swing out to get behind the cattle. Later we got an assessment of this skill from Lin Becerra: "The guys in the he-licopters could probably get on a horse and rope a damn cow just as well as the guys on horseback. The principle's still the same."

Just then, small dots of rust became visible below—the cattle. The pilot was an expert at positioning the helicopter just behind the animals in order to move them to the "road," a clearing that would lead the cattle to the pens. When some turned back, the pilot quickly moved the helicopter to round them up—the exact same technique used by the vaqueros on horseback. We were working a huge area stretching as far as we could see. If a few calves were particularly stubborn, the pilot would back the helicopter into a closer proximity, and the noise would move the animals forward. More than 90 percent of the cattle would be rounded up by the helicopter. The rest would be rounded up by vaqueros on horseback, the old-fashioned way.

The Kenedy Ranch Today

The Kenedy Ranch is located entirely in Kenedy County, bordered by a division of King Ranch on the south, Baffin Bay on the north, and Laguna Madre on the east. Raising cattle and horses is the main occupation of the county. Because the sandy terrain dries out so quickly, range management studies are underway to find grasses, like Bermuda grass, to add to or replace the native coastal cord grass and brush. About twenty-five acres are needed presently to support a cow and calf. The pastures remain without cross fencing; one pasture is said to still have more than 85,000 acres (Ward 1993, 82).

Today, the Kenedy Ranch is operated as two separate units in two different trusts. The northern portion of approximately 200,000 acres is owned by the John G. Kenedy Jr. Charitable Trust, so named by Kenedy's widow, Elena Seuss Kenedy, at her death in 1984. Administered by the Frost Bank of San Antonio, Texas, the trust leases the acreage, for grazing purposes only, to Mike East, a great-nephew of Sarita's deceased husband, Arthur L. East. Mike East is also a great-great-grandson of the founder of King Ranch, Captain Richard King; thus the relationship is another example of the continuing association between the King and Kenedy families after six generations (Ward 1993, 79).

Mike East raises mostly Santa Gertrudis cattle and runs from ten thousand to twelve thousand head. He does some crossbreeding, using various breeds. An aggressive vaccination program protects his herd, and animals brought to the Ranch from Mexico, from disease. Mexican cattle are dipped twice and quarantined for thirty days. Cutting horses are currently raised on the Ranch, and Mike East is active in state and national cutting horse competitions (Ward 1993, 82).

The southern half of the Kenedy Ranch, approximately 235,000 acres, is owned by the John G. and Marie Stella Kenedy Memorial Foundation, named by Sarita in honor of her parents. This property is under lease to Stuart Sasser, Frates Seeligson, and Tobin Armstrong. The lease includes both hunting and grazing rights. A lack of descendants, combined with the creation of the trust and foundation, may have achieved Mifflin Kenedy's wish—that the Kenedy Ranch would continue to be operated as a single unit (Ward 1993, 81, 82).

The Ranch's resident land manager, Joe A. Keepers, lives at La Parra Headquarters near Sarita. His duties include overseeing the operations by Exxon. Exxon Oil Company still holds exploration and production agreements, and there is production of both natural gas and hydrocarbon liquids on the Ranch.

A wide selection of wild game is plentiful on the Kenedy Ranch. Hunting rights are leased to a single individual who in turn sells hunting rights, to certain parts of the Ranch, to individuals, groups, or companies. Hunting-lease costs range from $1.00 to $1.50 an acre, depending on game supply. Turkey, quail, white-tailed deer, and javelina abound in good number. The Ranch is also home to the world's largest population of nilgai (Indian antelope). Deer are hunted mostly from pickup trucks cruising the Ranch roads, instead of from blinds. Bird dogs are used to hunt quail.

Today, some Kenedeños, such as the Gutierrez and Gonzales families, own their own homes. Sarita East bequeathed the dwellings and some money to their families at her death. Other Kenedeños live in housing provided by Mike East in Sarita.

Like the Kineños on King Ranch, the Kenedeños remain a steady work force, ensuring the success of the Ranch. Operations on both Ranches combine old and new methods. In 1991, Enemorio Serna described what his work was like:

> Morgan Chowder is the foreman. I've worked for Sarita East, Edgar Turcotte, Robert Hogan, Tom East [Jr.], and Mike East. I work on the Oleander Leaf Division. We go out for a week at a time to round up cattle. At first, I started with Longhorns, then Santa Gertrudis. Now I work with Beefmaster. They have different characteristics. The Beefmasters produce more and heavier beef, and bring more money. The Santa Gertrudis have more muscle.
>
> We bring the cattle in, separate them, put them in the chute, and ship from February to June. Today, roundups take three to six hours. We use huge gates that are hinged—we have about one hundred of them—and portable pens that will handle eight hundred cattle each. We ship by truck to San Antonio every week. We usually ship heifers at about a year—Mike [East] decides.
>
> We use more pickups and fewer horses. I only ride [horses]

> *now about twice a week. We use about fourteen men now; used to have thirty-five in a* corrida.
>
> *Water is still a problem because the wind takes the moisture out. The cattle feed on natural grass—about twenty acres to the cow. We use mineral blocks.*

The Kenedy Ranch has remained a viable operation throughout its long, fascinating, and sometimes turbulent history. Its founder, Captain Mifflin Kenedy, was an extraordinary character for his time.

The Kenedys had an avid interest in art and were collectors, an unusual pursuit for someone living in the near isolation of South Texas. An impressive collection of nineteenth-century artworks decorated their main residence at La Parra Ranch. An inventory of the Kenedy collection lists sixty-eight paintings and prints, mostly of European origin, since European art was at that time considered to be the greatest art in the world. Because of the generosity and foresight of Elena Kenedy, who was married to Mifflin Kenedy's grandson, John G. Jr., the Kenedy art collection now hangs in the Corpus Christi Museum of Science and History, Corpus Christi, Texas. Both King and Kenedy would prosper in huge proportions, and the association between the two families would continue into the late twentieth century.

By the time Mifflin Kenedy died in 1895, he was one of the largest ranch owners in Texas, and his intent was for the Kenedy Ranch to remain one entity. To keep his 400,000-acre ranch intact, he had purchased the inheritance rights of his stepchildren and continued operating as the Kenedy Pasture Company at La Parra Ranch. Kenedy died without a will, and his property was inherited by his son, John Gregory Kenedy Sr.; a daughter, Sarah Joséphine Kenedy Spohn; a grandson, George M. Kenedy (James Kenedy's son); and Mrs. Carmen Morell Kenedy, an adopted daughter (*Corpus Christi Caller,* September 23, 1984).

John Gregory Kenedy Jr. studied agricultural management at Texas A&M College and, in 1912, moved his bride, Elena Seuss, who was of German heritage, to the family compound at La Parra. His sister, Sarita, attended Sophie Newcombe College in New Orleans.

Upon John Gregory Kenedy Sr.'s death, the original Ranch was divided into two separate ranches, one for John Gregory Kenedy Jr. and one for Sarita. The siblings operated their properties separately, but the operations were always interrelated. There was never any doubt but that Sarita was in charge of her Ranch. She took a greater interest in management of the land than did her brother. She was very much involved in

Ranch operations and was a positive factor in the Ranch's success. She was known among the vaquero families as La Parra's "*patrona*." She was kind to the families of Ranch employees, helping to educate their children and caring for them when they were ill. Finally, in 1946, John leased his part of the Ranch to his sister, and she and her husband, Arthur East, operated the Kenedy Ranch as a single unit until Sarita's death in 1961 (Ward 1993, 80).

A Philanthropic Legacy

The Kenedy Ranch is best known for its large philanthropic gifts to worthy causes and organizations both inside and outside of Texas. Forceful leadership from several family members has helped to make this possible.

Sarita Kenedy East had exhibited strong leadership in the expansion of the Ranch's holdings by purchasing San Pablo Ranch near Hebbronville and Twin Peaks Ranch in Colorado. Because neither of Marie Stella Turcotte Kenedy's children had produced heirs, Marie asked them to leave ten thousand acres and the family home to the Oblate Order of the Roman Catholic Church following their deaths (*Corpus Christi Caller,* September 24, 1984). Mrs. Kenedy was known for her philanthropic bequests. She received from Pope Pius XII a Papal decoration of distinction, the medal Pro Ecclesia et Pontifice in recognition of outstanding deeds done for the Catholic church, for her donations of land and property. (*Corpus Christi Caller,* June 5, 1939).

The John G. and Marie Stella Kenedy Memorial Foundation exists as a charitable foundation. Following the family's pattern of charitable bequests, the foundation funds churches, parochial schools, hospitals, radio and television stations, and numerous other projects. The largest charitable foundation in South Texas, and one of the top ten in a state with more than eleven hundred foundations, it gives away millions of dollars. From 1982 to 1984, the foundation gave away $44.8 million in 143 grants. The money went to finance schools, hospital additions, churches, and a variety of public service programs (*Corpus Christi Caller,* August 28, 1984).

LEGAL BATTLES

Following Sarita East's death in 1961, her will was contested in the courts for more than twenty years. During this litigation, Alice National

Bank of Alice, Texas, served as trustee and had the responsibility of hiring managers to operate the Kenedy Ranch. Upon settlement of the foundation suit, a second charitable foundation was established in New York, named the Sarita Kenedy East Foundation. Approximately $13 million was placed in this trust, and the remaining assets were placed in the John G. and Marie Stella Kenedy Memorial Foundation in Texas. Assets of this trust were valued at about $100 million (*Corpus Christi Caller,* December 19, 1984). Under the terms of this trust, 10 percent of the trust income must be paid to the Catholic Diocese of Corpus Christi, and at least 10 percent of its charitable contributions must go to non-religious charities in Texas. Two-thirds of the six-member governing board of the John G. and Marie Stella Kenedy Memorial Foundation must be of the Catholic faith, and whoever is the Bishop of the Diocese of Corpus Christi is to be named to the foundation. These members elect directors who manage the holdings of the foundation (Ward 1993, 80).

King Ranch Today

King Ranch remains a private corporation in the hands of the sixth generation of Captain Richard King's descendants, with Stephen Justus "Tio" Kleberg as vice president of agribusiness. All shareholders are direct descendants of Captain King. King Ranch is still a leader in the ranching industry. Ranked 175 in the 1994 Texas 500 by *Texas Monthly* magazine, King Ranch is a profitable agribusiness deriving income from sources as diverse as sorghum and grain in Texas and citrus, sugarcane, sod, and rice in Florida. It is the largest cotton producer in Texas (Myers 1996, 27). The Ranch has agricultural properties in Florida, Kentucky, and Arizona, as well as two ranches in Brazil. A 15,000-head, computerized feedlot is located in Gonzales, Texas. Land management has become a major focus along with the cattle and horse operations (Erramouspe 1995, 10). Wildlife management and recreational hunting are highly developed, along with energy-related businesses in oil, natural gas, and independent power sources.

Nonetheless, to profitably manage 825,000 diverse acres in South Texas is no small feat. As in all major U.S. industries, significant changes from old-style management methods have been necessary to maintain integrity of ownership and continue acceptable profit margins. Profit, loss, and efficiency have become common terms for employees at all levels.

The new King Ranch Santa Cruz cattle breed was introduced to the industry in 1994. Following intricate investigative research, the mix of one-half Santa Gertrudis, one-fourth Gelbvieh, and one-fourth Red Angus was chosen. The first Santa Cruz calves were born in 1990 and, by careful selection, have been continuously upgraded. According to Hal Hawkins, King Ranch physiologist, King Ranch expects to use DNA mapping to link exceptional calves to specific sires in large, multiple-sire herds to further refine the breeding process. The breed is suited to environments similar to that of South Texas, but it also works in most other climates where cattle are produced (Wolfshohl 1995, 44).

The Kineños are still on King Ranch. They read *Running Words,* a crisp, well-designed Ranch bulletin, to keep up with important announcements, Ranch happenings, and news about each other. For more detailed, official information, they have *Wellspring,* a corporate newsletter published semiannually.

While the work is not as brutal as it once was, the average work week is still about seventy-two hours in the farming operation (Erramouspe 1995). Vaqueros no longer ride the fences to fend off poachers or rustlers. Security is headed up now by a former peace officer. Some vaquero family members have left the Ranch because of other job opportunities or because of a decrease in the labor force. Job descriptions are not the same, but the Kineños who have remained on the Ranch still work for its success with the same dedication and loyalty as their forefathers. Pride in their work and in the Ranch is still very much alive, as the following comments attest.

> *It'll always be the famous King Ranch. Everyone that I meet or talk to — as soon as they find out I work here, they are really impressed.* Catalina Maldonado

> *The majority of people will be here . . . I think that most of them will be happy here. I have been fortunate to experience all aspects of the Ranch.* David Maldonado

GROWING UP IS DIFFERENT

A major evolution has occurred in the lives of the Kineños in the past generation. Growing up today is not the same experience that it was for their parents, as Catalina Mandonado has discovered:

> *We never had a telephone. I never had it, so I didn't know what I was missing. I rode the bus every single day until I graduated from high school. I didn't bother to get a driver's license until I was eigh-*

teen or nineteen, because I didn't have a car to drive. Then I knew I could go buy myself a little car. Nowadays, teenagers can't live without a telephone and a car at the age of sixteen.

ANOTHER KIND OF LIFE

King Ranch vaqueros' fathers and grandfathers slept under the stars on an unyielding terrain. Now the vaqueros can come home at night. Their horses, once virtually their only means of transportation, have been relegated to a more limited, less prominent position. The pickup truck is more likely to be the vaqueros' preferred mount. Except for special occasions, meals around the chuck wagon and the camp house have been virtually replaced by meals at a favorite barbecue place, a mom-and-pop Mexican restaurant, or even McDonald's. Roundups are accomplished in a half-day, 90 percent by expert helicopter pilots and the rest by the vaqueros astride the still-famous King Ranch Quarter Horses. Preparing and moving the product from ranch to market has taken a different turn.

A BIT OF NOSTALGIA

Though today's vaquero family members understand the rationale and necessity for change, their responses to these new ways are very personal. Some changes are considered positive, but some leave a feeling of nostalgia for the way it was not so long ago.

Catalina Maldonado described the changes she has observed in the work place:

There've been a lot of changes. The biggest change is people. There were lots of older, more respectable-type people then. I got to work with Mr. [James] Clement [Sr.] and Mr. [L. A.] Walker Sr., and they would sit and tell stories just like my grandfather, so I enjoyed all of them. We were fortunate that we came out of the old school. I was the youngest one in the office for years, now I'm up there.

Another change—the camaraderie, the closeness is not the same. Mr. Clement was our president. He would pick up the phone and say, "Time to get in here for coffee," and you would drop what you were doing and get in there for coffee. The men had coffee at 10:00 and the women at 10:30. Paula [Smith], the receptionist, and I would go at 10:00 because we liked to hear the stories instead of listening to women talk about their babies and whatever. It gave you time to get together and find out what was going on with the other persons.

Since we've moved over here [Lauro's Hill], that's sort of been cut out. It's just different. It's a lot more professional. You come, you do your work, and do it well, and try to stay away from other offices. The people who've been here five years—they don't know any different.

Basically we're in transition. Now the oldest one here is like fifty-eight [years old], and back then the oldest was in the seventies.

Toni Maldonado is a kindergarten teacher at Santa Gertrudis School. She is married to David Maldonado, who is the director of Human Resources for King Ranch, Inc., and the grandson of Librado Maldonado Sr. Toni shared what she misses about the old days:

I miss driving up and seeing all the trucks, with people in the back, taking them off to the different parts of the Ranch with their water cans—going off to work. Truckloads of people. Now we no longer see that.

We don't see grandfather [Librado Maldonado] and the bulls. At one time, it was a very, very important job, and now it's gone. . . . One of the things I really miss—Jimmy [Vela] and Marty [Alegria] [former students at Santa Gertrudis School] tried high school one year, and they dropped out and came back to work here. During lunch they would walk over to the school to see their old teachers. When they walked down the hall you could hear their spurs jingling, and it was wonderful. Mr. Trant [superintendent] had to stop that, but I miss it.

Unfortunately, there is not the need for as many vaqueros as there once was. The new generation must look elsewhere for employment, as David Maldonado pointed out:

Toni [Maldonado] had those kids in school, and all they wanted to be was a King Ranch cowboy. They were lucky they got in before we changed everything. We're not hiring everybody who comes out of that school, or out of high school—we don't have room for them.

There is a big flow of applications and resumes, and a lot of phone calls from people wanting to work for King Ranch. We keep an open file on them for a year.

David Maldonado is the Director of Human Resources for King Ranch, Inc. He is a third-generation Kineño on his father's side and a fourth-generation on his mother's. His children represent the fifth generation of the Maldonado family on the Ranch.

A Different Education

Formal education holds a more prominent place in the lives of vaqueros today. Whether they acquire positions on the Ranch, or whether
they seek other lines of employment by choice or by necessity, their
skills have to be much different, much more sophisticated, than those of
their parents and grandparents. Children of the Kenedy Ranch vaqueros
attend school at Sarita in the Kenedy County-Wide Common School
District for grades pre-K through 6, then transfer to Riviera. Olga Serna
explained:

> *They are well-prepared and well-disciplined. They eat lunch at
> school and don't come home.*
>
> *The Sarita School Scholarship Fund was endowed by Sarita
> East. If Kenedeño children finish high school at Riviera with a
> good grade average, they get $500 a semester for college. The 1994
> Valedictorian was from Sarita. Our children do well.*

The Santa Gertrudis School, located near the New Colony, remains
open on King Ranch. It was established in 1917 by Henrietta King to provide primary and elementary education for the children who lived on
the Santa Gertrudis Division of the Ranch. A similar school was established on Norias in 1925.

Fully accredited by the Texas Education Agency and operated as an
independent school district since 1942, Santa Gertrudis School is housed
in an attractive, Spanish-style facility that was constructed in 1950. Its
white stucco exterior features a mural, with a Mexican motif, painted
across the façade in clear, soft hues. A front porch runs the width of the
school, which matches the architecture of the New Colony homes. The
school grounds are generously landscaped and neatly trimmed. A United
States flag flies prominently on a pole that was donated by Humble Oil
and Refining Company, the developer of the energy resources on King
Ranch. The school day still begins with a flag-raising ceremony.

The atmosphere at the school is reminiscent of a generation ago.
The setting is agrarian. The children are free to play in safety on the
fenceless playground in secure surroundings without fear or danger.
Their families are nearby, so they can go home for lunch—about 20 to
25 percent do so—or they can bring their lunch. Some outside students
are accepted. All students may eat breakfast at the school free of charge.
The school remains the center of community life; parents and other
family members are always welcome.

The Santa Gertrudis School is located within the gates of the Santa Gertrudis Division of King Ranch in Kingsville, Texas. It includes grades pre-K – 8.

The office of Mary Wright, the principal of Santa Gertrudis School, is neat and businesslike. Her straightforward manner suggested the breadth of her knowledge and abilities as she explained to us that Laureles is the only other school in operation on the Ranch, and its life expectancy is about a year. The school (grades pre-K through 2) is the last remnant of the Laureles Independent School District, which consolidated with Riviera in 1993. Remarking that the dropout rate at Laureles had been near 100 percent, she explained:

> They [vaquero children] had no expectations past the fence line. . . .
> It is slowly changing with higher expectations for kids at Laureles.
> The population is younger; parents are involved. The children
> have more self-confidence—they're more self-assured . . . . I was
> on the school board at Laureles, but was hired off. Tio [Kleberg]
> wanted model schools, and he said they would pay taxes to support
> them. The school was renovated, and gyms, playgrounds, and field
> trips added.
>   We're departmentalized in grades 4 – 8 here at Santa Ger-
> trudis. Students participate in academic UIL [University Inter-
> scholastic League] in grades 2 – 8. They have student council, sci-
> ence and art clubs, Junior Achievement, and a tininkling group

[a dance native to the Philippine Islands, in which there is a rhythmic stepping between two large poles as the poles are beaten together in cadence to music].

Junior high sports include basketball, baseball, and track. Like all other schools in Texas, they're under "no pass, no play." Four-H is a big program—they compete very well at the fair.

There is very low teacher turnover at the school. Toni Maldonado, a kindergarten teacher for almost twenty years, said: "They retire or they die. The school is like an extended family. Discipline is not a problem. Our strengths are our size, individual attention to each student, and our teachers."

The size of the Santa Gertrudis School, with its approximately 130 students, has been both a positive and a negative factor. Students have sometimes experienced culture shock in attempting to adjust from this small family atmosphere to that of the larger high school in Kingsville, where they may know almost no one. Some, however, have made the transition quite well.

There is one teacher for the four-year-olds, one teacher for each grade in grades K–3, and subjects are departmentalized with a home-room teacher in grades 4–8. Teachers of fine arts, special education, and physical education complete the staff. Spanish is taught as an elective in the seventh grade and a half-year in the eighth grade; English is by far the dominant language of the students in school, though Spanish is still the language of the Ranch.

The school operates on a year-round calendar, with students attending four nine-week sessions and then taking a three-week break for intercession. Attendance during the first vacation week is mandated if a student is failing a subject, enrichment classes are offered the second week, and, during the third week, all students are home. Parents participate in parenting classes and are encouraged to remain involved in their children's education.

The Santa Gertrudis School has a generously equipped computer room, with eighteen hardware units and featuring both work stations and labs. A remediation lab (CEI) with four units is currently using Recreational Education software, experimenting with retraining pathways of the brain. Three teachers work with the grades 5–6 lab and three with the grades 7–8 lab. Macintosh and Josten are the most prominent names on the computer hardware, but kindergartners use IBM programs, such as "Writing to Read." They are on-line with the principal's office and networked into the lab.

Sonia Maldonado Garcia described the differences in education at Santa Gertrudis School since she attended:

My two sisters go to Santa Gertrudis [School]. They work with computers and all that. They love it. I didn't have that opportunity. They're teaching completely different now to the way I was taught in school—I graduated in 1992. My sister, Samantha, is nine, and Veronica is thirteen. [Veronica] will probably go to a little private school just south of town for ninth through twelfth grade. It's Presbyterian.

THE LANGUAGE

No longer are schoolchildren punished for speaking Spanish at Santa Gertrudis School. In fact, many of them know very little of the language. David Maldonado explained:

When Lillie and Anise [David and Toni's daughters] were three or four-year-olds, they spoke a lot of Spanish, but after they started to school they didn't want to speak it anymore. I got to the point I wouldn't talk to them in English. I've noticed that when Toni's parents call—they don't speak much English—my daughters converse with them in Spanish. They know more than they lead us to believe . . . . I spoke very little English when I started school. It was very difficult for me, and it took me a long time to learn English. We used to get spankings for speaking Spanish in school— and now later they hired my wife to teach Spanish!

A SCHOOL FOR THE NEXT CENTURY

Since 1917, when the first formal school was opened at Santa Gertrudis, sons and daughters of vaqueros have attended elementary schools on the Ranches. If they remained in school, they transferred to Kingsville or Riviera upon completion of the eighth grade.

Today, they have a new, promising opportunity designed especially for them.

The February 2, 1994, issue of *The Kingsville Record* carried a story about a new approach to high school education initiated by King Ranch. The concept grew from the realization that students must be prepared for a very different kind of work today and must possess flexible skills that will enable them to adjust to fast-changing economic trends.

The Academy for Developmental Learning is the first of its kind in

Texas and marks a considerable departure from traditional educational concepts. Formed as a partnership between the Driscoll Independent School District, the Santa Gertrudis Independent School System, and Texas A&M University–Kingsville, the program is to be phased in over a four-year period. About sixty ninth-grade students entered the program in fall of the 1994–1995 school year. Students in the upper grades are attending schools elsewhere and will graduate from their current high schools. When the program is fully implemented in four years, all high school students from the two districts will be required to participate in this program.

Each student follows an individualized education plan. Grade levels are unstructured, and no grades (such as A, B, or C) are given. Evaluation is based on individual portfolios of student work. Instead of sequencing from grade 9 through 12, students move at their own pace. The idea is to change the system to fit the individual students' needs, rather than fitting the students into a prescribed system. Mastery is considered the cornerstone.

"They won't be able to move to the next level until they can apply the skills they have learned," according to Dr. Billy Bowman, Santa Gertrudis ISD superintendent (*The Kingsville Record*, February 2, 1994).

The Academy for Developmental Learning on the Texas A&M University–Kingsville campus will serve as a field-based site for teacher training and research. Along with selected elementary programs, it will form the basis for restructuring the Teacher Training Program. The desired result is that aspiring teachers will have a much more realistic, application-based preparation experience. The formal goals, which include 90-percent mastery on the state-required TAAS Test by the year 2000, guarantees student success regardless of learning level as well as active participation by parents and the community. Under this new educational program, it is expected that the sixth-generation vaqueros of King Ranch will in the future be better prepared to meet the demands of the changing workplace.

Commitment Continues

Through the new high school program, King Ranch continues to express, in tangible ways, its concern for the vaquero families that have worked on the Ranch for generations. But this is not the first educational assistance that the Ranch has offered to vaquero families. For years, the

Ranch has provided opportunities in higher education for vaquero sons and daughters through scholarships and work-study arrangements.

Many of these sons and daughters are pursuing higher education. Norma Martínez is a descendant of two of the oldest families on the Ranch, the Quintanillas and the Mendiettas. Five of her nine siblings have earned college degrees. She holds both a bachelor's degree and a master of science degree in geology, and is presently a senior environmental engineer with the Hoechst Celanese plant in Bishop, Texas.

Both Enemorio Serna and Chito Mendietta have had children earn college degrees. At the time of his interview, Enemorio's son was getting a ranch management degree at Texas A&I (now Texas A&M University–Kingsville). "Young people want to get their education," said Enemorio. "They work on the Ranch in the summer and take semesters off to get the money to go to school."

At the time of Chito's interview in 1994, he said: "I have three children, and they're still living with me. One graduated from Texas A&I, now Texas A&M, in 1991 and works there as an accountant. One girl's a junior and one's a sophomore at the University. They work for us. One does tours and one has other jobs."

David Maldonado benefited from his formal education as a business major at Texas A&I. "Tio Kleberg gave me the opportunity to work for the Ranch while I attended college," he explained. David's skills are important to the operation of the Ranch office. His work is a world apart from that of his grandfather, Librado Maldonado Sr., who spent most of his time grooming and showing cattle. David described his job responsibilities:

> I work in Human Resources. I manage the pension plan, make sure our retirees get their checks, and help with any problems they may have—they usually come in here. I administer the 401K savings plan we adopted in 1986, and I care for the personnel files. It's a very enjoyable job. I work with a lot of people I grew up with. It's like I never left home.

David's cousin, Sonia Maldonado Garcia, sometimes attends classes at Texas A&M University–Kingsville.

> Right now I'm majoring in ranch management. My Animal Science 101 instructor, Dr. Swakon—she was real good—and we hit it off.
>   I want to work on a ranch with animals. Doesn't have to be here, but I'd like it to be. I'd like to be a unit manager out here on

The Headquarters Office Building is located on the Santa Gertrudis Division of King Ranch in Kingsville, Texas. Its employees service many components of King Ranch that are located throughout the United States and Brazil.

this Ranch. There're not many girls who want to do that, but I would like to.

A Present-Day Vaquera

Beverly Jo "B. J." Myrick is a full-time vaquera. Though some other women work part time as vaqueras, she is the only full-time vaquera on King Ranch. An Anglo born in Jourdanton, Texas, to a dairy farm family, B. J. moved to King Ranch with her husband, Butch, who is a unit manager of the Encino and Norias Divisions. Eventually she was employed in her husband's unit.

Brought up working with dairy cattle and riding horses, B. J. helped her father with whatever tasks he had—vaccinating and branding calves, feeding, working cattle, baling hay, driving a combine, plowing, "just whatever needed to be done," said B. J.

B. J. remembers her first day working at Campbellton on the 74 Ranch, where there were about thirteen men working, some non–English speaking:

I got to the cook house about 6:00 in the morning. I didn't speak Spanish. First deal, the feed mixer broke; I fixed it. The hay baler broke—I also helped them fix it. Then I halter-broke two-year-old colts. Soon I was branding, dehorning, vaccinating—just whatever.

They [the men] don't care if you're male or female, if you can do the work. I knew how to do a lot of things, so I was accepted. I am not harassed. They respect me in all ways. Here it's like a big family. Everybody works together.

B. J. explained some of the reasons for her unusual skills.

Growing up on a farm is almost like a Ranch, but on a much larger scale. I would always rather help my father with his work than my mother. On a dairy farm, the cows have to be milked twice a day. In the summer, we would have to move irrigation pipes in the fields by hand. Some of the other jobs were cutting hay and putting it up for the winter time, plowing the field, planting grain, then harvesting the grain when the time was right. In the winter, we would hay and feed the cows. There were always windmills, fences, and equipment that needed [to be] fixed.

B. J. presently uses dogs to help in rounding up cattle from the brush on the Encino Division, just like in the old days.

We have Catahula cow dogs. We train them ourselves. They're good—worth a couple of [cow]hands in the brush. Dogs can get in some of the places we can't go in. They catch wind of them [the cattle], and we can find where they're laid up. I always take my dog Odie. I ride [horses] about 50 percent of the time—80 to 100 percent during weaning time.

Horses remain an integral part of B. J.'s Ranch work: "I ride Ranch horses. They're great. They're cuttin' horse breed—they're good all-around horses. Doc Toelkes sends 'em down after they're broke as two-year-olds."

As in the old days, working cattle is a dangerous occupation. With even the most experienced and well-trained rider, like B. J., injuries remain inevitable.

I got hurt several times. When I was sixteen years old, one horse kicked me on the jaw . . . broke a kidney loose, and I stayed in the hospital a couple of days. They said I had to take my boots off, but I kept them on the first night—I wasn't planning on staying over night. I rode up until three weeks before my little girl was born, and, three weeks after, [I] started ridin' again. The horse threw me, but I didn't go to the doctor until the next day because I was

not supposed to be on a horse. Finally went, and my arm was bro-
ken. Got a little cast here on my arm. After about three weeks, I
took it off myself, and never went back to the doctor.

    Another time . . . one early morning when I was training colts,
one fell over me against a roping box. Cracked three vertebrae.
Was in traction. Wore a back brace for a while. Should have left it
on three months, but I didn't. Now it hurts sometimes.

Spurning shopping and television, B. J. spends her time on the
range.

It's good working with my husband as boss. He decides what is to
be done that day. If he's not there, I look and see what needs to be
done. To me that makes a good hand.

    Working together all day is good—up to a point. We disagree
every once in a while. When we both get home, we talk about what
happened, have something in common. Some couples don't have
much in common to talk about.

B. J. and Butch's ten-year-old daughter, Bobbie Jo, and their five-
year-old son, Richard "Bud", work with them: "The kids are part of our
work, part of the team. They feed the dogs, open gates, help feed—there
are always things to do. They work with us. Our kids are brought up like
I was. I believe this teaches them responsibility."

    Though she is a present-day Anglo vaquera, B. J.'s day is not so dif-
ferent from that of the Mexican vaqueros of days gone by. Her day is star-
tlingly different, however, from the day of most women a generation ago.

I get up at about 4:45 or 5:00, but it's 4:30 A.M. when we start
weaning. Weaning has to be done at a certain time now. Back then
it was whenever you could get it done. Everything is on schedule
nowadays.

    I cook eggs and bacon sometimes. Sometimes just coffee. I
make lunches to take, have to hurry. I drop the kids off about 6:30.
The lady who works the gate keeps them before and after school 'til
we can pick them up.

    We gather the cattle with helicopters and on horseback. At
branding time, the heifers are vaccinated and dehorned; steers are
castrated, dehorned, vaccinated, and branded. When this is done,
[the heifers and steers] are put back with the cows and turned back
to the pastures. During weaning, they are gathered up again [and]
sorted by heifers and steers. The video steers are weighed while

loaded on trucks and sent to the buyers. The steers that remain are weighed and sent to Encino headquarters, where we process them, feed them for a couple of weeks, then turn them out on grass. The replacement heifers are sent to the Ranch at Gonzales, and the rest are sent to headquarters.

We get home late. Sometimes it's 9:00, and seven days a week during weaning. Sometimes I am too tired to cook, so we have sandwiches. We eat a sandwich for lunch break, also. Sometimes I've put meat in the smoker, or have stew that is ready in the crock pot.

Transition in the Office

There are notable changes in the way business is handled in the King Ranch offices. Catalina Maldonado, first cousin to David, daughter of Beto, and granddaughter of Librado Sr. and Ella, works at the Santa Gertrudis headquarters in the accounts payable department. She has worked for the Ranch since 1974, when she was a student in the Vocational Office Education (VOE) program at Henrietta M. King High School in Kingsville.

I worked in the personnel office many years ago, before David [Maldonado] was the manager. I worked in payroll a couple of years, worked for two accountants, then Jim Spear, who is an internal auditor for the Ranch—I worked for him twelve years.

Today, I pay the bills for King Ranch Florida, Running W Citrus that came on in January. We do all the bills for our Kentucky operation, Bluebonnet Warehousing in Galveston, Cannonade in Gonzales, Arizona, and King Ranch. There's lot of numbers, lots of keying in, lots of work. I caught onto the computer pretty quick. I use it and a calculator in this job. And the FAX machine—we didn't have one 'til shortly before we moved out here [Lauro's Hill]. Now, I don't know how we ever did without it. It's busy all day long.

B. J. Myrick talked about business operations at Encino:

The main change is in the offices. Long time ago, they had a Big Chief tablet and pencil to keep records. In the office [today] we've got computers and just punch it in. I do my own paperwork. Can use a typewriter, but not a computer. I get feed reports—how many pounds of what fed to whom. We have records of our cattle so we know where they came from, where they're going. Cattle are inventoried at all times—even their shots. It's punched in and comes up here to the big computer. Feed is ordered [and] brought from the feed mill. They deliver whatever we need.

Household Changes

The manner in which vaquero households are managed has changed drastically in just two generations. Electricity, indoor plumbing, air-conditioning, automatic washers and dryers, televisions, and microwave ovens abound. Many of the women work outside the home, on the Ranches or in town, and housekeeping chores have become minimized. "My mother always set the ironing board up in the living room," remembered Dora Maldonado Garcia. "It was an all day thing. There was no air-conditioning. I was good at ironing and am til this day. Now I just throw the clothes in the dryer—right quick."

But amidst all these household changes, one of the constants on the Ranch is the family tradition. Catalina Maldonado remembered her grandfather:

My grandfather, Librado [Sr.], told us many stories about the Ranch and about [our] family, in the evening after supper. My dad [Beto Maldonado] does that, too. He runs across pictures and letters, and he'll tell me the whole story about the picture. He can remember years and dates and stories.

Grandfather was kind, very friendly, loving, outgoing—lots of friends. My father is just like him.

My grandfather bought a house in town in 1977, and I got married and rented from him. Every time I paid him, he always said, "Are you sure you don't need this for something else?" Every single time he always kissed me . . . . The way you see my Dad— that's the way he is. I wish I could be like him and not get upset about things. He probably has raised his voice, but hardly ever. I talk with him almost every day, and every time he answers the phone, he's always in the best mood. He's got a real positive attitude about everything. I went with him one day on his tour, and I was pretty impressed. My parents never drank. My dad never really even cussed.

Now They Have Some Time to Play

Perhaps one of the most obvious changes in the lives of vaquero families today is the amount of leisure time they have. Heretofore, family celebrations were generally limited to church-related events such as weddings, baptisms, and Christmas holidays. Activities closely related to work, such as roping contests, or rodeos and storytelling around the campfire, were the main forms of recreation for the men. Visiting was the main recreation for women. But comparatively little time was spent on these pursuits because of the demands of the Ranch work.

Today more leisure time is available, and it is spent in a variety of ways. One big event is the King Ranch Rodeo held on the Saturday before the annual shareholders meeting in early summer. Only the shareholders, King Ranch personnel, and their immediate families participate. No outsiders are allowed.

B. J. Myrick has been a big winner at the King Ranch Rodeo:

You're all a family all year except for the Ranch rodeo. You want to beat the others in the rodeo. Want to be the best. Pride. Working for a good place like this is fun. I won Best All Around Cow Girl— first one given — in 1989. I compete with the guys at the rodeo, too. In everything. Team penning [cutting]. Won team branding against the men, too. Got a one, two, or three in every event every year. Last year was the only year I didn't get a buckle. Nobody else has as many — men or women. Big deal. Goes back to pride. Represent your division. Encino looks good. Butch [B. J.'s husband] won a couple of deals, too. I want to win a buckle and spurs this year.

The annual Service Awards Picnic is sometimes held in Kingsville at the J. K. Northway Pavilion, named for the Ranch's famed veterinarian. The 1995 picnic was held at the Cannonade Ranch in Gonzales. The Awards Picnic includes food, games, contests, and awards. Employees receive awards for five-year increments of service. These awards may be in the form of jewelry, a medallion, or some other gift the employee chooses.

The New Venture — Tourism on the Ranch

Since the days of Captain King, King Ranch has been known for its hospitality. Tradition has it that no person who came to King Ranch

Stephen J. "Tio" Kleberg (left) presents an award to Valentín Quintanilla Jr. Valentín is a retired third-generation vaquero and caporal on the Santa Gertrudis Division of King Ranch.

needing bed and board was ever refused. Strangers, friends, kings, and millionaires have been treated to the special food and conversation always available to be shared on the Ranch. The tradition continues into the 1990s through the efforts of the King Ranch Visitor Management Department.

The Visitor Management Department was created in 1990. Since that time, approximately fifty thousand visitors a year have passed through the white-washed stone gates with the black, wrought iron Running Ws at the Ranch entrance (Myers 1996, 30). Visitors come to see what is still one of the most famous ranches in the world.

The King Ranch Visitor Center provides an excellent opportunity for university students from vaquero families to work and relate their traditions while earning money for tuition. It is also the place where retired hands like Lolo Treviño, Beto Maldonado, Leonard Stiles, and Sylvia Paulk can share their vast knowledge of the Ranch.

For years, King Ranch's prize animals and a wide variety of agricultural products have been exported around the world. Now the world also comes to King Ranch: from Europe, especially Germany (the Klebergs were German immigrants), Mexico, Canada, and Japan. Visitors from Mexico nearly always include veterinary students coming to observe the model animal-care program directed by Dr. John P. Toelkes. Visitors from across the United States include a stream of "Winter Texans" who come south to escape the frigid northern winters and frequently stop on their way to their winter homesites. Sonia Maldonado Garcia described the tours of the Ranch that are offered by the Visitor Center: "Regular tours last an hour and a half or so. VIP tours are available for from two to seven people and last up to four hours. You can go anywhere on the Ranch you want to on these VIP tours, except the Main House. We have two special tour guides who do these—Leonard Stiles [former Santa Gertrudis foreman] and my grandfather [Beto Maldonado]."

The Visitor Management Department adds valuable hands-on information to what is already available to the public at the King Ranch Museum, located in the Henrietta Memorial Center, once an old ice factory, at 405 North Sixth Street in Kingsville. The ice factory, constructed in 1907 by Robert Kleberg and backed by Henrietta King, enabled the Rio Grande Valley to become a viable supplier of agricultural products to the rest of the nation. Thousands of pounds of ice were loaded on produce-laden railcars, which stopped briefly on tracks running parallel to the ice factory, enabling residents of other states to taste the luscious fruit and vegetables that abound in the Rio Grande Valley. Later the building was abandoned and headed for demolition. In 1969, King Ranch bought it and renovated it for use as a museum named for a granddaughter of Henrietta King (*Traveling Historic Texas*, 8).

Visitors arrive at the King Ranch Visitor Center, located just inside the main gate of the Ranch, seven days a week on climate-controlled charter buses or in their own automobiles. There they are greeted by docents who are more than likely members of vaquero families. Guests can either watch a short video or walk around the grounds to observe and become familiar with native vegetation. The *turistas* then either board a King Ranch tour bus, or are joined by a step-on guide on their charter buses, and are escorted around the black-topped Ranch roads through the Santa Gertrudis Division.

First, the guide gives a brief acccount of today's operation: 825,000 acres fenced with enough wire to reach from Kingsville to Boston, more than 300 water wells, 60,000 head of cattle, and 65,000 acres of farmland producing milo and cotton. The feed mill turns the milo into grain for 250,000 pounds of feed daily for the 16,000 cattle in the Ranch's feedlot.

Then the bus slows at Santa Gertrudis Creek, the original site of Captain Richard King's cow camp, which is marked with a Texas Historical Marker. Then it's on to see pastures of the Ranch's famous horses. Visitors may witness a lively exchange: "The colts are put in the pasture with an older horse. The older horse teaches them the ropes and settles them down when they get too wild. . . . The colts are just like a bunch of teenage boys. . . . They push and shove until they get into a fight, and then the older horse steps in and separates them before anybody gets hurt" (*Traveling Historic Texas*, 1).

During the ride, the *turistas* will also be able to view a diverse array of wildlife. They may see deer, wild turkey, feral (wild) hogs, javelina, dove, quail, caracaras—the possibilities are many. The vegetation includes lush green grasses and a myriad of spring wildflowers that turn to fall hues of brown and gold. Mesquite trees flourish, many reaching no more than six or seven feet in height, their brown, gnarled trunks supporting brilliant, lacy, green-leafed branches.

Sometimes visitors get to stop at the Plomo pens to watch vaqueros working cattle in a squeeze chute. These chutes are fitted with hydraulic gates that let one man do the work done by several not so long ago. Old-style roundups are rare today; cattle are worked like this in pens in the individual pastures. A display of heavy equipment used in brush control may be viewed from the bus: giant bulldozers with huge plows, chains, and disks. At the Plomo pens, *turistas* may also get a special treat of hot coffee and *pan de campo* cooked over coals in a Dutch oven by a King

Ranch cook and served by Lolo Treviño, a vaquero with more than forty years' experience. Lolo may tell you about matching wits with the 1946 Triple Crown winner, Assault, as Lolo trained the so-called Clubfooted Comet.

On occasion, Lolo may also include a demonstration of cattle handling while his guests drink their mugs of coffee. He uses a Miguel Muñiz rope made of horsehair. Lolo looks dapper in his tan cowboy-cut dress pants and shirt with pearl-topped buttons. His red bandanna is held by the tip of a cow horn, and his black boots and silver spurs complement his slim, straight, taut figure. His skin, browned by years of desert wind and sun, is accented by his short salt and pepper hair. A straw hat, with a handwoven, brown-and-black checked horsehair band with a narrow band of red, complete his outfit.

When Lolo sits atop his sorrel-colored King Ranch Quarter Horse and turns his attention to cutting and penning calves, he becomes the epitome of a professional cowboy. From the pen filled with mingling, bawling animals, he eyes the one to be cut out of the herd and goes swiftly to work. Using a vocabulary of guttural yelps only his horse and the cattle understand, he separates the calf and pens it. He is at least as adept as his three younger vaquero assistants; his age of sixty-four years seems impossible. So does his skill at putting the calf exactly where he wants it in very little time.

And Lolo is also keeping the vaquero tradition alive in other ways. While sixth-generation vaqueros learn of their heritage from the annual production of *Tales of the Wild Horse Desert,* the present generation of Captain Richard King's family learn their heritage by attending a week-long summer camp. Each year, they come from New York, California, or wherever they reside. They arrive to spend long days learning or adding to their knowledge of their Texas heritage. While the grownups attend an annual stockholders' meeting, seasoned vaqueros and their young assistants teach the younger King Ranch descendants the basics of Ranch work. The camp culminates in a *pachanga,* a fiesta, held on the east porch of the Main House, with plenty of food, music, and fun.

Lolo Treviño described what he teaches the summer camp attendees.

I've taught it for fourteen years. I teach the traditions: saddling, cleaning horses, how to put on blankets. I show them how to tie the saddle, walk the horse a little, then walk the horse again, and tie again. I teach how to hold the reins, to call before you approach a horse, and don't walk behind the horse. I tell them you have to slow a horse down when he gets excited.

My mother taught me. She said to be careful around flowers on the range—there could be holes under them. That's good to know when riding a horse.

The Ranch bus tour continues through pastures where visitors can view the famous Santa Gertrudis cattle that have stocked over eleven million acres on five continents. The guide points out that two Santa Gertrudis herds are maintained today: the commercial herd located on the Ranch's four divisions, and the top-of-the-line, A-herd located here on the Santa Gertrudis. Next, *turistas* see the King Ranch Santa Cruz, the new composite breed.

A camp house comes into view, once a home-away-from-home for vaqueros who, in the past, stayed out from two to three weeks at a time working cattle. Located behind the camp house are the feed mill and feed-lot, from which eleven hundred head are shipped to market each week.

The tour bus slows briefly at the Quarter Horse Barn and the youth projects barn, where a gray horse is always kept along with the sorrels in honor of the story about Jesse James leaving a gray horse for Captain King in exchange for a night's lodging. Nearby are the graves of Assault, Old Sorrel, and other equestrian celebrities who sleep near the Thoroughbred stables. Their epitaphs are starkly simple:

Old Sorrel
Chestnut Horse
Hickory Bill - Dr. Rose Mare
Foundation Sire
King Ranch Quarter Horse Family

Assault
Chestnut Horse
Bold Venture - Igual
March 26, 1943 – Sept. 1, 1971
Triple Crown Winner 1946

Next, the *turistas* learn that the Quarter Horse program receives less emphasis today, but that its high quality remains. King Ranch keeps about thirty Quarter Horse mares on the Ranch. Peppy San Badger, the leading sire of competition cutting horses, and his sire, Mr. San Peppy, are retired and are living their twilight years here on the Santa Gertrudis Division of King Ranch. A Thoroughbred breeding and boarding facility remains in operation in Lexington, Kentucky (Erramouspe 1995, 12).

The visitors see the more than one hundred houses in the New Colony, built in 1951 west of the Main House across from the Santa

Alberto "Beto" Maldonado conducts one of the many Ranch Loop Road bus tours from the King Ranch Visitor Center, located on the Santa Gertrudis Division in Kingsville, Texas. He continues to share his vast knowledge of the cattle and the operation of King Ranch with the *turistas* each year.

Gertrudis School. From the porches of these homes, the old-timers can sit in the evenings and savor the view of the same Santa Gertrudis Creek that drew Captain King to this site in the very beginning. But today, burnished red Santa Gertrudis and King Ranch Santa Cruz cattle accent the landscape, and sometimes the Longhorn steers make an appearance. Groups of cattle are gathered at huge cement watering holes in each pasture. Windmills and oil well pumps are scattered on the horizon. Visitors also pass by the Old Colony, the first permanent housing constructed for vaqueros on the Ranch in the late nineteenth century.

The tour winds to an end at the headquarters complex, which is located at the same spot where King and his wife, Henrietta, first lived in a crude jacal as honeymooners. A large frame dwelling that replaced the jacal burned in 1912. The tour bus drives by the Spanish-style Main House, fashioned around a courtyard, built originally to serve five families, including Robert King's children (Broyles 1980, 162). The house dominates the area. Built of white stucco with a red tile roof, it serves as the family seat. Also located on the grounds are an old school building, the maintenance shops built in 1931, a carriage house built in 1909, a former garage that serves as a party room, and an 1865 vintage barn. The oldest building in the complex is the white stucco Commissary, built in the 1850s. It once served as the location for Captain King's office, and, for years, it made food and supplies available to both vaqueros and owners (*Traveling Historic Texas*, 3).

Knowledgeable tour guides can answer almost any question. A retired vaquero, Beto Maldonado, remains involved with the Ranch as a regular tour guide, as does his granddaughter, Sonia Maldonado Garcia. Sonia explained:

> *I finished high school, and they asked me if I'd like to come work at the Visitor Center as a tour guide. My grandfather kind of wanted me to. I started in the office with the office manager, learned the cash register and how to help tourists coming through. Then I hopped on the buses and started learning the tours . . . . I have a commercial driver's license. Now some people ask for me. They think it's interesting when I talk about my family history—generations are going on out here on this Ranch—and they have a guide who is one of them.*
>
> *Some tours don't understand English. I have to speak in Spanish, and it's hard. Mostly we get my grandfather to do it. With mixed crowds I offer to stay after the tour and tell them as much as I can in Spanish. Most of the time they do.*

The Future

The future of the vaquero in the Wild Horse Desert will only be definitively known a generation from now, but we do know there will always be a need for vaqueros. A hundred years from now, the structures and faces of the industrial giants in the United States will have changed, perhaps in unrecognizable ways. The same may be true of these two ranching giants, the King and Kenedy Ranches. But in South Texas, cattle will still be produced, furnishing food for the nation. Men and land and herds will continue to be bonded in a relationship that has lasted five generations (Cypher 1995, 229). Those closest to these great transitions think about the future a lot. Sometimes they vocalize their predictions:

> *I think the people will stay on. I think most of the people here are happy. Basically we're in transition. What do I think will happen in ten years? This company will probably be just like any other*

company. But it'll always be the famous King Ranch. Catalina
Maldonado

*The majority of people will be here. There'll be some new ones,
some will leave, some will be retire.* David Maldonado

*There'll always be a need for ranching. It has a great future, but
will have to change to compete. Things are always changing . . .
have to keep up. You don't change a cattle breed overnight. Takes
lots of time. It's hard work.* B. J. Myrick

The Ranch owners and the vaqueros still maintain great respect for
each other. Their long journey together through history continues.
Their relationship is revealed in an account of Henrietta King's funeral
in *The King Ranch Papers* (Frost 1985):

> A great throng crowded to the simple funeral rite at the Big
> House on April 4th, at 3:30 in the sunny afternoon. When the
> service conducted by the Reverend S. E. Chandler was con-
> cluded, a cortege more than a mile long moved behind the
> black hearse down the gentle slope from the Santa Gertrudis on
> the road to town, to the cemetery of Kingsville which Henrietta
> King had planned and named Chamberlain Park in honor of
> her father.
>
> An honor guard unlike any other on the face of earth led
> the slow procession. The Ranch's cowboys, nearly 200 of them,
> wearing their range clothes, riding their range horses, accompa-
> nied La patrona, who had always been their partisan, upon her
> final journey.
>
> At her crowded gravesite, during the hymns, eulogies, and
> last prayers, grey-haired bankers from Manhattan rubbed shoul-
> ders with leather-faced choppers from the lonely *callos* of El Sauz.
>
> When the casket was lowered into the earth, there was a
> stir at the edge of the crowd where the bare-headed horsemen
> stood. They came reining forward in single file, unbidden and
> uncommanded save by their hearts, to canter with a centaur
> dash once around the open grave, their hats down at side salute
> to Henrietta King. (p. 64)

Perhaps Manuela Mayorga best summed up this remarkable rela-
tionship between the Ranch owners and the vaqueros when she quoted
Henrietta King: "King Ranch started with Spanish people and the King
Ranch will end with Spanish people."

Martín Mendietta Jr. is a fifth-generation vaquero at King Ranch, and his sons represent the sixth generation of Mendiettas. Martín's father, uncles, and other relatives have been caporals on the Santa Gertrudis Division for years.

Juan Guevara Jr. is a fourth-generation vaquero on the Kenedy Ranch, and his children represent the fifth generation of Guevaras. Employed in the Sarita Safari section at the time of the interviews, Juan helped to facilitate many of the interviews with retired vaqueros.

Ofelia M. Longória (left) with her granddaughter, Ofelia L. Moreno, at the Henrietta Memorial Museum in Kingsville, Texas. Mrs. Longória seems to have been the only female camp cook on King Ranch. She fed as many as ninety men a day at the Laureles cow camp.

Josefina Robles Adrián with her grandson, Oscar Cortez Jr., in front of the Commissary on the Santa Gertrudis Division of King Ranch. The Robles family is one of the oldest families on the Ranch. Josefina helped her father by doing the work of a vaquero on the *ranchito* at the Big Caesar Pasture on the Santa Gertrudis Division where she lived with her parents.

Maria Luisa Montalvo Silva grew up on the Laureles Division of King Ranch. She comes from a family of vaqueros and is one of the few vaqueras who worked with the men at the roundups. She says she is proud to be a Kineño.

Beverly Jo "B. J." Myrick is an Anglo working as a full-time vaquera on the Encino Division of King Ranch. She is married to Butch Myrick, the Division Manager. She richly described the life of a vaquera and how she is raising her two children on one of the world's largest ranches.

Enemorio Serna with his wife, Olga, who is from a third-generation vaquero family.
They live on the Kenedy Ranch. Enemorio is a second-generation vaquero. Olga
described life in the ranching community of Sarita, and Enemorio described both old
and new ranching methods.

Dora Maldonado Garcia (left) and her daughter, Sonia Maldonado Garcia, represent four generations of Maldonados on King Ranch. Sonia works for the King Ranch Visitor Management Department on the Santa Gertrudis Division.

David Maldonado with his two daughters, Anise (left) and Lillie, in 1986 after a successful hunting trip. David is a member of the Kineño Hunting Club on King Ranch.

Juan Garcia (left), Scott Masterson Kleberg, and José Angel Garcia Jr. Juan and José are sons of José and Nicolasa Garcia, and Scott is the son of Mary Lewis and Richard Mifflin Kleberg Jr. The children of vaqueros and owners were often friends and playmates.

Adán Muñoz Jr. (left) with his father Adán Muñoz Sr. Adán Sr. served Robert J. "Bob" Kleberg Jr. as a chauffeur, valet, dog handler, and gun bearer. Adán Muñoz Jr. was sheriff of Kleberg County 1989–1994, and is now special administrator assistant to the Texas State Attorney General's office.

Shown here with prized Quarter Horses, these present-day vaqueros on the Santa Gertrudis Division of King Ranch carry on the traditions of the vaqueros of the Wild Horse Desert.

Appendix A: Individuals Interviewed

Note: Interviews conducted in Spanish were translated into English.

Adrián, Josefina Robles (1923–   ); King Ranch; interviewed in Spanish, September 1994.

Josefina's family is one of the oldest on the Ranch. She gave us invaluable information on growing up there. One of the few recorded vaqueras, she did the same work as the vaqueros while she was growing up on a *ranchito* in the Big Caesar Pasture located near Bishop, Texas, where her father was employed.

Aguilar, Candy; King Ranch; interviewed in English, March 1994.

Candy is a present-day vaquero who works on the Santa Gertrudis Division using both old and new ranching methods, including the use of helicopters to round up cattle.

Alegría, José J. (c. 1931–   ); King and Kenedy Ranches; interviewed in English, March 1991.

José's father, Felipe Alegría Sr., worked as a vaquero at the Kenedy Ranch. At the time of the interview, José worked part time for King Ranch Visitor Management Department.

Alegría, Marty; King Ranch; interviewed in English, March 1994.

Marty is a present-day vaquero who works on the Santa Gertrudis Division using both old and new ranching methods, including the use of helicopters to round up cattle.

Allen, Clyde M. Jr.; interviewed in English, February 1996.

Clyde is the owner of Allen Furniture Store in Kingsville, which his father established in 1926. The store later included a funeral home that served both Anglos and Mexicans.

Alvarado, José O. (1925–   ); King Ranch; interviewed in English, March 1994.

José is a descendant of Francisco Alvarado, who died during the Union army raid on Santa Gertrudis during the American Civil War. Francisco and his son, Ramón, built the first jacales (houses) on the Ranch, and Francisco's great uncle, Ramón Ortiz, took care of the first mares Captain Richard King brought to the Ranch. José shared valuable pictures and history of the Alvarado family's association with King Ranch.

Becerra, Lin (c. 1946–   ); King Ranch; interviewed in English, March 1994.

At the time of his interview, Lin was a unit boss at the Santa Gertrudis Division. A graduate of Texas A&M University–Kingsville, he was in charge of the elite herd and the breeding of Santa Gertrudis bulls to Santa Gertrudis cows.

Bowman, Dr. Billy; King Ranch; interviewed in English, March 1994.

Dr. Bowman is presently the Superintendent of Schools for the Santa Gertrudis Independent School District. His office is located in the school on the Santa Gertrudis Division of King Ranch.

Buentello, Antonia Quintanilla (1908–   ); King Ranch; interviewed in Spanish, March 1991.

Antonia's father, Valentín Quintanilla, came to the Ranch in 1885. He was the son of Xavier Quintanilla and Teresita Pizana Quintanilla. Antonia's children represent the fourth generation of Quintanillas on the Ranch, and her grandchildren represent the fifth generation. The first Quintanilla on the Ranch, Antonio, is listed in the King Ranch Ledger Book as a horse hand in 1869. In 1872, Pedro Quintanilla is listed as a vaquero, and, on October 1, 1889, Sebastian Quintanilla is listed as horse caporal.

Buentello, Julian (1911–   ); King Ranch; interviewed in Spanish, March 1991.

Julian was a vaquero on the Ranch and the remuda boss in charge of horses before he retired. He knew the horses by name and temperament. Bob Kleberg relied on him to choose appropriate horses for his guests. Julian is also a good navigator, according to his wife, Antonia Quintanilla Buentello. She said that Julian has American Indian heritage that he believes is responsible for his uncanny ability to lead steers to the right pasture where they receive the herd. Julian also related stories of trail drives to Kansas City that were told to him by his vaquero father, Roman Buentello.

Cantu, Apolonia M.; King Ranch; interviewed in English, February 1995.

Apolonia was interviewed at Martín Mendietta's home in Riviera. She contributed information about the woman's role in providing spiritual leadership for the family.

Cortez, Oscar Jr.; King Ranch; interviewed in English, September 1994.

Oscar is a member of the Robles family, one of the oldest families on King Ranch. He is employed in King Ranch Visitor Management Department, located on the Santa Gertrudis Division, and attends Texas A&M University–Kingsville. He assisted in the interview with his grandmother, Josefina Robles Adrián.

Cuellar, Teresa Mayorga (1915–   ); Kenedy and King Ranches; interviewed in Spanish, with her grandson, Juan Guevara, facilitating and translating, September 1991.

Teresa's father, Macario Mayorga, was a famous vaquero on both the Kenedy and King Ranches. Her brother, George "Chorche" Mayorga, was also interviewed. She contributed stories about growing up on the Ranches.

Flores, Ricardo; King Ranch; interviewed in English, March 1994.

Ricardo is a present-day vaquero who works at the Santa Gertrudis Division using both old and new ranching methods, which include working with helicopters to round up cattle.

Garcia, Conrado; King Ranch; interviewed in English, April 1991.

At the time of the interview, Conrado was a cook's assistant to Felipe Garcia on the Santa Gertrudis Division. He remembers the chuck wagon when it was pulled by six mules, and how the cook rode the back left mule and reined the others from that position. His sister, Cecelia, was married to Ed Durham.

Garcia, Dora Maldonado (1949–   ); King Ranch; interviewed in English, March 1994.

Dora is the daughter of Dora and Alberto "Beto" Maldonado Sr. She described growing up in a Kineño family on the Santa Gertrudis Division. At the time of the interview, she worked in the King Ranch Insurance Department, in an office located on the Santa Gertrudis Division. She is married to Joe Garcia and is the mother of Sonia, Samantha, and Veronica.

Garcia, Felipe (1932–   ); King Ranch; interviewed in English, April 1991.

Felipe trained under a cook called Holotino "La Chista" Villarreal, who cooked for King Ranch for thirty years. At the time of the interview, Felipe was a cook for the Santa Gertrudis Division. His great-grandfather, Guadalupe Alegría, was killed by a bull on the Santa Rosa Ranch. Felipe shared valuable information about his past experience as a range cook with a chuck wagon and his present job as a camp house cook. He still makes camp bread every day. He shared recipes with the interviewers.

Garcia, Nicolasa "Nico" Quintanilla (1927–   ); King Ranch; interviewed in English, March 1994.

Nico gave valuable information about her wedding and the social customs on the Ranch. She worked for Mary Lewis Kleberg for many years. Her husband, José (Joe) Garcia, worked with Assault, King Ranch Triple Crown winner, and the other Thoroughbreds that were trained at the Santa Gertrudis Division.

Garcia, Sonia Maldonado (1974–   ); King Ranch; interviewed in English, March 1994.

Sonia is a fourth-generation Garcia family member on the Ranch and a member of a sixth-generation vaquero family, the Maldonados. She is the daughter of Dora Maldonado Garcia and Joe Garcia. She carries on the tradition of showmanship and interest in cattle established by her great-grandfather, Librado Maldonado. She also works for the King Ranch Visitor Management Department and attends Texas A&M-Kingsville.

Gonzales, Jesus Sr. (c. 1924–   ); Kenedy Ranch; interviewed in Spanish, December 1989.

Jesus worked with the wild horses that populated the Wild Horse Desert. He began as a cook's helper and later trained other cooks. He is married to Raffela Villarreal Gonzales.

Gonzales, Raffela Villarreal; Kenedy Ranch; interviewed in Spanish, December 1989.

Raffela is the wife of Jesus Gonzales Sr. She provided helpful information about herbs used to treat illnesses.

Guevara, Juan Sr. (1937–   ); Kenedy Ranch; interviewed in English, September 1991.

Juan is a third-generation vaquero who worked all aspects of the Kenedy Ranch. His mother died when he was very young, and he and his sister made candy and sold it to earn extra money. He is married to Stella Cuellar Guevara, and Juan Guevara Jr. is their son.

Guevara, Juan Jr.; Kenedy Ranch; interviewed in English, September 1991.

Juan is a fourth-generation vaquero, and his children represent the fifth generation. At the time of the interview he was employed with Sarita Safari. He was most helpful in facilitating many of the interviews with the Kenedeños.

Guevara, Stella Cuellar (1937–   ); Kenedy Ranch; interviewed in English, September 1991.

A fourth-generation member of the Mayorga and Cuellar families, Stella detailed growing up, the games children played, and her work with the owners on the Ranch. She is married to Juan Guevara Sr. and is the mother of Juan Guevara Jr.

Gutierrez, Seferino (1906–1990); Kenedy Ranch; interviewed in Spanish, December 1989.

At the time of his interview Seferino was retired and living in his house at Sarita, Texas. He was known as an excellent vaquero and an expert roper, perhaps the best on the Kenedy Ranch. He was also a horse trainer, and he explained the process in detail. His third- and fourth-generation family members exhibited much pride in him during the interview as he told his stories.

Hill, Bryan; King Ranch; interviewed in English, March 1994.

At the time of the interview, Bryan was working part time at the Santa Gertrudis Division in the Visitor Management Department. He also attends Texas A&M University–Kingsville.

Hinojosa, Hermila; King Ranch; interviewed in English, February 1995.

Hermila described the women's role in helping to provide spiritual guidance for the family. She was interviewed at Martín Mendietta Jr.'s home in Riviera, Texas.

Longória, Ofelia Montalvo (1926–   ); King Ranch; interviewed in Spanish, facilitated by her granddaughter, Ofelia L. Moreno, October 1994.

Ofelia is from one of the oldest families on the Ranch. She described being the only female camp cook and said that Bobby Cavazos chose her for the job. She cooked for about ninety people a day.

Maldonado, Alberto "Beto" Sr. (1930–   ); King Ranch; interviewed in English, October 1990.

Beto's father, Librado Maldonado Sr., was the master showman of the Santa Gertrudis and Jersey cattle. Beto accompanied his father to Morocco to introduce the Santa Gertrudis breed to the King of Morocco at the International Fair. Beto, like his father, became an expert at handling Santa Gertrudis cattle.

He was also in charge of record keeping for some three thousand of the famous King Ranch Quarter Horses. He is now employed on the Santa Gertrudis Division in the Visitor Management Department. He is married to Dora Maldonado.

Maldonado, Antonia "Toni"; King Ranch; interviewed in English, March 1994.

Antonia is presently a kindergarten teacher at Santa Gertrudis School. Toni described schooling on the Ranch and was helpful in contrasting today's work practices with those of earlier days. She is married to David Maldonado.

Maldonado, Catalina (1956–   ); King Ranch; interviewed in English; March 1994.

The granddaughter of Librado Sr. and the daughter of Beto and Dora Maldonado, Catalina was helpful in contrasting past and present office work at the Santa Gertrudis Division, where she is employed. She also gave valuable information about growing up on the Ranch.

Maldonado, David (1951–   ); King Ranch; interviewed in English, March 1994.

David began working with the show-string heifers in the Show Barn as a young boy with his grandfather, Librado Maldonado Sr., and later transferred to the Veterinary Department where he worked with his father, Plácido Maldonado III, and Dr. J. K. Northway. David described changes that technology has brought to the Ranch. Presently director of Human Resources for the Ranch, David was an invaluable resource in arranging and facilitating interviews with the Kineños. Married to Antonia "Toni" Maldonado, he represents the third generation on his father's side and fourth generation on his mother's side on the Ranch.

Maldonado, Dora (1930–   ); King Ranch; interviewed in English and Spanish, March 1994.

Dora is married to Alberto "Beto" Maldonado Sr. She shared details of life on the Santa Gertrudis Division and of raising her family there in the 1950s.

Maldonado, Plácido III (1921–1993); King Ranch; interviewed in English, May 1990.

At the time of his interview, Plácido was retired and living in town. He worked with his father, Librado Maldonado Sr., in the Jersey operation as a small boy. He also worked with the Thoroughbreds and as an assistant to the veterinarian, Dr. J. K. Northway. He was a second-generation Maldonado family member on the Ranch.

Martinez, Norma; King Ranch; interviewed in English, March 1994.

A senior environmental engineer with the Hoechst Celanese plant in Bishop, Texas, Norma holds B.S. and M.S. degrees in geology. She is descended from two of the oldest families on the Ranch, the Quintanillas and the Mendiettas. Five of the nine siblings in her family have earned college degrees. While conducting oral histories of some of her relatives, she learned that a church still stands in the village in northern Mexico, Cruias (Cruillas) in Tamaulipas, from which Captain King is said to have relocated the first Kineños.

Mayorga, George "Chorche" (1907–1993); King Ranch; interviewed in Spanish, facilitated by his daughter, Enriquiti Sanchez, March 1991.

George's father, Macario Mayorga, was a famous, prize-winning vaquero who represented King Ranch all over Texas and Mexico in rodeo competitions. George and his father both played the harmonica and accordion and sang both for entertainment and to keep the herd of cattle quiet. He contributed a copy of the words to "The Purple Bull," one of the songs they sang.

Mayorga, Manuela G. (1911–   ); King Ranch; interviewed in Spanish, facilitated by her daughter, Enriqueta "Keta" Sanchez, March 1991.

Manuela gave extensive information about the lives of the women on the Santa Gertrudis Division and the social customs of Ranch life. She recounted stories told by her mother and grandmother who were cooks for Henrietta King and Alice Kleberg, and she shared some of their recipes. She gave details of her wedding in 1929 and of her daughter Enriqueta's wedding in 1968.

Mendietta, Alfredo "Chito" (c. 1942–   ); King Ranch; interviewed in English, March 1994.

Alfredo was born on the Santa Gertrudis Division and is one of a long line of caporals from the Mendietta and Quintanilla families. He works with the cow program, including fences, water troughs, and all that is needed to care for the cattle. He is a unit manager in charge of 120 thousand acres and is heavily involved with technology on the Ranch, including the use of helicopters to round up cattle.

Mendietta, Gavina; King Ranch; interviewed in English, February 1995.

Gavina shared information about the altar in her home, as well as pictures of Martín Mendietta Sr. and stories about the family. She is the mother of Martín Mendietta Jr.

Mendietta, Martín Jr. (1931–   ); Kenedy and King Ranches; interviewed in English, October 1991.

Martín is a fifth-generation vaquero, and his sons represent the sixth generation. His father, uncles, and other family members have been caporals on King Ranch for years. He gave invaluable information on breaking horses and conducting range operations. He worked with the Thoroughbred horses and Santa Gertrudis cattle, succeeding his father as head of the cow outfit at the Santa Gertrudis Division for twenty years.

Moreno, Catarino (1902–   ); King Ranch; interviewed in Spanish, April 1990.

Catarino came to the Ranch in 1929 and helped build the houses at the Norias Division in 1939. He trained hunting dogs and was a shepherd. Wool from "his" sheep was woven into the famous Running W saddle blankets.

Moreno, Ofelia Longória; King Ranch; interviewed in Spanish, March 1994.

Ofelia brought her grandmother, Ofelia M. Longória, to her grandmother's interview and helped to facilitate the interview.

Muñiz, Miguel (1896–1990); King Ranch; interviewed in Spanish, December 1989.

At the time of the interview, Miguel was retired and living on the Ranch. He was formerly in charge of King Ranch Quarter Horses, including Peppy, Rey del Rancho, and Little Man. He broke horses used by Kleberg family members and Ranch foremen. In his later years, he was a master braider and plaiter, using horse hair to make ropes, bridles, and quirts. He was also well-known for his plaited hat bands. Examples of his work still exist.

Myrick, Beverly Jo "B. J."; King Ranch; interviewed in English, March 1994.

An Anglo and the only full-time vaquera working on King Ranch, B. J. gave valuable information on how Ranch work is done today. She described working and raising her two children on the Encino Division. She is married to Butch Myrick.

Quintanilla, Rafaela (1912–   ); King Ranch; interviewed in Spanish, October 1991.

Rafaela is married to Valentín Quintanilla Jr., whom she met in a nearby county. They raised their family on the Santa Gertrudis Division. Her father worked in the dairy operation.

Quintanilla, Valentín P. Jr. (1907–   ); King Ranch; interviewed in Spanish, October 1991.

Valentín is a second-generation vaquero. He was the caporal in charge of the *corrida* at the Santa Gertrudis Division for seven years, and later worked with one thousand purebred cattle at Santa Gertrudis.

Rodríguez, Nicolas Sr. (1897–); King Ranch; interviewed in Spanish, April 1990.

Nicolas's mother was killed in the Mexican bandit raids on the King Ranch in 1915. He recalled the role of Texas Rangers during the raids. He began his boy jobs at Caesar Kleberg's house at Norias Division, where Will Rogers was a frequent guest. Nicolas spent his years at Norias. He provided a lot of valuable information about the vaquero family and ranch housing.

Rodríguez, Raul Jr.; King Ranch; interviewed in English, March 1994.

Raul was a present-day vaquero on the Santa Gertrudis Division and worked in cooperation with the helicopters in rounding up cattle.

Rodríguez, Rosendo (1933–   ); King Ranch; interviewed in English, April 1990.

Rosendo is retired. At the time of the interview, he was head of the Commissary at the Norias Division. He also worked on the windmills, served as Ed Durham's driver, and assisted Bob and Helen Kleberg during their hunts. He also documented stories about the names and locations of historic pastures and landmarks on the Ranch. He is Nicolas Rodríguez Sr.'s son.

Salinas, Antonio (1913–   ); Kenedy Ranch; interviewed in Spanish, December 1990.

Antonio came to the Ranch at age twelve. He was first paid for his work by John Kenedy Jr. with a pair of boots. He worked for years driving trucks to deliver equipment and supplies. He was married to Marcella Salinas.

Salinas, Marcella (1913–deceased); Kenedy Ranch; interviewed in Spanish, December 1989.

Marcella was the wife of Antonio Salinas and was helpful in providing information on herbs used as medicine.

Sanchez, Enriqueta "Keta" Mayorga; King Ranch; interviewed in English, March 1991.

The daughter of George "Chorche" and Manuela Mayorga, Enriqueta is a member of a fifth-generation vaquero family. She described growing up on the Santa Gertrudis Division, including dating and wedding customs. She is married to Raul Sanchez, and her son, Raul Jr., works on the Ranch. His son was enrolled in the Ranch school on the Santa Gertrudis Division.

Serna, Enemorio Sr. (1931–   ); Kenedy Ranch; interviewed in English, March 1991.

Like his father before him, Enemorio is a vaquero on the Kenedy Ranch. He is nicknamed "Tequito," Little Tick, because as a child he would grab on to a horse and not let go. He is an expert rider. His experiences range from taming wild horses to working as a present-day vaquero using helicopters and portable pens. His grandfather was a *capitan* with the Mexican rebels. Enemorio is married to Olga Rodriguez Serna.

Serna, Olga Rodriguez (1932–   ); Kenedy Ranch; interviewed in English, March 1991.

Olga related her role as the wife of a vaquero and the mother of children growing up in Sarita, Texas, on the Kenedy Ranch. She talked about the Ranch community and the support role of women. She is married to Enemorio Serna.

Silva, Aurora; King Ranch; interviewed in Spanish, December 1989.

The wife of Manuel Silva, Aurora lived and raised her family on the Santa Gertrudis Division. She is known as an excellent seamstress.

Silva, Manuel Sr. (1905–   ); King Ranch; interviewed in Spanish, December 1989.

Manuel has been called the most skillful roper on King Ranch. He detailed his expertise as a roper. He also tamed and trained horses for twenty-seven years, which included the important job of gentling and handling the Thoroughbreds at the Santa Gertrudis Division for approximately a year before turning them over to the trainer. His father was an accomplished vaquero and a cow boss for many years.

Silva, María Garcia (1921–   ); King Ranch; interviewed in English, December 1989.

María raised her family on the Laureles Division. She is known as an excellent cook, especially for her light, flaky tortillas and her tamales. She is married to Rogerio Silva.

Silva, María Luisa Montalvo (1929–   ); King Ranch; interviewed in English, September 1994.

María's family is descended from Faustino Vela Tovar, who worked for Captain Richard King. She grew up on the Laureles Division and contributed excellent information about growing up there, as well as information on the woman's role.

Silva, Rogerio (1919–1996); King Ranch; interviewed in English, October 1991.

Rogerio was the caporal at the Laureles Division for years. He worked for the Ranch for fifty-six years and estimated that he had ridden 500,000 miles on horseback during his lifetime. He gave valuable information on the workings of the Ranch. He was married to María García Silva.

Stiles, Leonard; King Ranch; interviewed in English, March 1991 and October 1991.

Leonard is a former foreman at the Santa Gertrudis Division. Now retired, he works for the Visitor Management Department at the Santa Gertrudis Division. He facilitated a number of the interviews and provided information on the workings of the cow camps and the contributions of the vaqueros.

Treviño, Albert V. "Lolo" (1930–   ); King Ranch; interviewed in English, March 1994.

Lolo's ancestry goes back to the de la Garza family that owned the land before Captain Richard King purchased it. Lolo's ancestors named the creek, which runs through the Ranch, "Santa Gertrudis" after their daughter's saint. Lolo is retired and now works in the Visitor Management Department of the Santa Gertrudis Division. He shared his intricate knowledge of horsemanship and demonstrated cutting cattle. He is an expert plaiter and explained his technique.

Vela, Jimmy; King Ranch; interviewed in English, March 1994.

Jimmy is a present-day vaquero on King Ranch on the Santa Gertrudis Division. He works with the helicopters in rounding up cattle and also works the cattle the old way, on horseback.

Wright, Mary; King Ranch; interviewed in English, March 1994.

Mary is the principal of the Santa Gertrudis School on King Ranch. She manages a modern, up-to-date facility equipped with the latest technology for students in grades pre-K–8.

Appendix B: Individuals Referenced

Note: Except for those mentioned in the preface and introduction, these names are also found in the index.

Acuna, Martín; Kenedy Ranch. Martín was a Kenedy vaquero in the mid-1880s who was drowned while crossing a river while out on the trail taking cattle to northern markets.

Alaniz, Manuel; Kenedy Ranch. Manuel was a carpenter at the La Parra Division when the new ranch house was built in 1913.

Alegría, Felipe; Kenedy Ranch. Felipe was a vaquero around 1902 and was known for his roping ability, especially his ability to rope the front feet of horses while training them.

Alegría, José J. See Appendix A.

Alegría, José Maria; King Ranch. José cooked for many years at the Main House on the Santa Gertrudis Division. He was known for his small biscuits.

Alegría, Macario; King Ranch. Macario is the father of José Alegría who worked as a cook at the Main House on the Santa Gertrudis Division.

Alegría, Manuela; King Ranch. Manuela is the wife of Macario Alegría and the mother of José Alegría who was a cook at the Main House on the Santa Gertrudis Division.

Allen, A. C.; King Ranch. A. C., along with his partner John Fitch, contracted with Captain Richard King in 1875 to take a herd of cattle up the trail to sell at northern markets.

Alvarado, Abios. Abios was a fictional character in a story written by J. Frank Dobie that characterized one of the prominent vaquero families, the Alvarados. The story illustrates Captain King's trust in his Kineños.

Alvarado, Francisco "Pancho"; King Ranch. Francisco, who was born in 1800, was one of the first workers recorded in the Account Book for Rancho Santa Gertrudis, 1854–1855. He and his son, Ramón, built the first jacales on the Ranch in 1854. Francisco was killed in 1863 while protecting Henrietta King from Union troops after her husband, Captain Richard King, had fled. The Union troops surprised Mrs. King at King Ranch three days before Christmas.

Alvarado, Ignacio; King Ranch. Ignacio was a caporal who worked for Robert Justus Kleberg. His loyalty illustrated the dedication of the Kineños to King Ranch.

Alvarado, José; King Ranch. See Appendix A.

Alvarado, Porfirio (1861–1933); King Ranch. Porfirio, a caporal, was the grandson of Francisco Alvarado who died while protecting Henrietta King and her family from Union Troops.

Alvarado, Ramón; King Ranch. Ramón helped his father build the first jacales on King Ranch in 1854. Later, in the 1880s, he was one of the caporales.

Alvarado, Victor Rodríguez; King Ranch. Victor was Francisco Alvarado's grandson. His memories of the founding and early days of the Santa Gertrudis Division and King Ranch under Captain Richard King's leadership are recorded in the King Ranch Archives.

Alvarez, Helvita. A resident of Corpus Christi, Helvita was the aunt who raised Dora Maldonado.

Angeles, José; King Ranch. José was the uncle who took Manuela Mayorga to the church on her wedding day.

Armstrong, Charlie; King Ranch. Charlie is the son of John Armstrong and Henrietta "Etta" Larkin Armstrong, and he attended the wedding of Nicolasa Quintanilla and Joe (José) Garcia.

Armstrong, Henrietta "Etta" Larkin; King Ranch. Henrietta married John Armstrong and attended the wedding of Nicolasa Quintanilla and Joe (José) Garcia.

Armstrong, John; King Ranch. John married Henrietta "Etta" Larkin, and they attended the wedding of Nicolasa Quintanilla and Joe (José) Garcia.

Armstrong, Tobin. Tobin coleases, with Stuart Sasser and Frates Seeligson, the southern half of the Kenedy Ranch from the John G. and Marie Stella Kenedy Foundation for hunting and grazing rights.

Bass, Charles. Bass was a famous lawman who tracked down and arrested James Kenedy for murder in Dodge City, Kansas, in 1878.

Becerra, Lin; King Ranch. See Appendix A.

Benavides, Juan; King Ranch. Juan was on the Norias Division of King Ranch in 1952 when Catarino Moreno was injured.

Borden, A. P. A. P. was a leading Brahman cattle importer from Houston, Texas. In 1918, he sold to King Ranch fifty-two three-year-old bulls of three-fourths to seven-eighths Brahman blood. One of these bulls sired the famed bull named Monkey that became the foundation sire for the Santa Gertrudis breed developed by King Ranch.

Borglum, Lincoln; King Ranch. In 1979, when Dick Kleberg Jr. died, the family held a big barbecue in keeping with his prior request. The family presented the vaqueros with a medallion that was struck by Lincoln Borglum, the son of Gutzon Borglum, who was the designer and architect of Mt. Rushmore. Lincoln completed Mt. Rushmore following his father's death.

Bowman, Dr. Billy; King Ranch. See Appendix A.

Bueno, Demencio; Kenedy Ranch. A worker on the ranch, Demencio rescued John Gregory Kenedy Jr. and Elena Kenedy when their hunting car got stuck in the mud.

Burwell, Charlie; King Ranch. Charlie was a Texas Ranger and worked for the Texas Cattle Raisers Association (which became the Texas & Southwestern Cattle Raisers Association in 1921). He came to King Ranch in 1921 with the tick eradication crew and became the foreman at the Laureles Division in 1930.

Burwell, Mary; King Ranch. Mary was the daughter of Charlie Burwell. As a child, she was a playmate of María Luisa Montalvo Silva (see Appendix A).

Buentello, Antonia Quintanilla; King Ranch. See Appendix A.

Buentello, Julian; King Ranch. See Appendix A.

Buentello, Raul; King Ranch. Raul's father is Julian Buentello. Like his father and grandfather, Raul has an outstanding sense of direction, which makes him an excellent navigator.

Bush, George. Former U.S. president George Bush came to the Santa Gertrudis Division of King Ranch, before his presidency, to attend an auction and barbecue. He observed Librado and Beto Maldonado showing the Santa Gertrudis cattle.

Cantú, José; King Ranch. José was a caporal on the Santa Gertrudis Division and helped Beto Maldonado cover his first schoolbook.

Cantú, Julian; King Ranch. Julian was an expert horse boss who worked with Robert J. Kleberg Sr. after the death of Captain Richard King in 1885.

Carerra, Helena. Helena married Dora Maldonado's uncle, Johnny, on the same day that Dora and Alberto "Beto" Maldonado were married, February 6, 1949.

Cavazos, Antonia; King Ranch. Antonia was Manuela Gaytan Mayorga's mother. She raised her family on the Santa Gertrudis Division and worked to prepare food for Henrietta King and her guests.

Cavazos, Augustín. Augustín was a vaquero who was kicked to death by a horse he was trying to break while working at the Armstrong Ranch.

Cavazos, Bobby; King Ranch. While working at the Ranch as a boss, Bobby hired Ofelia M. Longória as a camp house cook at the Laureles Division.

Cavazos, Lauro F. Sr.; King Ranch. Lauro was a young vaquero and a defender of the Ranch in the 1915 Mexican bandit raid. Later, in 1926, he became the first Mexican American foreman at the Santa Gertrudis Division.

Cavazos, Lauro F. Jr.; King Ranch. Lauro grew up on the Santa Gertrudis Division where his father was foreman. He returned to King Ranch to visit in 1992 while he was serving as the United States Secretary of Education.

Cavazos, Narciso. Narciso received the San Juan de Carricitos Grant from the Spanish Crown in 1792. He is an ancestor of Lauro F. Cavazos Sr. and of Lauro F. Cavazos Jr.

Cavazos, Virginia; King Ranch. Virginia was Manuela Mayorga's grandmother and worked with her and her daughter, Antonia, on the Santa Gertrudis Division. She helped to prepare special enchiladas for Henrietta King and her guests.

Chandler, Morgan; Kenedy Ranch. Morgan was a *mayordomo* (boss) on the Ranch in about 1902.

Chandler, Reverend S. C. Reverend Chandler conducted Henrietta King's funeral at the Santa Gertrudis Division of King Ranch on April 4, 1925.

Cheeseman, Bruce. Bruce is the King Ranch Archivist and works at the King Ranch Museum and Archives located at the Henrietta Memorial Center in Kingsville, Texas. He was instrumental in providing information for this work.

Chowder, Morgan; Kenedy Ranch. Morgan was a foreman for whom Enemorio Serna worked on the Oleander Leaf Division.

Clark, Jasper "Jap"; King Ranch. Jasper was a cattle boss for Captain King. In 1883, he helped to round up cattle on the Santa Gertrudis Division for Captain King to show to a potential buyer.

Clegg, George. At the urging of Caesar Kleberg's young nephew, Bob Kleberg, George sold to Caesar the stallion known as the Old Sorrel, which became the foundation sire for King Ranch Quarter Horses.

Clement, James H. Sr.; King Ranch. James came to King Ranch in 1947. He rose through the ranks of the Ranch's management to become president and CEO in 1974. He was married to Ida Larkin. He died in 1994.

Connally, John. While Governor of Texas in 1976, John Connally was present when Librado Maldonado Sr. showed a prized Santa Gertrudis bull on the third floor of the Adolphus Hotel in Dallas, Texas.

Cortina, Juan. Mifflin Kenedy was asked to command a citizen's army called "The Brownsville Tigers" to defend Brownsville against Cortina's raids in 1860.

Coy, Paulino. Paulino was a Texas Ranger who served as Nicolas Rodríguez's godfather. Nicolas Rodríguez lived on the Norias Division of King Ranch.

Crosby, "Bing." The entertainer and movie star and his wife, Kathryn, visited the Santa Gertrudis Division of King Ranch where he was photographed with Librado Maldonado Sr.

Cuellar, Teresa Mayorga; Kenedy Ranch. See Appendix A.

Davila, Sofia; King Ranch. Sofia was a teacher at the Laureles Division of King Ranch. She taught in a one-room school, and Ofelia M. Longória was one of her students.

de la Garza Falcón, Blas María. Sometime in the 1760s, Falcón moved north from the Rio Grande to establish a stronghold in the wilderness near the Nueces River. He brought his family, scores of retainers, and a company of soldiers. Escandón awarded him private title to large land holdings that later became part of King Ranch.

Dern, Cecilia Garcia; King Ranch. Cecilia was on the Norias Division and helped Catarino Moreno when he was injured.

Doughty, A. C. "Mack"; King Ranch. When Captain King died and Robert Kleberg took over the management of King Ranch, along with Henrietta King, he kept James M. Doughty as his personal assistant, and he became superintendent of the Ranch in 1884. James's son, A. C. "Mack" Doughty, was made one of the foremen at the Santa Gertrudis Division in the 1890s.

Doughty, James M. James had been one of Captain Richard King's foremen and herd bosses on the trail to Kansas. He was in charge of the Ranch during Captain King's last illness. Robert Kleberg kept him as superintendent of range work after Captain King's death.

Durham, Ed; King Ranch. Ed served as the foreman of the Norias Division. His father, George Durham Jr., his grandfather, George Durham Sr., and his brother, Bland Durham, served as head men at the Sauz Division of King Ranch.

Earp, Wyatt. Earp was a famous lawman who tracked down and arrested James Kenedy for murder in Dodge City, Kansas in 1878.

East, Alice King Kleberg; King Ranch. Alice was born January 9, 1893, the daughter of Robert Justus Kleberg and Alice Gertrudis King Kleberg. She married Tom T. East. She was captured by Mexican bandits on March 17, 1916, at their ranch, San Antonio Viejo, and later released.

East, Arthur; Kenedy Ranch. Arthur married Sarita Kenedy in Corpus Christi, Texas, on December 8, 1910. He took over the management of the Ranch when John G. Kenedy Sr. died at age seventy-five in 1931. After Arthur East's death, his wife, Sarita, assumed the management of the Ranch.

East, Mike; Kenedy Ranch. Mike is a nephew of Arthur L. East (the husband of Sarita Kenedy) and the great-great-grandson of Captain King. He leases land from the John G. Kenedy Jr. Charitable Trust and is a foreman for whom Enemorio Serna worked.

East, Sarita (Sarah Josephine); Kenedy Ranch. Sarita was born in 1889 to John G. Kenedy and Marie Stella Turcotte Kenedy. She married Arthur East in Corpus Christi, Texas, on December 8, 1910. After her husband died, Sarita East took over the management of the Ranch. She died on February 11, 1961, in New York. In the settlement of her estate, the John G. and Marie Stella Kenedy Memorial Foundation was made owner of approximately 238,000 acres of the Ranch.

East, Tom T. Sr. Tom was the young cattleman who married Alice King Kleberg on January 30, 1915, at the Santa Gertrudis Division of King Ranch. They lived at the San Antonio Viejo, his ranch located seventy-five miles from Santa Gertrudis near Hebbronville in Jim Hogg County.

East, Tom Jr.; Kenedy Ranch. Tom was a foreman for whom Enemorio Serna worked. He is Mike East's father.

Fitch, John; King Ranch. John was Captain Richard King's foreman at the Agua Dulce Ranch in 1875. He, along with his partner, A. C. Allen, contracted with the Captain to take a herd of cattle up the trail for sale at northern markets.

Flores, Anselmo; King Ranch. Captain Richard King bought some of his first cows from Anselmo and Pedro Flores who lived in Tamaulipas, Mexico.

Flores, Pedro; King Ranch. Captain Richard King bought some of his first cows from Pedro and Anselmo Flores who lived in Tamaulipas, Mexico.

Garcia, Felipe; King Ranch. See Appendix A.

Garcia, Dora Maldonado; King Ranch. See Appendix A.

Garcia, Joe; King Ranch. Joe married Dora Maldonado, Dora and Beto's daughter, on February 6, 1949.

Garcia, José (Joe) Sr.; King Ranch. José was the exercise jockey for the Triple Crown winner Assault and the other Thoroughbreds that were raised at the Santa Gertrudis Division. He married Nicolasa "Nico" Quintanilla, and they raised their family on the Ranch.

Garcia, José (Joe) Jr.; King Ranch. The son of José Garcia Sr. and Nicolasa Quintanilla Garcia, Joe was raised at King Ranch. He is a jockey like his father and today races and trains horses at the Santa Anita track in California.

Garcia, Juan; King Ranch. Juan is the son of Nicolasa and José Garcia, and was a playmate of Scott M. Kleberg.

Garcia, Manuel; King Ranch. Manuel was Nicolas Rodríguez's father-in-law, and they worked together on the Norias Division of the Ranch.

Garcia, Nicolasa Quintanilla; King Ranch. See Appendix A.

Garcia, Samantha; King Ranch. Samantha is the daughter of Dora Maldonado Garcia and Joe Garcia. She attends the Santa Gertrudis School.

Garcia, Sonia Maldonado; King Ranch. See Appendix A.

Garcia, Veronica; King Ranch. Veronica is the daughter of Dora Maldonado Garcia and Joe Garcia. She attended the Santa Gertrudis School and is now at the Academy for Developmental Learning.

Gaytan, Antonia; King Ranch. Antonia, along with her mother, Virginia Cavazos, and her daughter, Manuela Mayorga, worked for Henrietta King. They would spend hours preparing enchiladas for Mrs. King and her guests.

Gonzales, "Chino"; King Ranch. Chino was a vaquero on the Santa Gertrudis Division where he worked in the *corrida* and as a caporal at the Thoroughbred barn.

Gonzales, Jesus; Kenedy Ranch. See Appendix A.

Gonzales, José; King Ranch. José is Antonia Cavazos's brother, who brought her to the Ranch to raise her five children after she became a widow.

Gonzales, Lucia; King Ranch. Lucia raised Helen (Helenita) Kleberg and rode in the carriage with her to her wedding.

Gonzales, Raffela; Kenedy Ranch. See Appendix A.

Guevara, Juan Sr.; Kenedy Ranch. See Appendix A.

Guevara, Juan Jr.; Kenedy Ranch. See Appendix A.

Guevara, Stella Cuellar; Kenedy Ranch. See Appendix A.

Gutierrez, Gumb; King and Kenedy Ranches. Gumb was Juan Guevara Sr.'s grandfather who worked on both the Laureles Division of King Ranch and on the Kenedy Ranch.

Gutierrez, Seferino; Kenedy Ranch. See Appendix A.

Hawkins, Hal; King Ranch. Hal is the physiologist at the Ranch and works with the development of the King Ranch Santa Cruz cattle breed.

Heaney, Pierpont; King Ranch. Pierpont was the daughter of a prominent physician in Corpus Christi, Texas. She married Captain King's grandson,

Richard King, in 1907, and they established their home in Corpus Christi.

Hernandez, Santos; Kenedy Ranch. Santos was one of the workers who built forms for the foundation of the ranch house at the La Parra Division in 1913.

Hirsch, Max; King Ranch. Max was a trainer that Bob Kleberg hired to train and manage his stable of racing horses that produced Assault and Middleground, among others.

Hobin, Robert; Kenedy Ranch. Robert was a foreman for whom Enemorio Serna worked on the Ranch.

Hughes, Michael; King Ranch. In 1969, Michael was the manager of King Ranch operations in Morocco. He arranged for the upkeep of the the Santa Gertrudis bulls that Librado Maldonado Sr. and his son, Alberto "Beto" Maldonado, brought to the International Livestock Fair in Morocco.

James, Jesse. Legend has it that a stranger came to King Ranch and was offered lodging by Captain Richard King. In return, the stranger left a gray horse for the Captain and told the vaquero to tell him that Jesse James left him a horse. Descendants of this horse are believed to be on the Ranch today.

Keepers, Joe A.; Kenedy Ranch. Joe is the Kenedy Ranch's resident land manager and lives at La Parra headquarters near Sarita.

Keenan, Fannie. This was an alias used by Dora Hand.

Kelly, James H. "Dog." Kelly was the mayor of Dodge City, Kansas, in 1878. He once threw James Kenedy out of his saloon. Later, James Kenedy accidentally killed Dora Hand, who worked at the saloon, and Kenedy was arrested for murder.

Kenedy, Carmen Morell; Kenedy Ranch. Carmen was Mifflin Kenedy's adopted daughter.

Kenedy, Elena Seuss; Kenedy Ranch. Elena was born February 7, 1889, in Saltillo, Mexico. She married John G. Kenedy Jr. in 1912 in San Antonio, and they lived on the La Parra Division of the Kenedy Ranch. She had a love of painting and music. She and her husband donated the land for the cathedral and surrounding buildings in Corpus Christi, Texas. Upon the settlement of her estate the John G. Kenedy Jr. Charitable Trust was created, which owns and operates 200,000 acres of the Ranch.

Kenedy, George. George was the son of James Kenedy, a grandson of Mifflin Kenedy, and was an heir to Mifflin Kenedy's estate.

Kenedy, James; Kenedy Ranch. James was the son of Mifflin Kenedy and Petra Vela Kenedy. He accidentally killed Dora Hand in Dodge City, Kansas in 1878. After his arrest for murder, his father assisted in his release, and James became the manager of the La Parra Division.

Kenedy, John G. Sr.; Kenedy Ranch. John was born to Mifflin Kenedy and Petra Vela Kenedy on April 22, 1856. He worked in New Orleans in a banking firm, then returned to help his father on cattle drives to Fort Dodge, Kansas. He married Marie Stella Turcotte in New Orleans in 1882. They had two children, John G. Kenedy Jr., born in Corpus Christi, Texas, on June 7, 1886, and Sarita

Kenedy, born in 1889. After Mifflin Kenedy's death on March 15, 1895, John Kenedy took over the management of La Parra Ranch and the Kenedy Pasture Company.

Kenedy, John G. Jr.; Kenedy Ranch. John was born June 7, 1886, in Corpus Christi, Texas, to John G. Kenedy and Maria Stella Turcotte Kenedy. He graduated from Texas A&M College and married Elena Seuss in 1912. He, Bob Kleberg Jr. and Major Tom Armstrong were close friends. Kenedy and his wife donated the land for the cathedral and surrounding buildings in Corpus Christi. Upon the settlement of their estate, the John G. Kenedy Jr. Charitable Trust was created, which owns and operates 200,000 acres of the Ranch.

Kenedy, Marie Stella Turcotte. Marie was married to John Gregory Kenedy Jr.

Kenedy, Captain Mifflin; Kenedy Ranch. Mifflin was born in 1818 to a devout Quaker family in Downington, Chester County, Pennsylvania. He arrived in Texas in August 1846 to run steamboats on the Rio Grande between Mexico and Texas. On April 16, 1852, Kenedy married the widow Petra Vela de Vidal. In 1860, Kenedy bought in to the Santa Gertrudis Ranch with Captain Richard King. In 1868, Kenedy sold his share in Santa Gertrudis Ranch and purchased Laureles Ranch near Flour Bluff. In 1882, Kenedy sold Laureles Ranch for $1.1 million and purchased La Parra, a 400,000-acre ranch south of the Santa Gertrudis that would become headquarters for his ranching operation.

Kenedy, Petra Vela de Vidal; Kenedy Ranch. Petra was born in Greece in 1825. Her family immigrated to Mier, Mexico. Her father, Gregorio Vela, was the provincial governor under the Spanish Crown for all of the territories between the Nueces River and the Rio Grande. She married Colonel Luis Vidal, who served in the Mexican army, and they had five children. She was widowed and later married Mifflin Kenedy on April 16, 1852. They settled in Brownsville, Texas, then later moved to Corpus Christi where they raised their children and managed the Kenedy Ranch.

Kenedy, Sarah Josephine Spohn; Kenedy Ranch. Sarah was the daughter of Mifflin Kenedy and Petra Vela. She and her husband, Dr. A. E. Spohn, lived in Corpus Christi, Texas.

Kenedy, Thomas; Kenedy Ranch. He was the son of Mifflin Kenedy and Petra Vela de Vidal. As a young man, Thomas was shot and killed in Brownsville, Texas, in a dispute over a young woman named Elvira Lima.

Kennedy, Bernard. Kennedy worked for Clyde M. Allen Sr. at the Allen Furniture Store in Kingsville, Texas, servicing the mortuary side of the business.

King, Alice Gertrudis; King Ranch. Alice was born on April 29, 1862, at Santa Gertrudis to Captain Richard King and Henrietta Chamberlain King.

King, Henrietta M. Chamberlain; King Ranch. Henrietta was born on July 21, 1832, in Boonville, Missouri. Her father, the Rev. Hiram Chamberlain, was an ordained Presbyterian minister and a worker in the Home Missionary Society, which brought the family to Brownsville, Texas, in 1850. She married Captain Richard King on December 10, 1854, in Brownsville and moved with him to the

Santa Gertrudis cow camp. There they began to develop the Ranch and raise their family.

King, Captain Richard; King Ranch. Richard King was born in New York City on July 10, 1824. He came to Texas in May 1847 to work as a river man on the Rio Grande between Texas and Mexico. King bought his first piece of King Ranch land, the Rincon de Santa Gertrudis grant, recorded on July 25, 1853, at Rio Grande City, county of Starr, state of Texas. He married Henrietta M. Chamberlain of Brownsville on December 10, 1854, in the First Presbyterian Church of Brownsville, with her father, The Rev. Hiram Chamberlain, performing the ceremony. She traveled with King to live on his new ranch on the Santa Gertrudis Creek where they began to develop King Ranch, which one day would include 1,250,000 acres.

King, Richard II; King Ranch. Richard was born to Captain Richard King and Henrietta Chamberlain King on December 15, 1860, in Brownsville, Texas. He was their first son and, at the time of his birth, he had two sisters, Henrietta (Nettie) and Ella.

King, Richard III; King Ranch. Richard was the son of Richard King II and Pearl Ashbrook King. He was born at Christmas time in 1884 at the La Puerta de Agua Dulce Ranch, which had been a wedding present to his parents from Captain Richard and Henrietta King on July 15, 1883.

King, Richard Lee (Don Ricardo); King Ranch. Richard was the son of Richard King III and Pierpont Heaney King. He was born in Corpus Christi, Texas, in 1909. As a young boy he played with Manuel Silva.

Kleberg, Alice King; King Ranch. Alice was born January 9, 1893. Her parents were Robert and Alice Kleberg. She married Tom T. East, a young cattleman, on January 30, 1915, and they lived on Tom's ranch, San Antonio Viejo, located south of Hebbronville in Jim Hogg County.

Kleberg, Caesar; King Ranch. Caesar was the nephew of Robert Justus Kleberg who married Alice Gertrudis King, the daughter of Captain Richard King, founder of King Ranch. Caesar worked at King Ranch for forty-six years and spent much of that time at the Norias Division. He was involved in game conservation and the beginning of Quarter Horse development on the Ranch.

Kleberg, Helen "Helenita"; King Ranch. Helen was born October 20, 1927, to Bob and Helen Kleberg. She was named for her mother, Helen Campbell Kleberg.

Kleberg, Janell; King Ranch. Janell is the wife of Stephen J. "Tio" Kleberg, vice president of Agribusiness for King Ranch, Inc. They live on the Santa Gertrudis Division of King Ranch. Mrs. Kleberg wrote the script for *Tales of the Wild Horse Desert,* a play depicting the history of King Ranch and the Kineños that is produced annually by the Drama Department at Texas A&M University–Kingsville.

Kleberg, Mary Lewis; King Ranch. Mary was married to Richard Mifflin Kleberg Jr. in November 1940, and they lived on King Ranch.

Kleberg, Richard "Dick" Mifflin Sr.; King Ranch. Richard was born in Corpus Christi, Texas, on July 7, 1887, and was the son of Robert Justus Kleberg and Alice Gertrudis King Kleberg. He obtained a law degree from the University of Texas at Austin and married Mamie Searcy of Brenham, Texas, on June 12, 1911. He and his wife then moved to the Laureles Division of the Ranch where he supervised operations. He was elected to the U.S. Congress on November 25, 1931, and served for thirteen years.

Kleberg, Richard Mifflin Jr.; King Ranch. Richard was born November 20, 1916, to Richard Mifflin Kleberg Sr. and Mamie Searcy Kleberg. He grew up on the Laureles Division of King Ranch with the Kineños. He married Mary Lewis Scott in November 1940 and managed Ranch operations along with Bob Kleberg.

Kleberg, Robert Justus Sr.; King Ranch. Robert was born on December 5, 1853, on a family farm near Meyersville, Texas. He studied law at the University of Virginia. He married Alice Gertrudis King on June 17, 1886, and, with the recently widowed Henrietta King, assumed the management of King Ranch. He helped to bring artesian wells to King Ranch, led the fight to control anthrax and Texas fever, helped to develop Corpus Christi as a port, and served as president of the Texas Cattle Raisers Association.

Kleberg, Robert Justus Jr.; King Ranch. Robert was born on March 29, 1896, to Robert Justus Kleberg and Alice Gertrudis King Kleberg. He took over the management of King Ranch from his father, Robert Justus Kleberg Sr., and was recognized for his leadership in the development of King Ranch fencing, land clearing, the breeding of the quarter horse, the development of the Santa Gertrudis cattle breed, negotiation of oil leases, and the development of the thoroughbred racing program.

Kleberg, Sarah Spohn; King Ranch. Sarah was born April 12, 1898, and was the youngest child of Robert and Alice Kleberg. She was named for Mifflin Kenedy's daughter, Sarah Josephine Kenedy Spohn. She married Dr. Joseph H. Shelton of Kingsville in 1932. Her first marriage was to Henry Belton Johnson Jr. in 1928.

Kleberg, Scott Masterson; King Ranch. Scott is the son of Mary Lewis and Richard Mifflin Kleberg Jr. As a child, he played with Nicolasa Garcia's children.

Kleberg, Stephen J. "Tio"; King Ranch. Stephen is vice president of Agribusiness for King Ranch, Inc. His parents are Richard Mifflin Kleberg Jr., and Mary Lewis Scott Kleberg.

Lewis, Gideon K. "Legs"; King Ranch. A Texas Ranger, Lewis met Captain Richard King in Corpus Christi, Texas, in 1852 at the Lone Star Fair, and from this meeting evolved their partnership in ranching on the Wild Horse Desert. At the time of his death in 1855, his estate owned one half interest with King in the Rincon de Santa Gertrudis and the de la Garza Santa Gertrudis grants.

Lima, Elvira. A resident of Brownsville, Texas, Elvira was separated from her husband, José Esparaza, when she accompanied Thomas Kenedy to a dance in Matamoros to celebrate his 35th birthday. Later that evening Thomas Kenedy was killed by Elvira's estranged husband.

Longória, Ofelia Montalvo; King Ranch. See Appendix A.

Longória, Reynaldo S.; King Ranch. Reynaldo was the husband of Ofelia M. Longória.

Lopez, José; King Ranch. José was a vaquero who worked in the brush rounding up cattle.

Lopez, Manuel; King Ranch. In 1968, Manuel was a cow camp cook who cooked for Enriqueta Mayorga's wedding at the Santa Gertrudis Division of King Ranch.

Maldonado, Alberto "Beto" Sr.; King Ranch. See Appendix A.

Maldonado, Alberto Jr.; King Ranch. Alberto is the son of Dora and Alberto "Beto" Maldonado, and is Sonia Maldonado Garcia's uncle. He lives in San Antonio and participates in the Christmas celebrations with the Maldonado family on the Santa Gertrudis Division of the Ranch.

Maldonado, Alicia; King Ranch. Alicia is the daughter of Librado and Ella Maldonado and the sister of Plácido III, Librado "Lee," and Beto Maldonado. She was raised on the Santa Gertrudis Division of the Ranch and still lives there today.

Maldonado, Anise; King Ranch. Anise is the daughter of David and Antonia "Toni" Maldonado. She attended the Santa Gertrudis School and now attends Texas A&M University–Kingsville.

Maldonado, Antonia "Toni"; King Ranch. See Appendix A.

Maldonado, Catalina; King Ranch. See Appendix A.

Maldonado, David; King Ranch. See Appendix A.

Maldonado, Dora; King Ranch. See Appendix A.

Maldonado, Ella Byington; King Ranch. Ella married Librado Maldonado Sr. in 1925 and lived on the Santa Gertrudis Division of King Ranch, where they raised their family.

Maldonado, Librado Jr. "Lee"; King Ranch. Lee was Librado Maldonado's son, and Lee's brother, Alberto "Beto" Maldonado, related stories of their growing up together on the Santa Gertrudis Division.

Maldonado, Librado Sr.; King Ranch. Librado was born on April 3, 1898, at the Lasater Ranch and came to King Ranch in 1925. He was the outstanding showman of King Ranch cattle, both Jersey and Santa Gertrudis breeds. He showed these cattle all over the United States and in Cuba and Morocco. He was the father of Plácido III, Librado Jr., Alicia, and Alberto "Beto" Sr., the grandfather of David, Dora, and Catalina, and the great-grandfather of Sonia Garcia and of Veronica, Samantha, Lillie, and Anise Maldonado.

Maldonado, Lillie; King Ranch. Lillie is the daughter of David and Antonia "Toni" Maldonado. She attended the Santa Gertrudis Division school and now attends the Academy for Developmental Learning.

Maldonado, Plácido III; King Ranch. See Appendix A.

Marshall, R. P.; King Ranch. R. P. was the director of Purebred Cattle Sales.

Martinez, Norma; King Ranch. See Appendix A.

Masterson, Bat. Masterson was a famous lawman who tracked down and arrested James Kenedy for murder in Dodge City, Kansas, in 1878.

Mayorga, Lupe Rivera. Lupe was the aunt who raised Macario Mayorga after his mother died.

Mayorga, Manuela; King Ranch. See Appendix A.

Mayorga, Macario; Kenedy, King, and East Ranches. Macario was a famous vaquero who competed in rodeos all over Texas and Mexico. He was the father of Teresa Mayorga Cuellar and George "Chorche" Mayorga.

Mendietta, Alfredo "Chito"; King Ranch. See Appendix A.

Mendietta, Gavina; King Ranch. See Appendix A.

Mendietta, Javier; King Ranch. Javier was one of the best vaqueros on King Ranch and was especially good at roping.

Mendietta, Manuel; King Ranch. Manuel, along with Ramón Alvarado, helped James M. Doughty's son, Mack Doughty, to learn King Ranch work when Mack became the foreman at the Santa Gertrudis Division of the Ranch. Robert Kleberg had begun to manage King Ranch with Henrietta King during this time, which was soon after Captain King's death in 1885.

Mendietta, Martín Sr.; King Ranch. Martín was a caporal on the Santa Gertrudis Division of the Ranch and was in charge of the barns where the Quarter Horses were kept and where the Thoroughbred mares were brought to foal. These barns were called "Martín's Barns."

Mendietta, Martín Jr.; King Ranch. See Appendix A.

Mendietta, Roberto; King Ranch. Roberto was a vaquero on King Ranch who worked for forty-eight years with his fellow vaqueros, Julian Buentello, Valentín Quintanilla Jr., and George "Chorche" Mayorga.

Mendietta, Sixto; King Ranch. Sixto was a cousin of Martín Mendietta Jr. and was a caporal on the Santa Gertrudis Division.

Montalvo, Pedro; King Ranch. Pedro was a vaquero on the Laureles Division and taught his grandaughter, Maria Luisa Montalvo and her friend, Mary Burwell, to ride as small girls.

Montez, Desiderio; Kenedy Ranch. Desiderio was a contractor for the Kenedy Ranch who brought about 160 Mexican American workers to the Ranch in 1925 to help clear brush from the pastures.

Moreno, Catarino; King Ranch. See Appendix A.

Morales, Encarnación; Kenedy Ranch. Members of Encarnación's family were already in the area when Mifflin Kenedy set up his headquarters at the La Parra Division. Many members of the Morales family have worked for the Kenedy Ranch for over one hundred years.

Morales, Guadalupe; Kenedy Ranch. Guadalupe was one of the *mayordomos* (bosses) on the Kenedy Ranch. He was in charge of constructing fences in 1940.

Morales, José María; Kenedy Ranch. José was a vaquero who went to work for the Kenedy Ranch in about 1880. He worked on the headquarters building at the La Parra Division. He once got into a dispute with his boss, Edgar Turcotte, about a saddle that John Gregory Kenedy Sr. had given him.

Mosely, Dick; King Ranch. Ofelia Longória worked for Dick Mosely at the Laureles Division.

Muñiz, José; King Ranch. José and his wife were attendants for Nicolasa Quintanilla and Joe (José) Garcia at their wedding on February 12, 1949.

Muñiz, Miguel; King Ranch. See Appendix A.

Muñoz, Adán Jr. Adán is the son of Adán Muñoz Sr. and a special administrator assistant in the Texas State Attorney General's office.

Muñoz, Adán Sr.; King Ranch. Adán grew up on the Ranch and was the closest vaquero to Bob Kleberg Jr. He served in a number of capacities for Bob every day, including chauffeur, valet, dog handler, and gun bearer.

Myrick, Beverly Jo "B. J."; King Ranch. See Appendix A.

Myrick, Bobbie Jo; King Ranch. Bobbie is the daughter of B. J. Myrick and Butch Myrick and is growing up on the Encino Division of the Ranch.

Myrick, Butch; King Ranch. Butch is a unit manager on the Encino and Norias Divisions and the husband of B. J. Myrick.

Myrick, Richard "Bud"; King Ranch. Richard is the son of B. J. Myrick and Butch Myrick and is growing up on the Encino Division of King Ranch.

Northway, Dr. J. K.; King Ranch. Dr. Northway came to King Ranch in 1916 as the veterinarian and played a major role in the development of the Santa Gertrudis cattle and the Quarter Horses and Thoroughbreds.

Ortíz, Damón. Damón was the brother of Victor Alvarado's grandmother. He drove twenty-five mares and a stallion from Mexico to Captain King's new rancho on the Santa Gertrudis Creek. These were some of the first horses that Captain King bought.

Paulk, Sylvia; King Ranch. Sylvia works at the King Ranch Visitor's Center on the Santa Gertrudis Division.

Quintanilla, Eugenio; King Ranch. Eugenio was David Maldonado's *padrino.* He worked in the veterinary department at King Ranch.

Quintanilla, Jamie; King Ranch. Jamie was a vaquero who, in 1993, was presented an award by Stephen J. "Tio" Kleberg for his contribution to the South Texas ranching tradition.

Quintanilla, José; King Ranch. José was Alberto "Chito" Mendietta's first cousin and his confirmation godparent.

Quintanilla Pérez, Elesa; King Ranch. Elesa was the wife of Valentín Quintanilla Sr., and they lived on a *ranchito* called Ormegas (The Ants) on the Ranch. A great hurricane came while Valentín was out "tying down" windmills to protect them from the wind, and Elesa barely got her children out of the house before it was destroyed. The *ranchito* was located on the Santa Gertrudis Division.

Quintanilla, Valentín Jr.; King Ranch. See Appendix A.

Quintanilla, Valentín Sr.; King Ranch. Valentín came to the Ranch in 1885 and married Elesa Pérez. Valentín was an excellent horseman, and when Dick Kleberg Sr. wanted to show off the vaqueros' horsemanship, he would ask

Valentín to ride for his guests. Valentín was also in charge of the Santa Gertrudis foundation sire, Monkey, and the twenty-five cows they put with Monkey.

Quintanilla, Venuseriano "Niño"; King Ranch. Venuseriano was Rogerio Silva's brother-in-law who helped to train him when he first went to work with the *corrida* on the Laureles Division.

Quintanilla, Xavier; King Ranch. Xavier is the father of Valentín Quintanilla Sr. His family is believed to have come to King Ranch with Captain King from the Mexican village of Cruias (Cruillas).

Ragland, Sam; King Ranch. Sam came to work for Robert Kleberg Sr. in 1892 as the livestock manager at the Santa Gertrudis Division. He served as range counselor for Robert Kleberg Sr. and his sons.

Richardson, Sid. A wealthy Texan from Dallas, Richardson attended the auctions and barbecues at the Santa Gertrudis Division of the Ranch where Librado Sr. and Beto Maldonado showed Santa Gertrudis cattle.

Robles, Aurora; King Ranch. Aurora was Josefina Robles Adrián's sister. She lived on a *ranchito* with her sisters and their father, Ramón, but did not work the cattle like her sisters Josefina and Carolina.

Robles, Carolina; King Ranch. Carolina was the sister of Aurora Robles and Josefina Robles Adrián and worked on the *ranchito* with Josefina and their father, Ramón.

Robles, Luis Sr.; King Ranch. Luis was one of the first vaqueros on the Ranch and was listed in the King Ranch Ledger as Captain King's bodyguard. He was also known as a good horseman. He was Josefina Robles Adrían's grandfather and Oscar Cortez Jr.'s great-great-grandfather.

Robles, Luis Jr.; King Ranch. Luis was the son of Luis Robles Sr. and lived on a *ranchito* with his brother Ramón and sisters Carolina, Aurora, and Josefina.

Robles, Ramón; King Ranch. Ramón was an early vaquero on King Ranch and was the son of Luis Robles. He was Josefina Robles Adrián's father and Oscar Cortez Jr.'s great-grandfather.

Rockefeller, Nelson. The New York governor Nelson Rockefeller attended the auctions and barbecues held at the Santa Gertrudis Division of the Ranch where Librado Sr. and Beto Maldonado showed Santa Gertrudis cattle.

Rodríguez, Manuel; King Ranch. Manuel was Nicolas Rodríguez's brother who was kidnapped during one of the raids.

Rodríguez, Manuela Flores; King Ranch. Manuela lived on the Norias Division of the Ranch and was killed in the 1915 Mexican bandit raid. She was the widowed mother of Nicolas Rodríguez.

Rodríguez, Marcela; King Ranch. Marcela lived on the Norias Division of King Ranch with her widowed mother, Manuela Flores Rodríguez, and her brother, Nicolas Rodríguez.

Rodríguez, Nicolas; King Ranch. See Appendix A.

Rodríguez, Rosendo; King Ranch. See Appendix A.

Rogers, Will. The famous humorist and actor often visited King Ranch to see his friends Caesar Kleberg and Robert Kleberg Sr.

Salazar, Jesse; Kenedy Ranch. Jesse was a vaquero on the Kenedy Ranch in the 1950s.

Salinas, Antonio; Kenedy Ranch. See Appendix A.

Salinas, Lucio; Kenedy Ranch. Lucio was the first Mexican American caporal of a *corrida* on the Kenedy Ranch. He succeeded Edgar Turcotte as caporal in 1916.

Salinas, Macedonio; Kenedy Ranch. Macedonio helped to build the forms for the foundation of the new ranch house at the La Parra Division.

Sanchez, Christopher; King Ranch. Christopher's father is Raul Sanchez, son of Enriqueta "Keta" Mayorga Sanchez and Raul Sanchez Sr. Christopher attends school at the Santa Gertrudis Division. A prospective vaquero, he represents the fifth generation of the Mayorga family on the Ranch.

Sanchez, Elvia; King Ranch. Elvia is the daughter of Enriqueta "Keta" Mayorga Sanchez and Raul Sanchez Sr. She worked at the summer camp held each June on the Santa Gertrudis Division for the stockholders' families.

Sanchez, Enriqueta "Keta" Mayorga; King Ranch. See Appendix A.

Sanchez, Raul Jr.; King Ranch. Raul is a fourth-generation vaquero in the Mayorga family. He is the son of Enriqueta "Keta" Mayorga Sanchez and Raul Sanchez Sr. He is also a welder on the Ranch.

Sanchez, Sylvia; King Ranch. Sylvia is the daughter of Enriqueta "Keta" Mayorga Sanchez and Raul Sanchez Sr. She worked at the summer camp held each June on the Santa Gertrudis Division for the stockholders' families.

Sasser, Stuart. Stuart coleases, with Tobin Armstrong and Frates Seeligson, the southern half of Kenedy Ranch from the John G. and Marie Stella Kenedy Foundation for hunting and grazing rights.

Seeligson, Frates. Frates coleases, with Stuart Sasser and Tobin Armstrong, the southern half of Kenedy Ranch from the John G. and Marie Stella Kenedy Foundation for hunting and grazing rights.

Serna, Enemorio "Tequito"; Kenedy Ranch. See Appendix A.

Serna, Olga; Kenedy Ranch. See Appendix A.

Shelton, Dr. Joseph H.; King Ranch. Dr. Shelton married Sarah Spohn Kleberg in 1932, and they were the parents of Robert Richard Shelton. Dr. Shelton delivered Manuela Mayorga's daughter on the Santa Gertrudis Division of King Ranch; his wife Sarah assisted with the birth.

Shelton, Robert Richard; King Ranch. Robert was born in 1932 to Sarah Spohn Kleberg Shelton and Dr. Joseph H. Shelton. After the death of his parents, he lived with his uncle and aunt, Robert and Helen Kleberg, and they raised him, along with his half-brother, B. K. Johnson, at the Santa Gertrudis Division of the Ranch.

Silva, Encarnación "Chon" Jr.; King Ranch. Chon married María Luisa Montalvo in 1945 and was a vaquero at the Laureles Division of the Ranch. Deceased 1985.

Silva, Juan; King Ranch. Juan was the blacksmith who rebuilt the split hoof of the Triple Crown winner Assault after the colt's injury, which was caused by stepping on a surveyor's stake.

Silva, María Luisa Montalvo; King Ranch. See Appendix A.

Silva, Manuel; King Ranch. See Appendix A.

Silva, Rogerio; King Ranch. See Appendix A.

Spear, Jim; King Ranch. Jim is vice president for King Ranch and works in the business office located on the Santa Gertrudis Division of the Ranch.

Stiles, Leonard; King Ranch. See Appendix A.

Tate, Captain Tom; King Ranch. A former Texas Ranger, Captain Tate became a King Ranch foreman and helped to protect the Norias Division after the attack by Mexican bandits in 1915.

Tate, Mrs. Tom; King Ranch. Mrs. Tate lived at the Norias Division and taught at the school there. She was kind to Macario Mayorga when he was a young boy.

Tijerina, Eulalia; Kenedy Ranch. Eulalia was José Morales's employer in about 1880 before José went to work for Mifflin Kenedy.

Toelkes, Dr. John P.; King Ranch. At present Dr. Toelkes is the veterinarian for the Ranch.

Trant, Donald; King Ranch. Donald was a superintendent of the Santa Gertrudis Independent School District.

Treviño, Alberto V. "Lolo"; King Ranch. See Appendix A.

Turcotte, Edgar; Kenedy Ranch. Edgar was a caporal with the *corridas* on the Kenedy Ranch in the early 1900s.

Turcotte, Jack; Kenedy Ranch. Jack was a relative of Marie Stella Turcotte Kenedy, the wife of John G. Kenedy, who was the son of Mifflin Kenedy. Stella Guevara babysat for the Turcotte family and traveled to Colorado with them for three months when she was a young woman.

Ubenze, Don; Kenedy Ranch. Don was the father-in-law of Nicolas Rodríguez. He helped Nicolas pack and load heavy items, such as tents, out on the range.

Vela, Gregorio; Kenedy Ranch. Gregorio was the provincial governor under the Spanish Crown for the territories between the Nueces River and the Rio Grande. He was the father of Petra Vela, who married Mifflin Kenedy on April 16, 1852.

Vidal, Adrián J.; Kenedy Ranch. Adrián was the son of Petra Vela Vidal and Captain Vidal before Petra married Mifflin Kenedy. Adrián was executed in Mexico; Captain Kenedy could not save him.

Villa, Faustino; King Ranch. Faustino worked with Captain King on the steamboats on the Rio Grande and later became a vaquero on King Ranch. He refused to accept a pension, saying he only wanted to be paid for what he earned.

Villa, Pancho. Enemorio Serna's grandfather was a capitan with Pancho Villa's Mexican rebels between 1915–1920.

Villarreal, Holotino "La Chista" (Little Bird); King Ranch. La Chista was a cook for the cow camps. He was called "La Chista" because he hopped around like a little bird. He cooked for the Ranch for thirty years in the *corrida* and in the kitchen on the second floor of the Commissary.

Walker, L. A. L. A. showed Buen Amigo, King Ranch's prize two thousand pound bull, at the International Fair in Chicago with Beto Maldonado in the 1950's.

Wright, Mary; King Ranch. See Appendix A.

Wright, Scott; King Ranch. Scott is the Area 1 cattle manager for the Ranch.

Glossary

"Alissia"—a song George Mayorga played on the harmonica around the chuck wagon in the evenings

altarcito—small altars in vaquero homes, usually decorated with brightly colored crepe-paper flowers, candles, pictures of saints, and other objects of a religious nature

amarosa—an herb used to treat stomach distress

armadillo—a burrowing mammal with an armorlike covering of bony plates that is indigenous to Texas and Central and South America

arras—a small container of dimes presented to a couple during their wedding ceremony to signify prosperity; also, a gift made by a husband to his wife upon marriage

bandanna—cotton handkerchief, often red, used by cowboys to protect their faces and necks against sun and grit

bandito—robber

bluing—a blue liquid added to laundry rinse water to make clothes look whiter

bolo—Mexican string tie

boy jobs—tasks around the home and ranch performed by boys beginning at age seven or eight

branding—using a hot iron to burn marks of identification into the hide of an animal

brush—thick undergrowth of vegetation

buñuelos—Mexican dessert made of fried, puffed tortillas sprinkled with brown sugar and cinnamon; a fritter

buttones—leather loop that fits over the saddle horn and is attached to the end of a rope. Developed on King Ranch to free the rope if an animal gets hung

cabresto—braided horsehair rope

cabrito—goat meat prepared as a delicacy

Caesar Pens—large shipping pens built by King Ranch near Kingsville to hold cattle before shipping them by rail to northern markets *calles*—streets

capitan—captain, caporal

caporal—cow boss

caracara—a large, vulture-like hawk native to South America

carne asada—barbecue

carne guisada—beef stew

caudillo—second in command to the caporal

cenizo—herb for treating coughs

chiquito—small boy

chorizo—seasoned pork sausage

chuck wagon—kitchen on wheels for storing, transporting, and serving food
    on the trail

churn—container in which sour milk or cream is beaten, stirred, and shaken
    to form butter

clabber—thickly curdled sour milk

cocinero—cook

cojines—the kneeler at a wedding

comanche—an herb used to cure fevers

compadre—a close friend, a buddy

commissary—a store on the ranches that provided food items and other
    supplies

comadre—godmother of one's child or mother of one's godchild

conquistadores—Spanish conquerors of Mexico, Peru, and other parts of the
    Americas in the 16th century

corrida—cow camp; basic work unit of the Ranches in which ten to thirty men
    work together

cuacos—horns

cuadrillao—laborer working in a team

culling—removing non-producing cows from the herd from horseback

cutting—separating individual animals from the herd on horseback for
    culling, branding, or inoculation

Dansa loches—a popular dance during celebrations attended by the Kineño
    and Kenedeño families

despacio—slowly

el abogado—lawyer

El Cojo—the lame one

el ocho—a popular dance during celebrations attended by the Kineño and
    Kenedeño families

"El Rancho Grande"—song cowboys sometimes sang while guarding the cattle
    at night

enchilada—Mexican dish made of a tortilla rolled with a meat mixture inside
    and covered with a spicy, red pepper sauce

Encino—the name of the smallest division of King Ranch, located south and
    east of Falfurrias, Texas; also, Spanish for live oak

feedlot—pens for short-term, intensive feeding of cattle to fatten them for
     market

fiesta—party. See also *pachanga*

hacienda—ranching tradition that originated in Spain, was adopted in Mexico
     and later in South Texas; also, a large ranch, estate, farm, or plantation

heeler—small loop tossed, usually in the brush, so that the back legs of an
     animal are caught and the animal is thrown

istafrate—an herb used to treat colic

jacal—straw hut; wall construction was later improved to include mesquite
     logs laid horizontally with a mixture of clay, lime, and sacahuiste grass
     used to fill the crevices

javelina—collared peccary common in South Texas

La patrona—a female employer; boss

lariat—rawhide rope braided with four, six, eight, or twelve strands; later was
     made of hemp and then of nylon. See also reata

lasso—rope loop

Laureles—largest of the four divisions of King Ranch, located east of Kingsville,
     Texas, bounded on the south by Baffin Bay, on the north by Nueces
     County, and on the east by the Gulf of Mexico; named for a Spanish land
     grant that was probably named for stands of laurel trees on the land

Laurel Leaf Division—one of two divisions of La Parra, headquarters of
     Kenedy Ranch

Las Pastorelas—a traditional Mexican play with a religious theme, typically
     performed during the Christmas season

levántate—get up

los amigos—friends

madrina—godmother

mangana—rope or lariat

manta—coarse cotton cloth

manzanilla—an herb used to treat stomach aches

mas carote—cubes of cattle feed

mayordomo—boss of a "foot section" charged with jobs other than cattle work

mesquite—thorny, shrublike trees common in Mexico and South Texas

Mifflin Kenedy Division—one of two divisions of La Parra, headquarters of
     Kenedy Ranch

muy bien—very good

negro—an herb for treating coughs

New Colony—a cluster of homes built in the 1930s on the Santa Gertrudis
     Division of King Ranch for the vaquero families

nilgai—Indian antelope

Norias—the name of the southernmost and second-largest division of King
     Ranch, with its eastern boundary located on the coast of the Gulf of
     Mexico; also, Spanish for wells

nuda—an herb used to treat stomach problems

Old Colony—a cluster of ninety-two ranch-style frame houses and five brick houses built on the Santa Gertrudis Division of King Ranch for the vaquero families

oxen—castrated bulls of a domestic breed of cattle used as draft animals

pachanga—party or fiesta

padrino—godfather

padrinos—close family or friends who furnish items for a wedding, such as cake and the kneeler

paisanos—from the same country; fellow countrymen

pan de campo—camp bread made on the King and Kenedy Ranches

pan de polvo—sweet bread

parteras—midwives, who delivered most of the babies on the Ranches

partidas—cattle drive holding pens; also used to mean "cattle drives"

patrón—landowning class

pase—enter, come in

paso doble—a common dance during celebrations attended by the Kineño and Kenedeño families

postadores—intermediary between two families whose son and daughter want to marry

purple sage—a prairie plant used to treat coughs

Quarter Horse—a breed developed in America and noted for its ability to run at a fast pace for up to a quarter of a mile

quinceañera—a celebration of the approaching womanhood of girls, held on their fifteenth birthday

¿Quién viene?—Who goes there?

ranchero—a person who works on or owns a ranch

ranchito—homesteads located in remote areas of the Ranches, usually near windmills

rancho—a small ranch

reata—rope. See also lariat

remuda—a group of fifteen to twenty-five horses used for working cattle

remudero—person in charge of the horses

rosemary—an herb used to treat coughs and colic

roundup—gathering of cattle for branding, inoculating, and separating for breeding or market

rub board—a device made of ridged metal framed with wood that was slipped into galvanized wash tubs of soapy water for scrubbing clothes; predates automatic washing machines

sacahuiste—prairie grass that was cut in short pieces, mixed with clay and lime, and used as a filler between mesquite logs in the construction of jacales

Saint Reyes—a celebration of the Catholic Church held on January 6 *sancho*—pet lamb

Santa Gertrudis—ranch headquarters and third-largest division of King Ranch, named for Santa Gertrudis Creek where Captain Richard King established his first cow camp; also, the name of the first American cattle breed, which was developed on King Ranch.

segundo—second in command to the *mayordomo*

siesta—nap

sorrel—chestnut or light brown color

staffeleto—plant used to treat cuts

tamales—native Mexican dish made of minced meat and red pepper seasoning rolled in cornmeal, then wrapped in corn shucks and steamed

Thoroughbred—pure bred, pedigreed; a breed of horses used for racing

tirones—anchor posts used in fence building

toronjil—an herb for making tea, considered a treatment for nerves

tortilla—flat, small, unleavened rounds of bread; staple of the Mexican diet

"Una noche"—a song George Mayorga played on the harmonica around the chuck wagon at night

valentín—female lamb; sometimes used as a nickname for nilgai

vaquera—cowgirl

vaquero—cowboy

viejo—very old friend; my old man

viverierda—an herb used to treat stomachaches

Wild Horse Desert—the land stretching from the Rio Grande north to the Nueces River in South Texas

yerbaníz—an herb for making a tea, considered helpful in losing weight

Bibliography

BOOKS

Adams, Ramon F. *Come an' Get It*. Norman: University of Oklahoma Press, 1952.

Atherton, Lewis. *The Cattle Kings*. Bloomington: University of Indiana, 1961.

Brown, Dee. *Cowboys: Trail Driving Days*. New York: Scribner's, 1952.

Brown, Mark. *Cowboys: Before Barbed Wire*. New York: Holt, 1956.

Cheeseman, Bruce. *My Dear Henrietta*. Kingsville, Tex.: King Ranch, Inc., 1993.

Corpus Christi Caller-Times. King Ranch: 100 Years of Ranching, 1853–1953. Corpus Christi, Tex.: *Corpus Christi Caller-Times*, 1953.

Cypher, John. *Bob Kleberg and the King Ranch*. Austin: University of Texas Press, 1995.

Dary, David. *Cowboy Culture*. Lawrence: University Press of Kansas, 1989.

Denhardt, Robert M. *The King Ranch Quarter Horses*. Norman: University of Oklahoma Press, 1970.

Dobie, J. Frank. *Cow People*. Boston: Little, Brown and Co., 1964.

———. *A Vaquero of the Brush Country*. Austin: University of Texas Press, 1985.

Frissell, Toni. *The King Ranch, 1939–1944*. New York: Morgan & Morgan, 1975.

Frost, Dick. *The King Ranch Papers*. Chicago: Aquarius Rising Press, 1985.

Goodwyn, Frank. *Life on the King Ranch*. New York: Crowell, 1951.

Graham, Joe S. *El Rancho in South Texas*. Denton: University of North Texas Press, 1994.

Harper, Minnie Timms, and George Dewey Harper. *Old Ranches*. Dallas: Dealey and Lowe, 1936.

King, Edward, and T. Wells Champney. *Texas 1874*. Lincoln, Mass.: Cordovan Press, 1947.

Lea, Tom. *The King Ranch*. 2 vols. Boston: Little, Brown and Co., 1957.

Lehman, Valgene W. *Forgotten Legions: Sheep in the Rio Grande Plain of Texas*. El Paso: Texas Western Press, 1969.

Lomax, John. *Cow Camps and Cattle Herds*. Austin: Encino Press, 1967.

Michaud, Stephen G., and Hugh Aynesworth. *If You Love Me You Will Do My Will*. New York: W. W. Norton & Co., 1990.

Montejano, David. *Anglos and Mexicans and the Making of Texas, 1936–1986.* Austin: University of Texas Press, 1987.

Morgan, Sarah. *Dining with the Cattle Barons Yesterday and Today.* Waco: Texian Press, 1981.

Munson, Sammye. *Our Tejano Heroes.* Austin: Panda Books, 1989.

Myers, Sandra L. *The Ranch in Spanish Texas 1691–1800.* El Paso: Texas Western Press, 1969.

Nixon, Jay. *Running W, Stewards of a Vision (A History of King Ranch).* Hong Kong: Everbest Printing Co., 1986.

Nordyke, Lewis. *Cattle Empire.* New York: William Morrow, 1949.

O'Conner, Louise. *Crying for Daylight: A Ranching Culture in the Texas Coastal Bend.* Austin: Wexford Publishing, 1989.

Robertson, Brian. *Wild Horse Desert: The Heritage of South Texas.* Edinburg, Tex.: Santander Press, 1985.

Smith, Diane S. *The Armstrong Chronicle: A Ranching History.* San Antonio: Corona Publishing Co., 1986.

Steiner, Stan. *The Ranchers.* Norman: University of Oklahoma Press, by arrangement with Alfred A. Knopf, 1985.

Ward, Delbert R. *Great Ranches of the United States.* San Antonio: Ganado Press, 1993.

Ward, Fay E. *The Working Cowboy's Manual.* New York: Bonanza Books, 1983.

Welch, June Rayfield. *The Glory That Was Texas.* Waco: Texian Press, 1975.

Witliff, William O. *Vaquero—Genesis of the Texas Cowboy.* San Antonio: University of Texas Institute of Texan Cultures, 1972.

Bulletins

Alvarado, Victor Rodríguez. *Memoirs.* Translation. Kingsville, Tex.: King Ranch Archives, Henrietta Memorial Museum, 1937.

Cheeseman, Bruce. "Richard King: Pioneering Market Capitalism on the Frontier," in *Ranching in South Texas: A Symposium,* ed. Joe S. Graham. Grunwald Printing Co., 1994.

Davis, Cary, Carl Haub, and JoAnne Willette. *U.S. Hispanics: Changing the Face of America.* Washington, D.C.: U.S. Department of Health and Human Services, June 1983.

Goodwyn, Frank. *Folk-Lore of the King Ranch Mexicans.* Reprint. Publications of the Texas Folk-Lore Society, vol. 9, 1931.

Kleberg, Robert J., Jr. *The Santa Gertrudis Breed of Beef Cattle.* Kingsville, Tex.: King Ranch, 1954.

The Mexican Texans. San Antonio: University of Texas Institute of Texan Cultures, 1986.

National Endowment for the Humanities and Southwest Texas State University. *No Traveller Remains Untouched, Journeys and Transformations in the American Southwest.* Bulletin for a traveling exhibition, 1995, pp. 29–38.

PERIODICALS

Alexander, Sandy. "Retired Cowboy Feels He Was Destined for Job." *Kingsville Record.*

"America's Cowboys: A History." *Cobblestone,* vol. 3, no. 7 (July 1982), 4–48.

Associated Press. "Study Cites Hispanics' Lack of Education." *Dallas Morning News,* July 4, 1991.

Barnhardt, Lee Ann. "Learning at the Center of New High School Concept." *Kingsville Record,* February 2, 1994, 1, 3.

"Big As All Outdoors." *Time* (December 1947), 89–96.

Bray, Ralph G. "Great American Ranch." *Texas Farming and Citriculture* (September 1940), 18–26, 56, 59.

Broyles, William, Jr. "The King Ranch." *Texas Monthly* (October 1980), 150–173.

"Cattle Showman Librado Maldonado Known in Falfurrias." *Falfurrias Facts,* February 17, 1983.

Cohen, Sharon. "Hispanics Seeking the 'Dream Up North' in Rural Midwest." *Texarkana Gazette,* August 4, 1991.

Currie, Barton W. "A Farm As Big As Delaware." *Country Gentleman* (Philadelphia), August 28, 1915, 1, 4, 24.

Dobie, J. Frank. "The Mexican Vaquero of the Texas Border." Reprint. *Southwestern Political and Social Science Quarterly,* vol. 8, no. 1 (June 1927).

———. "The Magician on Horseback." *Mexican Life,* vol. 30, no. 5 (May 1955), 11–14.

Erramouspe, Roxanne. "Today's King Ranch." *The Cattleman,* vol. 82, no. 4 (September 1995), 10–32.

"The Fabulous Klebergs of Texas." *Fortune,* June 1969.

Frazier, Kendall. "King-Sized Changes." *National Cattlemen* (April 1987), 13–17.

Frost, Dick. "La Madonna Goes to the Big Rancho in the Sky," in *The King Ranch Papers.* Chicago: Aquarius Rising Press, 1985.

"King Ranch Today." *Western Horseman* (May 1980).

"Lauro Cavazos." *Dallas Morning News,* August 20, 1989.

Lea, Tom. "The Mighty Ranch of Richard King." *Life* (July 8, 1957), 37–44.

Markley, Melanie, and Stephanie Asin. "School Districts' Makeup Shifts." *Houston Chronicle,* July 8, 1991.

Markus, Kurt. "Five Generations of Horsemen." *Western Horseman* (April–May 1980), 37–45.

"Minorities a Majority in 51 Cities." *USA Today,* September 17, 1991.

Morrison, Dan. "The Right Gear." *Texas Highways* (September 1994), 7–13.

Mullen, Joan. "A High School and University in One." *ATPE News* (September/October 1994).

Murphy, Charles J. V. "The Fabulous House of Kleberg: A World of Cattle and Grass." 3 parts. *Fortune* (June, July, and August 1969).

Myers, Cindi. "Texas Giant." *Historic Traveler* (January 1996), 26–37.

Nash, Susan Hawthorne. "Mystique in the Mesquite." *Southern Living* (February 1994), 86–93.

Norvell, Scott. "Vaquero Tradition Immortalized in Exhibit." *Corpus Christi Caller-Times,* September 18, 1989.

Quellhorst, Sherry. "Retired Ranch Employee Branding Iron Specialist." *Kingsville Record,* August 2, 1989.

Rhoad, A. O. "The Santa Gertrudis Breed." *Journal of Heredity,* vol. 40, no. 5 (May 1949).

Rhoad, A. O., and R. J. Kleberg, Jr. "The Development of a Superior Family of the Modern Quarter Horse." *Journal of Heredity,* vol. 37, no. 8 (August 1946).

Rosenblatt, George L. "Home on the Range." *Texas Highways* (September 1994).

Ruiz, Marco A. "Lonesome Legacies." *Dallas Morning News,* September 1, 1991.

Smallwood, Lanette. "Alberto 'Lolo' Trevino, King Ranch Celebrity." *Traveler* (March 1994), 38–39.

Stanush, Barbara. "Only in the Wild Horse Desert Would You Find King Ranch." *San Antonio Express-News,* July 25, 1992.

Stutz, Terrence. "Minority Students Now a Majority, State Report Says." *Dallas Morning News,* September 6, 1991.

Tedford, Deborah. "Muñoz Named Candidate for Marshall." *Houston Chronicle,* April 15 1995.

"The Texas 500." *Texas Monthly* (1994).

Traveling Historic Texas (February/March 1991), 1–8.

"The Voice of South Texas Agriculture." *Texas Farming and Citriculture* (September 1940).

Wolfshohl, Karl. "Birth of a New Breed." *Progressive Farmer* (February 1995), 44–50.

"The World's Biggest Ranch." *Fortune* (December 1933), 48–109.

Unpublished Sources

Cheeseman, Bruce S. "La Patrona of Santa Gertrudis." Paper presented at the annual meeting of the Southwestern Social Science Association, Fort Worth, Tex., 1990.

———. "History of Santa Gertrudis School." Unpublished manuscript, King Ranch Archives, Kingsville, Tex.

Kenedy Ranch Ledger Books. Corpus Christi: Corpus Christi Museum of Science & History.

King Ranch Archives. Account Book of Employee Wages, October 1, 1889– October 1, 1892.

King Ranch Archives. Account Book of Household Expenses, November 12, 1867–July 31, 1868.

King Ranch Archives. Account Book of Household Expenses, August 1, 1868–November 13, 1869.

King Ranch Archives. Account Book for *Las Conchas,* May 22, 1872–February 10, 1873.

King Ranch Archives. Account Book for *Rancho Santa Gertrudis,* 1854–1855.

King Ranch Archives. R. King & Company, Journal No. 3, November 5, 1867–February 28, 1870.

King Ranch Archives. Trail Drive Account Book, Expenses on 1875 Kansas Trip by John Fitch.

King Ranch Archives. Letter from J. B. Murphy to Captain Richard King, March 1, 1878.

Kleberg, Robert J., Sr. "Address of Robert J. Kleberg, Chairman of the Executive Committee of the Texas Industrial Congress, Delivered March 9 [1911], at San Benito, to the Farmers of Southwest Texas." King Ranch Archives, Kingsville, Tex.

Neely, Lisa A. "Folklore of Los Kineños." Graduate paper in Gothic Literature, Texas A&I University, November 30, 1993.

Villarreal, Roberto M. "The Mexican-American Vaqueros of Kenedy Ranch: A Social History." Master's thesis, Texas A&I University, 1972.

Young, Andrew Herbert. "Life and Labor on the King Ranch: 1853–1900." Undergraduate paper, Texas A&I University, 1992.

Index